An inventory of UK estuaries

Volume 3
North-west Britain

Compiled by A.L. Buck

Joint Nature Conservation Committee
Monkstone House
City Road
Peterborough PE1 1JY
UK

© JNCC 1993

ISBN 1 873701 38 1 vol. 3. North-west Britain
ISBN 1 873701 35 7 Set of seven vols.

05961884

PPR

An inventory of UK estuaries

This report should be quoted as:

Buck, A.L. 1993. *An inventory of UK estuaries. Volume 3. North-west Britain.*
Peterborough, Joint Nature Conservation Committee.

All sections of this report are authored by A.L. Buck unless otherwise indicated.

An inventory of UK estuaries is being produced in seven volumes. The inventory is
compiled by the Coastal Review Unit of JNCC's Coastal Conservation Branch.
Further reports are in preparation.

© JNCC 1993

ISBN 1 873701 35 7 Set of seven vols.
ISBN 1 873701 36 5 vol. 1. Introduction
ISBN 1 873701 37 3 vol. 2. South-west Britain
ISBN 1 873701 38 1 vol. 3. North-west Britain
ISBN 1 873701 39 X vol. 4. North and east Scotland
ISBN 1 873701 40 3 vol. 5. Eastern England
ISBN 1 873701 41 1 vol. 6. Southern England
ISBN 1 873701 42 X vol. 7. Northern Ireland

Design by Professional Communications Ltd.
Cover design by Nature Conservation Bureau.
Printed by W. Lake.

Sandscale Haws on the Duddon Estuary, which supports a breeding population of the natterjack toad *Bufo calamita*.
(Peter Wakely, English Nature)

Contents

1 Foreword

Professor Peter Evans
Chairman, Department of Biological Sciences, University of Durham

Viewed worldwide, estuaries are a scarce natural resource, even though some in the deltas of great rivers are of immense size. The British Isles are fortunate in holding a large number and variety of types of estuary, particularly when compared with the rest of temperate and Mediterranean Europe. Yet we have not used most of our estuaries either wisely or sustainably, probably for two reasons: first a lack of knowledge of the natural resources they contain and second a lack of understanding of the effects of the human uses to which they have been, or are being, put.

Pollution problems up-river have readily been apparent to anglers and recreational users alike and there have been long-standing campaigns to improve water quality in many of our rivers. These have begun to bear fruit. Many of the larger estuaries have not attracted such concern from the general public in relation to their water quality. People have increasingly turned their backs on the river corridors as they near the sea and looked further afield for clean recreational areas. As a result discharges of industrial and domestic wastes into estuaries have continued on a large scale, though restrictions are gradually being introduced (or even self-imposed by environmentally aware industrial concerns).

Even less obvious to the general public has been the steady loss of intertidal land within estuaries, to land-claim for industrial development and to dredging for the creation of wider and deeper shipping channels and berths needed to accept the larger vessels in which we import more raw material as our own accessible resources of many minerals and chemicals decline. Intertidal and even permanent shallow-water areas of estuaries have been buried under domestic rubbish and other solid wastes, or sometimes permanently flooded for water storage schemes. To these established, though often not sustainable, uses are being added new demands: barrage schemes for power generation, harbour developments for pleasure craft and many others.

Knowledge of the natural resources of the British estuaries has been slow to accumulate. Even one of the most obvious of the biological resources, the bird populations, had not been counted in more than a few of the smaller estuaries before the 'Birds of Estuaries Enquiry', now organised by the BTO, WWT, RSPB, and JNCC, was launched in 1969. The very idea of attempting a count of all the birds using the shores of the Wash in Lincolnshire and Norfolk was considered impractical before a Cambridge Bird Club team, of which I was a member, attempted the task in the mid-1950s. Quantification of other resources has proven even more difficult: fishery catch statistics do not necessarily permit identification of spawning and nursery areas, yet for several species these lie in estuaries and are vital for the continued health of our fish stocks. The role of algae and other plants in stabilising estuarine shores against erosion is only now becoming understood in a more quantitative way though it had been appreciated for more than half a century that planting of the cord-grass *Spartina* provided an extra line of defence against erosion of soft shores.

Now we are faced with the reality of sea level rise and the need for rethinking coastal defences. People have come to appreciate the value of the wildlife resources of estuaries, and industries located on estuaries increasingly appreciate the advantages of developing a 'green image' backed by actions such as the reduction of waste discharges to confirm it. This, therefore, is a particularly appropriate time to launch this *Inventory of UK estuaries*, building on the excellent publication *Nature conservation and estuaries in Great Britain* which appeared in 1991. That book, edited by Dr Davidson, who is a co-author of several of the chapters in these present inventory volumes, was the last major review published by the former Nature Conservancy Council. I am proud to have persuaded my fellow Council members in the mid-1980s to commission that work which has, I believe, influenced attitudes to estuary use in a most positive way.

I well recall, during the Examination in Public of the Teesside Structure Plan in 1975, appealing for a national planning policy to be developed for estuarine use. It was considered impossible at that time. But today there is great enthusiasm including guidance from government for coastal conservation and management, in part as a result of our growing international responsibilities for example in relation to the management of the North Sea, the implementation of the Ramsar Convention on Wetlands of International Importance and the acceptance of the EC Directives on the Conservation of Wild Birds (1979) and Habitats and Species (1992). The need for detailed information to enable sensible estuarine management plans to be formulated not only in a local but also a national and international context has never been greater. I commend these volumes to all interested in the planning, sustainable development, management and conservation of UK estuaries. It is an authoritative base-line from which to prepare for the 21st century.

Peter Evans

Durham, January 1993

2 Introduction

N.C. Davidson & A.L. Buck

Coastlines change continually under the forces of wave, tide, current and wind. In some places along the coast the hard rocks laid down millions of years ago or the softer, more recent, glacial deposits are being eroded. These eroded sediments are transported by currents, often for considerable distances, out into deeper water or along the shore. Much of this sediment is deposited along the coastline: coarse sediments forming shingle and sand beaches, and fine particles forming mudflats in sheltered bays, inlets and river estuaries. All these types of estuary act as 'sediment sinks' that trap much of the sediment moving along the coast. Where the estuary is formed by a river discharging into the sea, particles carried downstream by the rivers are deposited in the reduced currents and shelter of the river mouth, adding to the sediments of marine origin.

In time these sediments build up in estuaries, become stable and parts may become vegetated to provide a complex of habitats. Saltmarsh vegetation colonises intertidal flats that have accumulated to levels above mid-tide height. Where sand is blown onshore there is development of sand dunes, or where larger deposits move onshore shingle ridges develop. In the event of restricted drainage within sand dunes or shingle ridges, or even within saltmarshes, saline lagoons can form. This variety of coastal habitats is often in a state of change, adjusting to the short-term effects of winds, tides, waves and currents, and are shaped by the more gradual changes over periods of thousands of years as sea levels rise and fall.

The inflow of water from rivers and the sea brings a continual influx of nutrients. In river estuaries the freshwater brought down the river meets the saline water from the sea. In some estuaries these water bodies mix well, with tidal movements and variations in river flow creating large variations in water salinity over short periods of time.

The complex of estuarine habitats that develops under these conditions supports a variety of plants and animals which have adapted to exploit the nutrient-rich but continually changing tidal conditions. Relatively few species have evolved to cope with the extremes of constantly changing salinity and tidal levels of river estuaries but those that have often occur in great densities. As a result the estuarine mudflats and saltmarshes in temperate regions such as the United Kingdom are amongst the most productive ecosystems in the world. This rich plant and invertebrate life provides an abundant food supply for predators such as fish, which often use the shelter of estuaries for spawning and as nursery areas. Some species of birds and mammals feed on these fish, whilst many others feed directly on the saltmarsh vegetation and on the abundant molluscs, crustaceans and worms living in soft sediments. The relatively mild winter weather conditions of estuaries in the United Kingdom make them additionally attractive wintering grounds for migratory waterfowl from a large area of the northern hemisphere.

The coastline of the United Kingdom is particularly well endowed with estuaries, and these vary greatly in their geomorphological origins, size, shape, extent of freshwater influence, and the complex of marine and coastal habitats that occur there. These estuaries are widely recognised as one of the greatest natural assets in the UK.

UK estuaries vary greatly also in the extent to which they have been used, changed or destroyed by people exploiting their natural resources. People have used estuaries for many centuries and for many purposes. Some uses, such as ports, exploit the shelter offered by the physical structure of the estuary. Others, for example barrages, control or exploit tidal movements. Many traditional practices depend on sustainable use of the rich natural resources such as fish and shellfish found in estuaries. A recent trend has seen estuaries as the focus for leisure activities, in water, land and air. These range from organised activities such as sailing regattas to informal uses such as walking and the quiet enjoyment of these often spectacular wild landscapes and their wildlife.

Effective conservation of estuaries for their wildlife requires the maintenance of the diversity of the estuarine network throughout Britain and internationally, and the sustainable management of individual estuaries in this network. Yet many parts of estuaries have already been destroyed through human activities leading to land-claim and degradation. Such pressures continue and damage can arise through the subtle interaction of the human urge to control estuaries (e.g. by constructing sea defences against flooding) and the estuaries' natural movement in response to rising sea levels.

There is increasing recognition that managing and maintaining our coasts and estuaries for the future depends on co-operation between the groups of users, coastal managers and decision makers. This co-operation is increasingly being sought through processes of integrated coastal zone planning and management (CZM). Many CZM initiatives are focused on estuaries since it is often here that there is most overlap and potential conflict between people and the natural estuarine resource.

In developing estuary management plans there is a need for sound baseline information on the natural resource and how it is being used. Such information is needed both in detail for the estuary under consideration and more broadly so as to set a particular feature or site in its wider national and international context. To provide this British national context as a baseline for the development of sustainable use objectives, the Nature Conservancy Council (NCC) undertook an Estuaries Review which published *Nature conservation and estuaries in Great Britain* as a national overview of estuaries, their wildlife, their conservation and their human uses (Davidson *et al.* 1991).

An inventory of UK estuaries follows on from this national overview, and provides a summary of resource, wildlife, conservation status and human use features on each of the 163 estuaries identified by the Estuaries Review around the coasts of the United Kingdom. Much of the information presented in the inventory was collated between 1988 and 1991 during the work of the Estuaries Review. Where possible, however, we have included more up-to-date information. Where this more recent information is given the relevant dates are indicated in each display. The inventory thus provides a 'snap-shot' in time for the state of the UK estuarine resource at the end of the 1980s.

An inventory of UK estuaries takes the form of a series of standardised dossiers, taking each estuary (as defined by the Estuaries Review) in turn. Each of these reports gives a summary of the key features of interest or significance for estuary management from a nature conservation perspective. An inventory entry is designed to give initial summary information about a feature and to help direct users to more detailed sources of information should this be required. The inventory is not, however, intended to provide comprehensive listings of plant and animal species recorded on the estuary. Nor can it provide more than the initial basis for the development of practical coastal zone management initiatives such as integrated estuary management plans.

The inventory provides part of a sound information base for estuary management. Taken together with the national overview provided by *Nature conservation and estuaries in Great Britain,* the information in the inventory permits estuary managers to set the resource on a particular estuary in its national and international context - an important stage in the identification of management issues. The inventory should also help understanding of the great importance of the UK estuarine resource by the many user-groups and those involved in decision-making. Its availability for use in matters of development planning and control ensures that there is a readily available single source of summarised information, eliminating the need to search through a great variety of sources in many different styles of presentation. In addition the snap-shot information in the summary provides an easy-to-use basis for broad-scale monitoring of change in the estuarine resource and its human uses.

An inventory of UK estuaries is being published in six regional volumes, most including 20-30 estuary reports. The regions are shown in Figure 1. Boundaries have been chosen largely on topographical grounds to provide meaningful geographical zones. For England and Wales these boundaries coincide broadly with the known divisions of major coastal sediment cells.

There is also an introductory volume (volume 1). This provides more detail of the rationale of the inventory, explanations of the approach to site definition and selection, details of the information sources used for the inventory, and summary tables listing estuary locations and characteristics updated and corrected from those in Davidson *et al.* (1991). Users of the inventory are strongly urged to consult this volume for definitions before undertaking detailed interpretation of site reports. Since many people who have helped with the Estuaries Review and inventory work have contributed to more than one volume we have included a full Acknowledgements

section in this introductory publication rather than in each regional volume.

We give below a brief overview of the overall estuarine resource in this North-west Britain coastal area covered by Volume 3, then a short key to using and interpreting the information entries in each site report, followed by the site reports.

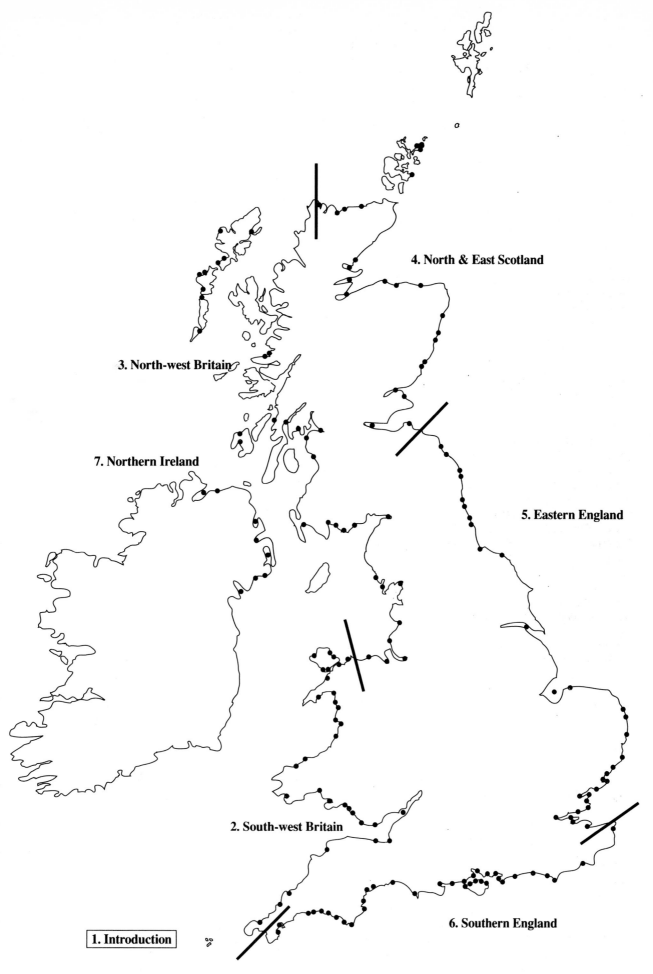

Figure 1 The regional volumes comprising *An inventory of UK estuaries*. Each estuary is marked by its centre grid reference.

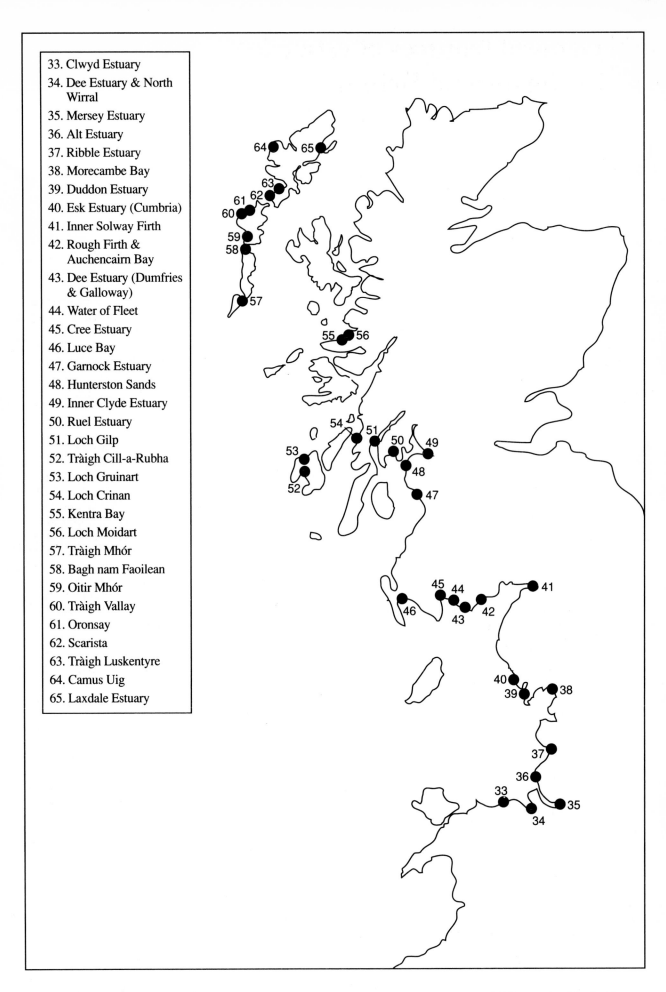

Figure 2 The locations and names of the 33 estuaries covered by Volume 3 of *An inventory of UK estuaries*. See the site map in each regional report for the precise boundaries of the site identified as the core estuary.

3 General features of estuaries in North-west Britain

A.L. Buck & N.C. Davidson

Resource distribution and size

This volume covers the 33 estuaries on the north-west coast of Britain between Great Orme in North Wales and Cape Wrath on the north coast of Scotland. The estuaries within this region fall mainly into two groups. In the southern part of the region are the river estuaries and embayments from the Dee Estuary & North Wirral north to the Solway Firth and along the southern shoreline of Dumfries and Galloway. This Liverpool Bay and Solway Firth area includes an interlinked network of large estuaries. North and west of Luce Bay is a coastline formed mostly of older, harder rocks with landforms strongly influenced by glaciation. Here coastlines are strongly indented and large areas of soft sediments are scattered amid the sounds, embayments and sea lochs of shores that are generally rising relative to sea level. In this region there are many sea lochs with insufficient soft shores for inclusion in this inventory, but the estuaries identified within this area are smaller and occur on the west coast of Scotland and the Western Isles. Figure 2 shows the names and locations of the estuaries covered by this volume.

Eighteen estuaries in the northern part of this North-west Britain region are of fjord or fjard geomorphology, and most of those in the southern part are of coastal plain type. There are smaller numbers of embayments, bar built estuaries and linear shores, and the Inner Solway Firth is of complex origin. Tidal ranges are highest in the southern part of the region. All the estuaries here are macrotidal (i.e. with tidal ranges greater than 4 metres), the largest being at the mouth of the Mersey Estuary (8.9 m), Morecambe Bay and Solway Firth (8.4 m) and the Duddon Estuary (8.1 m). There is a general trend for the tidal ranges to decrease northwards, where the estuaries are generally mesotidal (i.e. with tidal ranges of between 2 and 4 metres) although seven sites just qualify as macrotidal. Tràigh Cill-a-Rubha at the sheltered head of Loch Indaal on the island of Islay has a particularly small tidal range of 1.5 metres.

The largest estuaries within this region are Morecambe Bay (45,462 ha) and the Inner Solway Firth (42,056 ha). The other large estuaries (over 5,000 ha) are mostly within the Liverpool Bay area, namely the Dee Estuary and North Wirral (16,101 ha), the Ribble (11,924 ha) and Mersey Estuaries (8,914 ha). In the north of the region only the Inner Clyde Estuary (5,485 ha) and Oitir Mhór in the Western Isles (5,519 ha) exceed 5,000 ha. In addition only three estuaries in this area (Inner Clyde Estuary, Bagh nam Faoilean and Oitir Mhór) have more than 1,000 ha of intertidal area. The remaining sites, although small, include some of the most unspoilt estuaries in Britain.

The areas and lengths of key features of each estuary are listed in Table 1, and Table 2 provides a summary of the size of the estuarine resource in the North-west Britain region.

Wildlife features

Coastal habitats and aquatic estuarine communities

Estuaries are composed of a mosaic of inter-related subtidal, intertidal and terrestrial habitats, with the relative composition and variety of these habitats depending on a great many physical, chemical and biotic factors. Overall, almost three-quarters of the total area of estuarine habitat in this North-west Britain region is intertidal and in many estuaries this is chiefly represented by sandflats and mudflats. The intertidal flats, especially soft mudflats, of estuaries support important populations of marine worms, molluscs and other invertebrates, often living in high densities and with high biomass. These in turn provide an abundant food supply for estuarine predators, notably fish and migratory waterfowl.

The glacial offshore sediment sources around the Liverpool Bay area contribute to the sediment availability. Many parts of the intertidal flats in these high tidal range estuaries are composed of mobile sediments, since much of the fine silt that would otherwise deposit to form mudflats is held in suspension by high current velocities. This characteristic contributes substantially to the geomorphological interest of such estuaries. Soft mudflats in these estuaries are confined to their more sheltered inlets and bays. In many of the estuaries throughout this region the intertidal flats are a mosaic of both sandflats and mudflats, but in the exposed fjords and fjards of the Western Isles the tidal flats are predominantly sandy.

The intertidal flats of most North-west British estuaries are composed of mosaics of mud and sand. In terms of size, tidal flat distribution is dominated by Morecambe Bay, which contains 29% of the tidal flats in North-west Britain, and is the largest area of tidal flats of any estuary in the UK. Between them, the six largest estuaries in the region (Morecambe Bay, Dee Estuary and North Wirral, Mersey, Ribble and Duddon Estuaries and the Inner Solway Firth) have over 80% of the total area of tidal flats in North-west Britain. This region is of great significance in terms of its tidal flats, for North-west Britain contains almost 40% of the total area of tidal flats in Great Britain.

Saltmarshes play a major role in estuarine processes, both through the cycling of nutrients within the estuary and through their role as 'soft' sea defences dissipating wave energy. In this North-west Britain region saltmarshes are widespread, occurring on 31 estuaries, but they generally form only a very small proportion of the intertidal area. Only in Morecambe Bay, Inner Solway Firth, Ribble Estuary and the Dee Estuary and North Wirral are there extensive areas of saltmarsh, and in the Ribble Estuary these occupy over 20% of the intertidal area of the estuary. In total, eight estuaries in the region (Dee Estuary and North Wirral, Mersey and Ribble Estuaries, Morecambe Bay, Duddon Estuary, Inner Solway Firth, Cree and Ruel

Table 1 Areas, shoreline and channel lengths and mean spring tidal range measurements for estuaries in North-west Britain.

Estuary	Area (ha)	Intertidal area (ha)	Saltmarsh (ha)	Shoreline (km)	Channel length (km)	Tidal range (m)
33. Clwyd Estuary	422	386	43	19.1	8.1	6.7
34. Dee Estuary & North Wirral	16,101	12,981	2,108	108.5	36.8	7.6
35. Mersey Estuary	8,914	5,606	847	102.9	15.6	8.9
36. Alt Estuary	1,413	1,413	1	14.0	5.2	8.0
37. Ribble Estuary	11,924	10,674	2,184	107.5	28.4	7.9
38. Morecambe Bay	45,462	34,339	3,253	266.5	40.3	8.4
39. Duddon Estuary	6,092	5,056	537	65.5	22.6	8.1
40. Esk Estuary (Cumbria)	1,134	1,049	158	42.2	11.4	7.7
41. Inner Solway Firth	42,056	27,550	2,925	213.6	46.3	8.4
42. Rough Firth & Auchencairn Bay	1,290	1,289	135	44.4	14.4	6.7
43. Dee Estuary (D & G)	1,144	825	77	28.6	11.7	6.7
44. Water of Fleet	790	790	28	19.9	7.2	6.7
45. Cree Estuary	4,728	3,340	445	24.3	63.2	6.7
46. Luce Bay	1,228	1,196	36	27.5	8.5	5.3
47. Garnock Estuary	204	161	30	14.7	5.6	3.2
48. Hunterston Sands	291	291	0	16.4	0	2.9
49. Inner Clyde Estuary	5,485	1,841	67	129.7	41.9	3.0
50. Ruel Estuary	426	184	7	15.4	6.7	3.0
51. Loch Gilp	245	143	0	6.8	3.4	3.1
52. Tràigh Cill-a-Rubha	639	288	40	8.6	3.0	1.5
53. Loch Gruinart	973	876	51	18.7	8.1	3.1
54. Loch Crinan	280	168	47	15.3	6.2	3.7
55. Kentra Bay	338	313	41	13.4	4.9	4.3
56. Loch Moidart	881	469	24	34.9	10.1	4.3
57. Tràigh Mhór	242	210	0	6.5	0	3.7
58. Bagh nam Faoilean	2,144	1,264	35	37.5	10.9	4.1
59. Oitir Mhór	5,519	4,028	114	292.4	13.3	4.1
60. Tràigh Vallay	1,113	823	15	22.9	6.9	4.1
61. Oronsay	1,278	825	6	29.9	6.3	4.1
62. Scarista	290	290	40	7.5	0	3.8
63. Tràigh Luskentyre	344	344	32	11.5	4.1	3.8
64. Camus Uig	438	214	10	18.0	5.5	3.6
65. Laxdale Estuary	559	390	96	12.8	4.7	4.1

Table 2 Total areas and lengths of the regional estuarine resource in North-west Britain.

Total area (ha)	Subtidal area (ha)	Intertidal area (ha)	Intertidal flats (ha)	Saltmarsh (ha)	Shoreline (km)	Channel length (km)
164,387	44,771	119,616	106,184	13,432	1,797.4	461.3

Estuaries) contain nationally important saltmarshes. That is, they support a full and representative sequence of plant communities covering the variation found in Great Britain. The total area of saltmarsh in the region (13,432 ha) is over 30% of the British saltmarsh resource.

In the northern part of the region, there has been much less human interference with saltmarshes, and these northern marshes are important for the presence of natural transitions to non-tidal vegetation, notably grasslands. Transitional grassland communities occur on twelve estuaries in this region, which total 63% of British estuaries with this feature.

The cord-grass *Spartina anglica* is now found in estuaries in the Liverpool Bay and Solway Firth areas, and in two estuaries (Rough Firth and Auchencairn Bay and Water of Fleet) *Spartina* now forms over half the saltmarsh area. In contrast to some estuaries in southern England where areas of *Spartina* are now decreasing, *Spartina* is still spreading in many of these places although it forms a much smaller proportion of saltmarsh area than in the south. On at least seven estuaries in the region *Spartina* was deliberately planted between 1921 and 1951 to encourage dune stabilisation. Now attempts to control *Spartina* are occurring on four estuaries. However, in most of the estuaries on the Scottish coast there is little or no *Spartina* present.

There are particularly extensive sand dune systems on the west coast of Britain, where the high-energy environment and the conditions of prevailing and dominant winds combine to form large accumulations of sand. Sixteen estuaries in North-west Britain have associated sand dune systems, of which eight are of national importance. These include the Sefton Coast dune system which extends from the Alt to the Ribble Estuary, North Walney and Sandscale on the Duddon Estuary, Ravenglass on the Esk Estuary, Torrs Warren on Luce Bay, Killinallan Dunes on Loch Gruinart, Baleshare Machair to the west of Oitir Mhór and Northton Bay on Scarista. Overall nineteen estuaries have at least a small area of sand dunes within their habitat mosaic.

There is only one substantial shingle structure associated with estuaries in North-west Britain, namely Walney Island which lies between the Duddon Estuary to the north and Morecambe Bay to the south. Walney Island is a barrier island, a product of erosion and the reworking of glacial boulder clay, and has become vegetated towards its southern end. A sand dune system has developed over the north of the island. Many other estuaries within North-west Britain have patches of bare intertidal shingle, and shingle is found on over half (nineteen) of the estuaries in this region.

Coastal saline lagoons are scarce in North-west Britain, and associated with only two estuaries in the region. Within Morecambe Bay there is a saline lagoon system at the southernmost tip of Walney Island; and on the Duddon Estuary, Hodbarrow Lagoon is a large pool separated from the sea by an artificial sea wall.

The largest areas of coastal grazing marshes and other lowland grasslands are outside the North-west Britain area covered in this volume, but twelve of the estuaries have some associated grazing marsh remaining. The grazing

marshes of those estuaries within the Liverpool Bay area are often sited on former intertidal areas of the estuary which have undergone land-claim, for example large areas on the Dee & North Wirral and Ribble Estuaries. In contrast, the grasslands associated with the estuaries on the north-west coasts of Scotland are chiefly areas of machair. These form part of the very extensive mosaic of dune grasslands and wetlands especially along the western shores of the Outer Hebrides, most of which are not directly associated with estuaries.

The aquatic estuarine benthic communities of many of the estuaries within this North-west Britain region have been recorded and several sites are known to be of great marine biological and conservation importance. The diversity of both soft substrate and hard substrate communities within this region is generally lower than that of estuaries in South and South-west England, with the largest recorded diversity (more than five communities) in the Duddon Estuary, Inner Solway Firth, Rough Firth and Auchencairn Bay and Dee Estuary (Dumfries and Galloway). In general the estuaries on the west coast of Scotland and the Western Isles support lower numbers of aquatic estuarine communities, but these sites include Tràigh Cill-a-Rubha within the Loch Indaal Marine Consultation Area, and Bagh nam Faoilean, which supports a rich example of the sand/muddy sand community and rocky shore communities considered to be of national marine biological importance.

Plant and animal species

At least four estuaries within the North-west Britain region support nationally rare species of vascular plants. The extensive sand dune systems associated with the Ribble and Duddon Estuaries support two of the four estuarine populations of the nationally rare endemic dune helleborine *Epipactis dunensis;* Morecambe Bay supports a population of goldilocks *Aster linosyris* on coastal grassland; and holy-grass *Hierochloe odorata* and sticky catchfly *Lychnis viscaria* have been recorded on the Inner Solway Firth.

The nationally scarce endemic Isle of Man cabbage *Rhynchosinapis monensis* is locally common on sandy beaches in the North-west of Britain. All of the six estuaries on which it occurs are in this North-west Britain region, from the Alt Estuary northwards to the Garnock Estuary. Other nationally scarce plants have also been recorded on Loch Gruinart and the Duddon Estuary, and at least seven species have been found on the Inner Solway Firth. In addition, a site within the Dee Estuary and North Wirral is the only known site in England where Mackay's horsetail *Equisetum* x *trachyodon* has been found.

The terrestrial invertebrate faunas of saltmarshes on estuaries in North-west Britain are generally rather poorly known compared with those of southern and eastern England. However, the Altcar sand dunes of the Alt Estuary, the Ainsdale and Formby Dunes of the Alt and Ribble Estuaries, and the Sandscale Haws dunes of the Duddon Estuary are of note for their invertebrate assemblages. The variety of habitats on South Walney within Morecambe Bay are also known to support a number of coastal moths, and the saltmarshes and shingle of the Solway Estuary are of note for a number of beetles and flies.

The estuaries of North-west Britain support a variety of adult fish species and are spawning and nursery areas for others. Tràigh Luskentyre supports a good salmon fishery and the tidal creeks of the Duddon and Mersey Estuaries are the most northerly nurseries in Britain for sea bass *Dicentrarchus labrax*. The Cree Estuary is also of importance for smelt *Osmerus eperlanus* which uses the estuary for spawning, one of only three locations in Scotland. There are also recent records of smelt in the upper parts of the Dee Estuary and North Wirral.

The extensive dune and marsh systems of North-west Britain are the major stronghold for the natterjack toad *Bufo calamita*. The dunes associated with five of these estuaries (Inner Solway Firth, Esk, Duddon, Ribble and Alt Estuaries) together support at least 81% of the British population. There are also smaller populations on the dunes association with Morecambe Bay and the Dee Estuary and North Wirral. In addition the sand dunes of the Sefton Coast (Ribble and Alt Estuaries) support an isolated population of the nationally rare sand lizard *Lacerta agilis*, amounting to an estimated 5% of the British population.

Many estuaries in the UK are of great importance to migratory and wintering waterfowl (waders and wildfowl), and the habitat mosaics of estuaries in this part of North-west Britain provide feeding and roosting sites for many waterfowl species. Many of these birds, which come from a vast area of arctic and boreal breeding grounds between Canada and Siberia, are wholly or largely dependent on estuaries during their non-breeding period. The estuaries from the Liverpool Bay area north to the Solway Firth region generally support large waterfowl populations, while the smaller, sandier estuaries along the more northern shores support smaller total numbers of waterfowl. Overall the estuaries in North-west Britain hold over 527,000 waterfowl in midwinter (January), some 30% of the British estuarine population in that month. The relatively mild winter weather on these west coast estuaries can be of critical importance to the survival of wintering waterfowl during periods of severe weather. At such times waterfowl move west to estuaries, including those in the Liverpool Bay area, to escape freezing weather in continental Europe and eastern Britain.

Since migratory waterfowl depend on a network of estuaries during their year, many birds move between estuaries, even during the winter period, so that the total number of individuals using a site is considerably higher than those present at any one time. Average peak winter counts of waterfowl suggest that at least 870,000 birds may be using the estuaries covered by this volume during the winter period, and as the bird populations of several sites in the extreme north-west of this region are not regularly counted sites, this figure is an underestimate.

Eleven of these estuaries in North-west Britain attain international importance by supporting over 1% of the flyway population of at least one waterfowl species. Seven of these estuaries are currently also of international importance for supporting over 20,000 waterfowl during winter. Numbers of wintering waterfowl exceed 100,000 on four of these estuaries (Dee Estuary & North Wirral, Ribble Estuary, Morecambe Bay and Inner Solway Firth), making this one of the most important parts of the British coastline for waterfowl.

There is over 1% of the flyway population of at least 20 species or biogeographic populations of waterfowl on some of the estuaries in North-west Britain. These species are: whooper swan *Cygnus cygnus*, pink-footed goose *Anser brachyrhynchus*, Greenland white-fronted goose *Anser albifrons flavirostris*, barnacle goose *Branta leucopsis* (both Greenland- and Svalbard-breeding populations), shelduck *Tadorna tadorna*, wigeon *Anas penelope*, teal *Anas crecca*, pintail *A. strepera*, oystercatcher *Haematopus ostralegus*, grey plover *Pluvialis squatorola*, lapwing *Vanellus vanellus*, knot *Calidris canutus*, sanderling *C. alba*, dunlin *C. alpina*, black-tailed godwit *Limosa limosa*, bar-tailed godwit *L. lapponica*, curlew *Numenius arquata*, redshank *Tringa totanus* and turnstone *Arenaria interpres*. A further two estuarine sites in North-west Britain (Clwyd Estuary and Garnock Estuary) support nationally important populations of waterfowl. Of particular interest is the entire Svalbard-breeding population of barnacle geese wintering on the Solway Firth, and the two estuaries on Islay (Tràigh Cill-a-Rubha and Loch Gruinart) are of great importance as roosting sites for many of the Islay-wintering populations of Greenland white-fronted goose and barnacle goose. Many of the other estuaries in the region contribute to the geographical network upon which waterfowl depend, and together provide wintering grounds for at least 49,000 birds.

Outside the wintering period, many estuaries throughout the North-west Britain region have additional importance as staging and moulting areas in autumn and spring for migratory waterfowl populations. During these periods birds pass through rapidly so that many more individuals depend on these estuaries than are present at any one time. Overall this part of the estuarine resource, especially from the Dee Estuary and North Wirral to the Inner Solway Firth, may be the most important in Britain for spring migrant waders, especially sanderling, ringed plover, turnstone, knot and Iceland-breeding dunlin. In autumn some of the largest concentrations of migrant and moulting waders in Europe occur on this coast, particularly in Morecambe Bay, the Ribble Estuary and the Dee Estuary and North Wirral.

The saltmarshes, shingle banks and coastal grazing marshes around the estuaries also support breeding populations of waders (chiefly redshank, oystercatcher, lapwing and ringed plover *Charadrius hiaticula*). The most diverse assemblages are on the Inner Solway Firth (seven species), Morecambe Bay, Bagh nam Faoilean, Oitir Mhór, Tràigh Vallay and Oronsay (six species). The machair grasslands and marshes associated with these latter four estuaries on the Uists in the Western Isles support particularly large numbers of breeding waders, including internationally important breeding populations of ringed plover.

Groups of grey seals *Halichoerus gryphus* regularly use several estuaries within the region. A non-breeding group using the Dee Estuary and North Wirral has increased in number to over 300 individuals in the 1980s, and smaller numbers of seals are regularly recorded in the Mersey, Ribble, Morecambe Bay and Duddon Estuaries. Otters *Lutra lutra* are common on estuaries in North-west Britain, and are known to live on 20 of the 25 estuaries north of the Inner Solway Firth. In the Liverpool Bay area they have been recorded upstream of the tidal limit on the

Clwyd Estuary, Dee Estuary and North Wirral and Morecambe Bay only.

Conservation status

The important and diverse wildlife and landscape features of much of the UK estuarine resource has been recognised by many parts of estuaries and their surroundings being designated under a variety of local, national and international measures, both statutory and non-statutory. The estuaries of North-west Britain are typical of this pattern in which there are often many overlapping site designations covering parts of an estuary. In addition to this site-based approach through which much of estuarine conservation has traditionally been delivered, some of the estuaries covered in this report (Dee Estuary and North Wirral, Mersey and Ribble Estuaries, Morecambe Bay, Duddon Estuary and Inner Solway Firth) are now also included in a variety of coastal zone planning and management initiatives.

Sites of Special Scientific Interest (SSSIs), the major statutory designations for the delivery of site-based wildlife conservation, cover many parts of the intertidal and associated terrestrial areas of North-west Britain. At least one SSSI is associated with all but four (Clwyd Estuary, Loch Gilp, Bagh nam Faoilean, and Camus Uig) of the estuaries covered by this volume, although SSSIs, like most other designations, cover only parts of each estuary. On some estuaries, such as the Dee Estuary (Dumfries & Galloway) and Water of Fleet, SSSIs cover little of the core estuary area.

In all there are 60 SSSIs in this region, 18% of estuarine SSSIs in Great Britain. Morecambe Bay currently has the largest number of SSSIs (thirteen) associated with an estuary in this area. SSSIs on Morecambe Bay are typical of those on many estuaries – a mixture of small SSSIs notified for their geological and geomorphological features and a few larger sites of biological or mixed interest covering tidal flats, saltmarshes and associated terrestrial habitats. Other estuaries in the region covered by four or more SSSIs are the Dee Estuary and North Wirral, the Ribble Estuary and the Inner Clyde Estuary. SSSIs associated with estuaries in this region cover a total of 138,998 ha (36% of the British estuarine SSSI area), with by far the largest areas of SSSI being on Morecambe Bay, the Inner Solway Firth, the Dee Estuary and North Wirral, and the Ribble Estuary.

Seven of the 42 declared estuarine National Nature Reserves (NNRs) in Britain are on the intertidal or terrestrial habitats of the estuaries covered by this volume. These include several areas of intertidal flats or saltmarshes, e.g. Ribble Marshes (Ribble Estuary), Caerlaverock (Inner Solway Firth) and North Walney (Duddon Estuary). Others include the extensive Ainsdale Sand Dunes (Alt and Ribble Estuaries), Roudsea Woods and Moss (Morecambe Bay) and Moine Mhor adjacent to the upper reaches of Loch Crinan.

One estuary within the region also falls within the non-statutory Marine Consultation Areas (MCAs), namely Tràigh Cill-a-Rubha which lies at the head of Loch Indaal MCA.

Local Nature Reserves are statutory designations made by local authorities (in consultation with country conservation agencies) with objectives similar to those of NNRs but in the local interest of the site and its wildlife. Of the 33 designated LNRs which occur on estuaries, four lie within the region: Hilbre Island (Dee Estuary and North Wirral), Ravenmeols Hills (Alt Estuary), Ainsdale and Birkdale Hills, Lytham St Anne's Dunes (Ribble Estuary) and Drigg Dunes & Gullery (Esk Estuary).

Two international designations are particularly relevant to estuarine habitats and their birds. The Ramsar Convention designates wetlands of international importance especially as waterfowl habitat (Ramsar sites) and Special Protection Areas (SPAs) designated under the EC Directive on the conservation of wild birds. For estuarine waterfowl populations both designations often apply. Parts of the Dee Estuary and North Wirral, Alt Estuary, Inner Solway Firth, Tràigh Cill-a-Rubha and Loch Gruinart have been designated as Ramsar sites and SPAs, and the Ribble is also a designated SPA. There are proposals for Ramsar/SPA sites which would include parts of the Mersey Estuary, Morecambe Bay, Duddon, Esk and Cree Estuaries, Luce Bay, Inner Clyde Estuary, Tràigh Mhór, Bagh nam Faoilean, Oitir Mhór, and Oronsay. There are proposals for a single Ramsar/SPA site incorporating both the Ribble and Alt Estuaries, for single Ramsar/SPA sites can include more than one estuary since international site boundaries are set to cover areas linked by known movements of bird populations.

Other wildlife conservation sites include County Wildlife Trust reserves on six estuaries, RSPB reserves on or adjacent to the Dee Estuary and North Wirral, Morecambe Bay, Duddon Estuary, Inner Clyde Estuary and Loch Gruinart, and the Wildfowl and Wetlands Trust reserve at Caerlaverock on the Inner Solway Firth.

There are, in addition, several landscape conservation designations that partly cover estuaries in North-west Britain. The Lake District National Park overlaps with three estuaries (Morecambe Bay, Duddon and Esk Estuaries) and parts of Morecambe Bay and the Inner Solway Firth fall within Areas of Outstanding Natural Beauty. Twelve of the fifteen estuaries within National Scenic Areas (a Scottish landscape designation) are within the North-west Britain region. In addition there are Country Parks adjacent to three estuaries in North-west Britain (Dee Estuary and North Wirral, Mersey Estuary and Morecambe Bay) and there are National Trust properties on eight estuaries in the North-west Britain region.

Features of human use

Many parts of the coastline of North-west Britain are largely natural and little affected by damaging human activities. Rather few people live close to many of the estuaries covered in this volume. A major exception is the Mersey Estuary (> 500,000 population). Elsewhere, only the Liverpool Bay estuaries of the Dee Estuary and North Wirral, Ribble Estuary and Morecambe Bay and the Inner Clyde Estuary have nearby urban populations exceeding 50,000 people, and the majority of the remaining estuaries have nearby populations of less than 5,000 people. Hence there are few parts of the estuarine resource in North-west Britain that have been subjected to the major urban and industrial pressures characteristic of estuaries close to

large conurbations. The more typical human uses of many estuaries in North-west Britain are the exploitation of natural resources and recreation.

Few estuaries in North-west Britain have been subjected to substantial sea defence measures such as construction of sea walls. This is due, in part, to land areas rising relative to sea level (isostatic rebound after the last ice age), particularly in North-west Scotland. As a result, the erosion problems which often lead to the construction of major sea defences are not as significant in North-west Britain as they are, for example, in South-east England. Also, as many estuaries are incised steeply into hard rock systems, they are not surrounded by substantial low-lying areas that need defending. Only four estuaries in the region have artificial sea defences along more than 50% of their shoreline, namely the Dee Estuary and North Wirral, Ribble Estuary, Hunterston Sands and the Inner Clyde Estuary. In many areas there are long stretches of natural transitions from intertidal to terrestrial habitats.

Despite this overall pattern of low-intensity use of estuaries, there are a number of places where intensive human use occurs and where there has been substantial loss and damage to the estuarine resource. For example, there have been very extensive areas of historical land-claim on some estuaries such as the Dee Estuary and North Wirral, where around 6,000 ha have been claimed since 1730 (some 27% of the former total area of the estuary), and the Ribble Estuary, where 2,230 ha have been claimed since 1800 (16 % of the former total area). Substantial further land-claim of saltmarshes for agricultural use has historically created coastal grazing marshes on a number of estuaries e.g. the Ribble Estuary, but as has occurred on many sites considerable parts of the resource have been subsequently further altered through intense agricultural use or urban spread.

Heavy industrial activities are concentrated on the larger estuaries, notably the Mersey Estuary where extensive dock systems, power stations and a series of industrial sites stretch along both shores of the estuary; Morecambe Bay where there are large industries at Barrow-in-Furness, Ulverston, Heysham and Brine Wells; and the Inner Clyde Estuary, the shores of which are dominated by industry, large ports and oil terminals. At least twelve other estuaries have small ports and harbour facilities. In the past, several of these more industrial estuaries in North-west Britain have suffered chronic pollution from sewage and industrial discharges. The Mersey and Garnock Estuaries are typical examples, with both recently showing signs of improvement.

Other urban and infrastructure developments have, and are, altering estuarine features. Three of the estuaries on which housing and car-park developments were taking place in 1989 were in North-west Britain: the Mersey Estuary, in association with re-development of some of the now disused docks, the Duddon Estuary and the Inner Solway Firth. There have also been a number of further proposals for such developments in this region.

The coastlines of North-west Britain are largely undeveloped, and are popular spots for tourism and recreation. A wide variety of leisure pursuits, from general beach use and bathing to water-based recreation, take place on parts of these estuaries, especially during the summer months. This is particularly true for the estuaries of the Liverpool Bay area which are easily accessible and close to large population centres, and recreational pursuits along these shores can be intensive in some areas. On some sites these activities can be detrimental to the habitats and wildlife of the estuary. For example attention has been focused recently on damage to dune systems on the Sefton Coast by recreational activities, and on disturbance to waterfowl on the Dee Estuary and North Wirral. To avoid this, on some sites, such as the Sefton Coast, the use of the sand dunes and beaches for leisure pursuits has to be carefully managed. Further north, along the coast of Scotland, estuaries are still used for recreation, but this is usually at much lower intensity.

Alongside recreation there are a variety of traditional land uses which exploit the natural plant and animal resources of these west coast estuaries. Stock grazing of saltmarshes, especially by sheep, is widespread, as is grazing of stable sand dunes. Other resource use includes fish-netting, shrimping, dredging for mussels, mollusc cultivation and cockle fisheries, e.g. on Morecambe Bay and the Inner Solway Firth. There are also fish farms on two estuaries within the region (Oitir Mhór and the Ruel Estuary).

As in South-west Britain, the high tidal ranges of estuaries in the southern part of this North-west Britain region have focused attention on the possibilities of creating tidal power barrages across the mouths of these estuaries. In 1989 potential for tidal power generation had been identified on the Duddon Estuary, the Wyre Estuary of Morecambe Bay and the Mersey Estuary, and an earlier proposal for a barrage on the Inner Solway Firth had not been dropped entirely. There was also a proposal for a leisure barrage associated with housing and marina development on Loch Gilp. Active investigations for the tidal power barrages on the Duddon and Mersey Estuaries were continuing in 1992.

Whilst this is only a brief overview of some of the key features of the estuaries of North-west Britain and their human uses, it is clear that this network of estuaries is both of great interest and value for wildlife and has a wide variety of human uses. Despite some areas of considerable degradation and past land-claim, and some proposals such as barrages that would further alter the ecosystem processes on important parts of the resource, many estuaries in this part of Britain have been subject to largely sustainable human exploitation. There is great opportunity therefore for all those involved in using and managing these estuaries to collaborate, through such approaches as integrated coastal zone management. Such future management can ensure that this wild and beautiful part of Britain's estuarine heritage continues to be used in sustainable ways that allow for the retention of its varied wildlife.

4 Using the inventory

A.L. Buck

This section provides some brief descriptions and keys to interpreting the presentations of information in the site reports. Full descriptions of the methodology, information sources and presentations are given in Volume 1 (Introduction) of the inventory.

The rationale for site definition and selection follows that developed by Davidson *et al.* (1991). It should be noted that some of the information collated by Davidson *et al.* (1991) has been updated and corrected in some instances, and that the core estuary sites as presented in the inventory now include some adjacent intertidal areas treated separately in the Estuaries Review (also see below).

A short key to the inventory

Inventory sites are numbered and presented in clockwise sequence from Land's End. Note, however, that the numbering of estuaries in Northern Ireland follows on from those in Great Britain. Where data was collected or measured from sources other than the Estuaries Review or Coastal Review Unit, these sources are identified below. Information refers to the period 1988-1990 unless otherwise stated.

Site map

Sites were selected for inclusion in the Estuaries Review and inventory using a definition of an estuary based on that developed by NERC (1975): a partially enclosed area at least partly composed of soft tidal shores, open to saline water from the sea, and receiving fresh water from rivers, land run-off or seepage.

For the inventory only sites with a tidal channel longer than 2 km or sites with a shore width of over 0.5 km at low water along a shoreline greater than 2 km are included. The upstream limit is normally taken as the Normal Tidal Limit (NTL), the upper shoreline limit is an interpreted high water mark approximating to the highest astronomical tides (EHWS), and seaward limits are set as either a 'bay closing line' or 'across mouth' (XM) or an 'along shore' (AS) set by the low water mark. On sites that are not isolated from their neighbours, an arbitrary boundary 'between adjacent estuaries' (BAE) has been set, usually at the mid-point of the shore between the sites, or where the intertidal zone is at its narrowest. Note that the low water mark is that shown on 1:50,000 O.S. maps - mean low water in England and Wales, low water spring tides in Scotland.

The approach used for the Estuaries Review and inventory has been to locate a 'core site' of intertidal and subtidal habitats. The core site boundary is shown on the site map. For a few estuaries we have, in addition, defined adjacent areas of 'associated intertidal' habitat where this is outside the inventory estuary mouth but has a functional link to the estuary, for example where the area forms part of an estuarine structure when considered at larger scale, or where there are links through area use by mobile wildlife.

It is difficult to define standard geographical zones for the inclusion of terrestrial habitats associated with estuaries. For this reason we have followed the Estuaries Review in collating information for an 'associated terrestrial' zone that varies in extent between sites, but which includes functional units of maritime-influenced wildlife habitat and areas of human use that closely affect the core estuary.

Estuary size characteristics and description

Measurements of *total area* and *intertidal area* have been rounded to the nearest 1 ha.

Shore length and *channel length* measurements have been rounded to the nearest 0.1 km.

Tidal ranges have been derived from High and Low Water for Mean Spring Tides for the site closest to the defined estuary mouth, from Hewitt & Lees-Spalding. (1988).

Human population gives numbers of people living in towns reaching within 1 km of the tidal shore, from the results of the 1981 population census. Population figures greater than 5,000 have been rounded off to the nearest 1,000.

Water quality descriptions are from the DoE River Quality in England and Wales Survey 1991, (National Rivers Authority 1991) and the Water Quality Survey of Scotland 1985 (Scottish Development Department 1987).

Wildlife features

All *coastal habitat* areas are rounded to the nearest 1 ha. Areas for sandflats and mudflats were not measured separately, and are given as a combined figure. Saltmarsh areas are derived from NCC's *Saltmarsh survey of Great Britain* (Burd 1989).

Aquatic estuarine communities. The classification of aquatic estuarine communities - subtidal and intertidal marine communities of substrates not vegetated by higher plants - was prepared by the Estuaries Review using methodology developed by the Marine Nature Conservation Review (MNCR). The Estuaries Review classification was prepared before completion of all relevant survey work by MNCR so this classification should be treated as preliminary. It is being developed further by MNCR. Information on the presence of these benthic communities (rather than the substrates on which they occur) was not available during the review for all sites, although further work is in progress. The benthic plant and animal communities are divided into two broad categories: those on soft substrates and those on hard substrates, and are further divided into communities describable largely on their physico-chemical characteristics. Some of the communities occur on both the intertidal and subtidal parts of estuaries. Communities are as follows:

Soft substrates

1. Gravel/shell gravel community
2. Maerl beds
3. Exposed sand community
4. Clean sand community
5. Common mussel beds
6. Horse mussel beds
7. European oyster beds
8. Surface algal community
9. Current-swept sand community
10. Sand/muddy sand community
11. Muddy gravel community
12. Muddy 'offshore' sand community
13. Normal/variable salinity muddy community
14. *Zostera* and *Ruppia* beds
15. Variable/reduced salinity mud community
16. Reduced salinity mud community

Hard substrates

17. Exposed rocky shore community
18. Moderately exposed rocky shore community
19. Sheltered rocky shore community
20. Variable salinity rocky shore community
21. Reduced (variable) salinity rocky shore community
22. Reduced salinity rocky shore community
23. *Sabellaria* reef community
24. Current-exposed sheltered rocky shore community
25. Exposed rock community
26. Sheltered rock community
27. Hydrozoan/bryozoan turf community
28. Slipper limpet beds
29. Artificial substrata community
30. Variable salinity rock community
31. Variable salinity clay community
32. Reduced (variable) salinity rock community
33. Reduced salinity rock community

Birds. Major sources of information on wintering waders and wildfowl are the BTO/JNCC/RSPB Birds of Estuaries Enquiry (BoEE) co-ordinated by the British Trust for Ornithology, and the National Wildfowl Count (NWC) operated by the Wildfowl and Wetlands Trust. Information in the inventory is calculated from five year peak monthly counts for waterfowl for the winters 1986/87 - 1990/91. The proportions of international and national populations of individual species are shown where these are of national or international importance ($\geq$1% of the relevant population except where this value is <50 birds).

Information for some estuaries or parts of estuaries not regularly covered by the BoEE is included from the BTO/WSG Winter Shorebird Count from midwinter 1984/85. Breeding bird data comes from the JNCC/Seabird Group's Seabird Colony Register and a variety of other national, regional and local surveys (see Volume 1 for details).

Additional wildlife features. Information presented here includes: nationally rare plants i.e. those found in fifteen or fewer 10 km squares in Great Britain (from the Rare Plants Database); Red Data Book (RDB) terrestrial invertebrates (from JNCC's Invertebrate Site Register - ISR); and a variety of other recorded features of conservation interest, for example rare fish, amphibians, reptiles and mammals. Note that 'recently recorded' species of terrestrial invertebrate have been recorded since 1970.

Conservation status

The presence of both statutory and non-statutory wildlife and landscape conservation sites is shown. Known proposals for Sites of Special Scientific Interest, National Nature Reserves, Local Nature Reserves, 'Ramsar' sites and Special Protection Areas are also indicated where these were in their final stages of preparation for designation during completion of the inventory.

Abbreviations to the designations are as follows:

NCR	Nature Conservation Review site
GCR	Geological Conservation Review site
SSSI (B)	Site of Special Scientific Interest (biological)
SSSI (G)	Site of Special Scientific Interest (geological and/or geomorphological)
SSSI (M)	Site of Special Scientific Interest (mixed biological and geological/geomorphological)
NNR	National Nature Reserve
LNR	Local Nature Reserve
Ramsar	Wetland of International Importance (Ramsar Convention)
SPA	Special Protection Area (EC Directive on the conservation of wild birds)
AONB	Area of Outstanding Natural Beauty (Countryside Commission)
CWT	County Wildlife Trust reserve
RSPB	Royal Society for the Protection of Birds reserve
ESA	Environmentally Sensitive Area (MAFF)
NP	National Park (England and Wales only)
WWT	Wildfowl and Wetlands Trust centre/reserve
NT	National Trust land
NSA	National Scenic Area (Scotland only)
HC	Heritage Coast (Countryside Commission)
Other	Marine Nature Reserves, Areas of Special Protection, Country Parks etc.

Human use

Features of human use data were collected and collated largely between February and June 1989 (from a wide variety of sources chiefly through members of NCC's regional staff with responsibility for conservation management for each estuary). Activities listed as 'Present' and/or 'Proposed' indicate that status only during that period. Proposals include both those developments subject to consent applications and those subject to less formal public discussion and/or investigation. When more recent information is available, changes since 1989 in present activities or the status of proposals are noted in the text, as are major proposals that have arisen since 1989.

Categories of human use. The bar chart shows, for each broad use category, the percentage of activity types in that category known to occur in 1989. For a fuller explanation of this analysis see the introductory volume of the Inventory.

Further reading

Further reading lists selected references containing further information on the estuary and its wildlife. Note that not all this further reading refers to detailed scientific studies: some sources are general or are historical descriptions of life on these estuaries or are even part of the extensive fictional literature that describes estuaries.

References

Buck, A.L. In prep. *An inventory of UK estuaries.*
    Volume 6. Southern England.
    Peterborough, Joint Nature Conservation Committee.

Burd, F. 1989. *Saltmarsh survey of Great Britain.*
    Peterborough, Nature Conservancy Council.
    (Research and survey in nature conservation, No. 17.)

Davidson, N.C., & Buck, A.L. 1993.
    An inventory of UK estuaries. Volume 1. Introduction.
    Peterborough, Joint Nature Conservation Committee.

Davidson, N.C., Laffoley, D.A., Doody, J.P., Way, L.S.,
    Gordon, J., Key, R., Drake, C.M., Pienkowski, M.W.,
    Mitchell, R., & Duff, K.L. 1991.
    Nature conservation and estuaries in Great Britain.
    Peterborough, Nature Conservancy Council.

Hewitt, R.L., & Lees-Spalding, I.J. *eds.* 1988.
    The Macmillan & Silk Cut Almanac.
    London, Macmillan.

National Rivers Authority. 1991. *The quality of rivers,*
    canals and estuaries in England and Wales.
    Bristol, National Rivers Authority.
    (Water quality series, No. 4)

Natural Environment Research Council. 1975.
    Estuaries research.
    NERC Publications Series 'B', No. 9.

Scottish Development Department. 1987.
    Water quality survey of Scotland 1985.
    Edinburgh, HMSO.

5 | The estuaries

A.L. Buck

Upper Solway Flats and Marshes. The geomorphology of the saltmarshes within the Solway Estuary is outstanding.
(Peter Wakely, English Nature)

33	Clwyd Estuary

Centre grid: SJ0080   District: Colwyn, Rhuddlan
County: Clwyd   CCW region: North Wales

Review site location

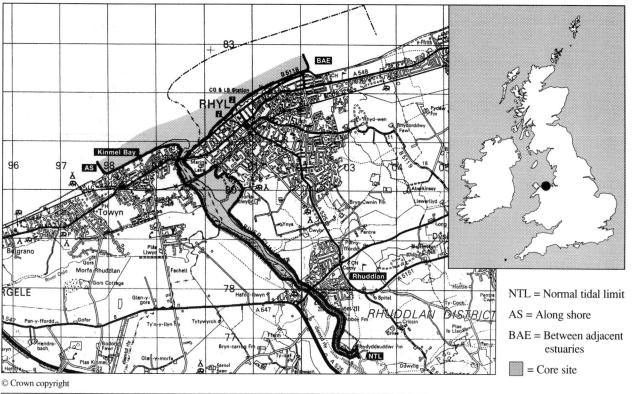

© Crown copyright

NTL = Normal tidal limit

AS = Along shore

BAE = Between adjacent estuaries

▨ = Core site

Total area (ha)	Intertidal area (ha)	Shore length (km)	Channel length (km)	Tidal range (m)	Geomorph. type	Human population
422	386	19.2	8.2	6.7	Coastal plain	23,000

Description

The Clwyd is a small estuary on the north coast of Wales, and is contiguous with the Dee Estuary and North Wirral review site to the east. The Clwyd has a long history of land-claim and flood prevention works, and the entire length of the tidal channel is canalised with flood prevention embankments. Water quality has been classified as grade A.

The mouth of the estuary at Rhyl is restricted and displaced north-eastwards by a small spit, behind which the estuary drains almost completely at low tide to expose narrow mudflats. On either side of these mudflats there are small areas of saltmarsh, which have a diverse vegetation.

The mouth of the estuary opens out into a large expanse of sand beaches along Kinmel Bay and Rhyl. These beaches once graded into an extensive sand dune system, but buildings now cover most of this.

Wintering bird populations on the estuary are dominated by waders, and the Clwyd regularly supports nationally important populations of sanderling. The marine lake at Rhyl (adjacent to the review site) is filled from the estuary and is a good feeding ground for waders when it is drained in winter.

Wildlife features

Coastal habitats

	Subtidal	Saltmarsh	Sandflats	Mudflats	Sand dunes	Rocky shores	Shingle	Lowland grassland	Lagoon	Other
	●	●	●	●						
Area (ha)	36	43	343							

● = major habitat   ◍ = minor habitat

Aquatic estuarine communities

Soft substrate

1	2	3	4	5	6	7	8	9	10	11	12	13	14	15	16
		●										●		●	●

Hard substrate

17	18	19	20	21	22	23	24	25	26	27	28	29	30	31	32	33
																●

Birds

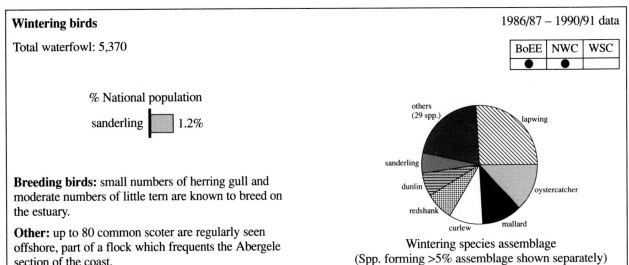

Wintering birds   1986/87 – 1990/91 data

Total waterfowl: 5,370

	BoEE	NWC	WSC
	●	●	

% National population

sanderling ▭ 1.2%

Breeding birds: small numbers of herring gull and moderate numbers of little tern are known to breed on the estuary.

Other: up to 80 common scoter are regularly seen offshore, part of a flock which frequents the Abergele section of the coast.

others (29 spp.), lapwing, sanderling, dunlin, oystercatcher, redshank, mallard, curlew

Wintering species assemblage
(Spp. forming >5% assemblage shown separately)

Conservation status

● = designated   ◍ = proposed

	NCR	GCR	SSSI (B)	SSSI (G)	SSSI (M)	NNR	LNR	Ramsar	SPA	AONB	CWT	RSPB	ESA	NP	WWT	NT	NSA	HC	Other
																			●
No.																			4

There are no statutory designations present on the estuary, but the River Clwyd Estuary, Foryd Sand Dunes and Kinmel Bay Sand Dunes have been notified as Sites of Nature Conservation Importance to the District and Borough Council, and are afforded protection under Local and County Structure Plans. There is also an area of common land on the western shore of the estuary.

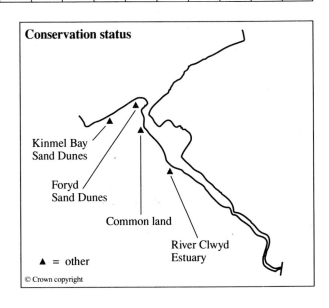

Conservation status

Kinmel Bay Sand Dunes

Foryd Sand Dunes

Common land

River Clwyd Estuary

▲ = other

© Crown copyright

Human activities

Present	Proposed	Activity
		Coast protection & sea defences
●		Linear defences
●		Training walls
●		Groynes
●		Brushwood fences
		Spartina planting
●		Marram grass planting
		Barrage schemes
		Weirs & barrages for river management
		Storm surge barrages
		Water storage barrages & bunds
●		Leisure barrages
		Tidal power barrages
		Power generation
		Thermal power stations
		Import/export jetties (power generation)
		Wind-power generation
		Industrial, port & related development
●		Dock, port & harbour facilities
●		Manufacturing industries
		Chemical industries
		Ship & boat building
		Others
		Extraction & processing of natural gas & oil
		Exploration
		Production
		Rig & platform construction
		Pipeline construction
		Pipeline installation
		Import/export jetties & single-point moorings
		Oil refineries
		Mothballing of rigs & tankers
		Military activities
		Overflying by military aircraft
		Others
		Waste discharge
		Domestic waste disposal
●		Sewage discharge & outfalls
●		Sewage treatment works
		Rubbish tips
		Industrial & agricultural waste discharge
		Thermal discharges (power stations)
		Dredge spoil
		Accidental discharges
		Aerial crop spraying
		Waste incinerators
		Others
		Sediment extraction
		Capital dredging
		Maintenance dredging
		Commercial estuarine aggregates extraction
		Commercial terrestrial aggregates extraction
		Non-commercial aggregates extraction
		Hard-rock quarrying
		Transport & communications
		Airports & helipads
●	●	Tunnels, bridges & aqueducts
		Causeways & fords
	●	Road schemes
		Ferries
●		Cables
		Urbanisation
		Land-claim for housing & car parks
		Education & scientific research
		Sampling, specimen collection & observation
		Nature trails & interpretative facilities
		Seismic studies & geological test drilling
		Marine & terrestrial archaeology
		Fossil collecting

Present	Proposed	Activity
		Tourism & recreation
		Infrastructure developments
		Marinas
●		Non-marina moorings
		Dinghy & boat parks
●		Caravan parks & chalets
		Leisure centres, complexes & piers
		Aquatic-based recreation
●		Power-boating & water-skiing
		Jet-skiing
●		Sailing
●		Sailboarding & wind-surfing
		SCUBA & snorkelling
●		Canoeing
		Surfing
		Rowing
		Tourist boat trips/leisure barges
●		Angling
●		Other non-commercial fishing
●		Bathing & general beach recreation
		Terrestrial & intertidal-based recreation
●		Walking, including dog walking
●		Bird-watching
		Sand-yachting
●		4WD & trial-biking
		Car sand-racing
●		Horse-riding
		Rock-climbing
		Golf courses
		Clay-pigeon shooting
		Others
		Airborne recreation
		Overflying by light aircraft
		Radio-controlled model aircraft
		Others
		Wildfowling & hunting
●		Wildfowling
●		Other hunting-related activities
		Bait-collecting
●		Digging & pumping for lugworms & ragworms
		Hydraulic dredging for worms
		Others
		Commercial fisheries
●		Fish-netting & trawling
●		Fyke-netting for eels
●		Fish traps & other fixed devices & nets
●		Crustacea
		Molluscs – Hand-gathering
		Dredging
		Hydraulic dredging
		Cultivation of living resource
●		Saltmarsh grazing
		Sand dune grazing
		Agricultural land-claim
		Fish-farming
		Shellfish farming
		Bottom & tray cultivation
		Suspended cultivation
		Crustacea farming
		Reeds for roofing
		Salicornia picking
		Others
		Management & killing of birds & mammals
		Killing of mammals
		Killing of birds
		Adult fish-eating birds
		Adult shellfish-eating birds
		Gulls
●		Geese
		Wildlife habitat management
		Spartina control
		Habitat creation & restoration
		Marine
		Intertidal
●		Terrestrial
		Habitat management
		Others

Features of human use

Most activities are of a recreational nature and as the town of Rhyl, which dominates the mouth of the estuary, is a seaside and holiday resort, these activities are most intensive during the summer months. Angling, fishing, sailing and wind-surfing are concentrated along the coast, and water-skiing occurs in the marine lake and inside the estuary mouth. Walkers and horse-riders use the sea front and the embankments on either side of the river, and trial-biking occurs on a small area of Kinmel dunes.

Exploitation of the natural resources includes fixed- and gill-netting and trawling for fish, fyke-netting for eels, trawling for Crustacea, shrimping and bait-digging. The saltings on either side of the estuary are grazed by sheep and cattle, and wildfowling occurs on the river downstream of Rhuddlan.

Industrial activity on the estuary is limited, with the one harbour just inside the estuary mouth used mainly by fishing and pleasure craft. There is also a scrapyard on the west bank which has encroached on 1 ha of the intertidal area.

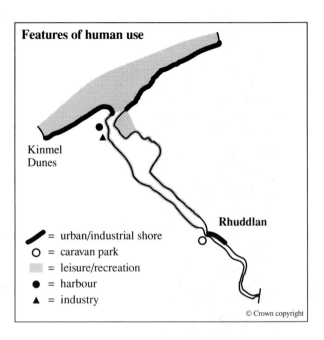

Categories of human use

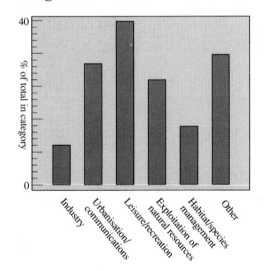

Further reading

Ashell, J., Duckworth, J., Smart, S., & Holder, C. In prep. *The sand dune vegetation survey of Great Britain. Site report, Kinmel Bay.* Peterborough, Joint Nature Conservation Committee.

Ashell, J., Duckworth, J., Smart, S., & Holder, C. In prep. *The sand dune vegetation survey of Great Britain. Site report, Rhyl to Prestatyn.* Peterborough, Joint Nature Conservation Committee.

Burd, F. 1986. *Saltmarsh survey of Great Britain.* Unpublished report, Nature Conservancy Council.

Parsons, J. 1976. *An ecological survey of the Clwyd Estuary.* Ph.D. thesis, Salford University.

Parsons, N., & Pugh-Thomas, M. 1979. Notes on the ecology of the Clwyd Estuary, North Wales. *Journal of Natural History, 13*: 725-734.

34 Dee Estuary & North Wirral

Centre grid: SJ2674
Counties: Merseyside, Cheshire, Clwyd

Districts: Wirral, Ellesmere Port, Neston, Chester, Alyn & Deeside, Delyn
EN/CCW regions: West Midlands, North-west England, North Wales

Review site location

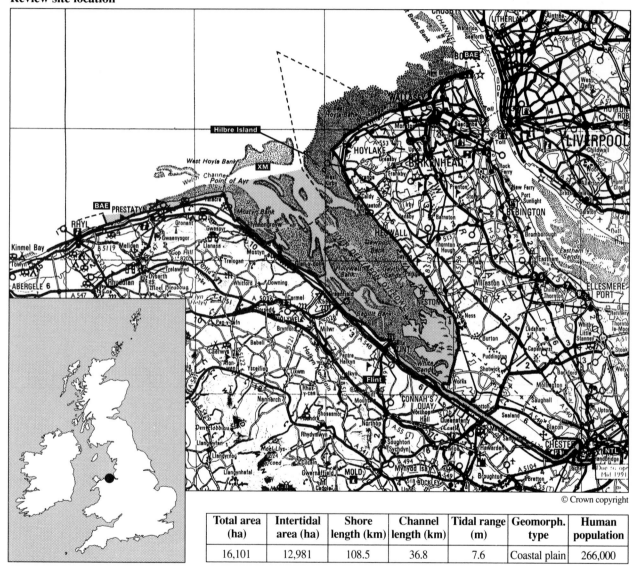

© Crown copyright

Total area (ha)	Intertidal area (ha)	Shore length (km)	Channel length (km)	Tidal range (m)	Geomorph. type	Human population
16,101	12,981	108.5	36.8	7.6	Coastal plain	266,000

NTL = Normal tidal limit

BAE = Between adjacent estuaries

XM = Across mouth

= Core site

34.1

Description

The Dee Estuary lies between the Wirral peninsula and the North Wales coast, and is adjacent to the Mersey Estuary and the Clwyd Estuary review sites. The Dee is a large, funnel-shaped, sheltered estuary, and its upper reaches have been canalised from Flint to Chester. Water quality within the estuary has been classified largely as grade A, apart from a small section on the eastern shore north of Neston which was grade B.

Much of the estuary consists of a large intertidal sand and mudflat, rich in invertebrates, and extensive areas of saltmarsh where the canalised Dee broadens out into the main body of the estuary. Much of the saltmarsh is dominated by pioneer and low-mid marsh vegetation communities, and *Spartina* is also a significant feature. There are relatively few areas of transition communities, as much of the former upper saltmarshes have been subject to land-claim.

On either side of the mouth of the estuary there are long stretches of sandy beaches, behind which there are areas of sand dunes. To the east the dunes grade into brackish dune slacks and reed-bed, where the wet slacks form important breeding grounds for amphibians, and to the western shore the dune ridges and slacks grade into brackish marsh, and support a varied invertebrate fauna which is particularly rich in moths.

The Dee Estuary also has a stretch of cliffs along its eastern shore from Hoylake to Heswall. Rising to 15 metres high, these clay cliffs and banks have a rich flora and fauna. The estuary also includes the rocky shores of Hilbre Island, lying 1.5 km from the north-west corner of the Wirral peninsula.

The Dee is of particular importance for wintering waders and waterfowl, for it regularly supports nine internationally important populations and five nationally important populations of waterfowl. There is, however, some movement of waterfowl between the Dee and the Mersey Estuary.

Wildlife features

Coastal habitats

Subtidal	Saltmarsh	Sandflats	Mudflats	Sand dunes	Rocky shores	Shingle	Lowland grassland	Lagoon	Other
●	●	●	●	●	◉		●		●

Area (ha)	3,120	2,108	10,873

● = major habitat   ◉ = minor habitat

Aquatic estuarine communities

Soft substrate

1	2	3	4	5	6	7	8	9	10	11	12	13	14	15	16
												●		●	

Hard substrate

17	18	19	20	21	22	23	24	25	26	27	28	29	30	31	32	33

Birds

1985/86 – 1990/91 data

Wintering birds

Total waterfowl: 118,800

BoEE	NWC	WSC
●	●	

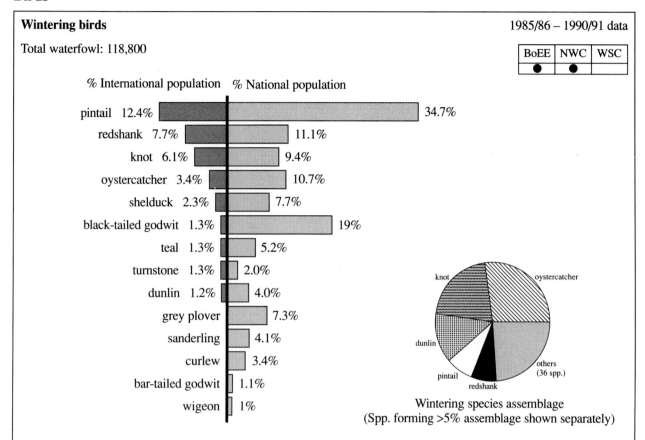

% International population   % National population

pintail 12.4% — 34.7%
redshank 7.7% — 11.1%
knot 6.1% — 9.4%
oystercatcher 3.4% — 10.7%
shelduck 2.3% — 7.7%
black-tailed godwit 1.3% — 19%
teal 1.3% — 5.2%
turnstone 1.3% — 2.0%
dunlin 1.2% — 4.0%
grey plover — 7.3%
sanderling — 4.1%
curlew — 3.4%
bar-tailed godwit — 1.1%
wigeon — 1%

Wintering species assemblage
(Spp. forming >5% assemblage shown separately)

Breeding birds: there are small breeding colonies of black-headed gull and little tern, and a moderate-sized colony of common tern on the estuary. Moderate numbers of lapwing also breed on the grasslands adjacent to the estuary, and small numbers of redshank breed on the saltmarshes.

Other: many migrating waders use the Dee Estuary in spring and autumn, and it is also a moulting ground in autumn.

Additional wildlife features

Red Rocks is the only known site in England where Mackay's horsetail *Equisetum* x *trachydon* has been found, and the invertebrate fauna recently recorded on the estuary includes the RDB 3 fly *Thereva valida*, the RDB 3 belted beauty moth *Lycia zonaria* and 12 Notable species.

The Dee Estuary is a major sea bass *Dicentrarchus labrax*

nursery and smelt *Osmerus eperlanus* occur in the estuary. There are also recent records of the rare allis shad *Alosa alosa* in the Dee. There is also a small breeding population of the natterjack toad *Bufo calamita* adjacent to the estuary.

In addition around 15% of the Welsh population of grey seals use the sandbanks of the Dee as a haul-out site.

Conservation status

● = designated   ◉ = proposed

	NCR	GCR	SSSI (B)	SSSI (G)	SSSI (M)	NNR	LNR	Ramsar	SPA	AONB	CWT	RSPB	ESA	NP	WWT	NT	NSA	HC	Other
	●	●	●		●	◉	●	●	●			●							●
No.	1	1	4		1	1	1	1	1			4							4

There are several Sites of Special Scientific Interest within the Dee Estuary. Gronant Dunes and Talacre Warren (470 ha), North Wirral Foreshore (2,110 ha), Red Rocks (11 ha) and Dee Estuary (13,060 ha) are biological SSSIs, of which Dee Estuary is a Nature Conservation Review site and is proposed as a National Nature Reserve. Dee Cliffs (18 ha) is an SSSI for its biological and geological interest and is a Geological Conservation Review site.

The Dee Estuary has been designated as a Ramsar site and a Special Protection Area. Hilbre Island is a Local Nature Reserve and Red Rocks are managed as a reserve by the Cheshire Conservation Trust. The RSPB have reserves at Point of Ayr, Gayton Sands, Oakenholt Marshes and Shotwick Fields which are adjacent to the estuary, and Wirral Country Park lies along part of the eastern shore.

In addition there are numerous areas around the estuary which have been identified as Sites of Nature Conservation Interest (not shown).

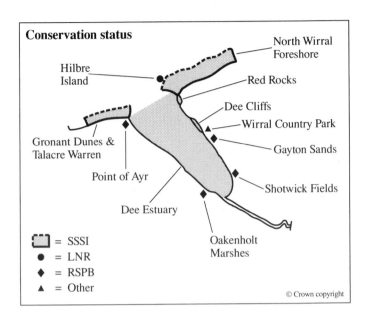

A steelworks in the upper reaches of the estuary. Industry is a major feature of the Dee. (Pat Doody, JNCC)

Human activities

Present **Proposed**

●		**Coast protection & sea defences**
		Linear defences
●		Training walls
		Groynes
		Brushwood fences
●		*Spartina* planting
		Marram grass planting

●		**Barrage schemes**
		Weirs & barrages for river management
		Storm surge barrages
	●	Water storage barrages & bunds
		Leisure barrages
●		Tidal power barrages

●		**Power generation**
●		Thermal power stations
		Import/export jetties (power generation)
		Wind-power generation

●		**Industrial, port & related development**
●		Dock, port & harbour facilities
●		Manufacturing industries
		Chemical industries
		Ship & boat building
		Others

●		**Extraction & processing of natural gas & oil**
		Exploration
	●	Production
		Rig & platform construction
		Pipeline construction
		Pipeline installation
		Import/export jetties & single-point moorings
		Oil refineries
		Mothballing of rigs & tankers

		Military activities
●		Overflying by military aircraft
		Others

●		**Waste discharge**
●		Domestic waste disposal
●		Sewage discharge & outfalls
●		Sewage treatment works
		Rubbish tips
		Industrial & agricultural waste discharge
		Thermal discharges (power stations)
●		Dredge spoil
		Accidental discharges
		Aerial crop spraying
		Waste incinerators
		Others

●		**Sediment extraction**
●		Capital dredging
●		Maintenance dredging
		Commercial estuarine aggregates extraction
		Commercial terrestrial aggregates extraction
		Non-commercial aggregates extraction
		Hard-rock quarrying

		Transport & communications
		Airports & helipads
●	●	Tunnels, bridges & aqueducts
●		Causeways & fords
●	●	Road schemes
		Ferries
●		Cables

		Urbanisation
		Land-claim for housing & car parks

		Education & scientific research
●		Sampling, specimen collection & observation
●		Nature trails & interpretative facilities
		Seismic studies & geological test drilling
		Marine & terrestrial archaeology
		Fossil collecting

		Tourism & recreation
		Infrastructure developments
●		Marinas
●		Non-marina moorings
●		Dinghy & boat parks
●		Caravan parks & chalets
●		Leisure centres, complexes & piers
		Aquatic-based recreation
●		Power-boating & water-skiing
		Jet-skiing
●		Sailing
●		Sailboarding & wind-surfing
		SCUBA & snorkelling
●		Canoeing
		Surfing
		Rowing
●		Tourist boat trips/leisure barges
●		Angling
		Other non-commercial fishing
●		Bathing & general beach recreation
		Terrestrial & intertidal-based recreation
●		Walking, including dog walking
●		Bird-watching
●	●	Sand-yachting
●		4WD & trial-biking
		Car sand-racing
●		Horse-riding
		Rock-climbing
●		Golf courses
		Clay-pigeon shooting
		Others
		Airborne recreation
●		Overflying by light aircraft
●		Radio-controlled model aircraft
		Others

		Wildfowling & hunting
●		Wildfowling
●		Other hunting-related activities

		Bait-collecting
●		Digging & pumping for lugworms & ragworms
		Hydraulic dredging for worms
		Others

		Commercial fisheries
●		Fish-netting & trawling
●		Fyke-netting for eels
●		Fish traps & other fixed devices & nets
●		Crustacea
●		Molluscs – Hand-gathering
		Dredging
		Hydraulic dredging

		Cultivation of living resource
●		Saltmarsh grazing
		Sand dune grazing
		Agricultural land-claim
		Fish-farming
		Shellfish farming
		Bottom & tray cultivation
		Suspended cultivation
		Crustacea farming
		Reeds for roofing
		Salicornia picking
		Others

		Management & killing of birds & mammals
●		Killing of mammals
		Killing of birds
		Adult fish-eating birds
		Adult shellfish-eating birds
		Gulls
●		Geese

		Wildlife habitat management
●	●	*Spartina* control
		Habitat creation & restoration
		Marine
		Intertidal
●	●	Terrestrial
●		Habitat management

●		**Others**

Features of human use

There are a large number of leisure activities on the Dee, particularly water-sports with three yacht clubs, seven sailing clubs and a marina at various locations over the estuary. Land-based pursuits are centred on the sands at the estuary mouth, with 4WD, trial-biking and horse-riding. Beach recreation is widespread along the sandy beaches, and is most intensive where there is road access to the beach.

Industry is a major feature of the Dee Estuary with docks at Mostyn and jetty facilities at Shotton, and at least five chemical industries concentrated along the shores of the inner estuary. There is also a steelworks and paper mill at Shotton, and coal mining occurs at the Point of Ayr.

Exploitation of the natural resources includes saltmarsh grazing, sand dune grazing, seine-, trammel and drift-netting for fish, trawling for shrimps, cockling and bait-digging, which is not intensive. A wildfowling club shoots over the marshes, but there are some no-shooting areas within the estuary.

In 1989 there were proposals for a water storage barrage, the Flint By-pass road scheme, urbanisation for the Deeside Waterfront Development which may involve some land-claim, sand-yachting and *Spartina* control. Since then sand-yachting has begun on the North Wirral foreshore and the proposals for a water storage barrage have been dropped. There have been more recent proposals for an oil and gas terminal at Point of Ayr, and three proposals for gas-fired power stations at Shotton/Connah's Quay which would involve thermal discharges into the estuary.

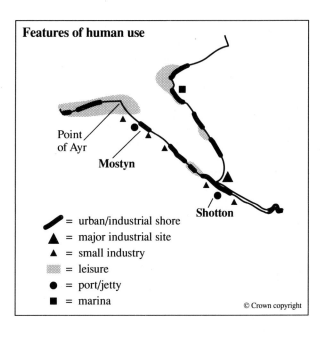

Features of human use

= urban/industrial shore
▲ = major industrial site
▲ = small industry
░ = leisure
● = port/jetty
■ = marina

© Crown copyright

Categories of human use

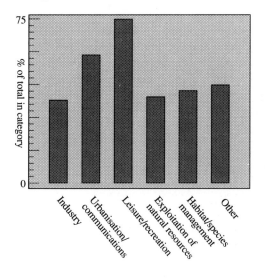

% of total in category

Industry | Urbanisation/communications | Leisure/recreation | Exploitation of natural resources | Habitat/species management | Other

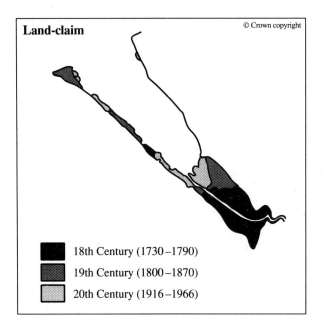

Land-claim

© Crown copyright

■ 18th Century (1730–1790)
■ 19th Century (1800–1870)
░ 20th Century (1916–1966)

Land-claim

On the Dee there has been a history of land-claim, principally for agriculture, and since 1730 there has been a loss of 6,000 ha, 27% of the total area of the estuary. This has extensively altered the pattern of saltmarsh accretion on the estuary, causing the growth of new saltmarsh out over the upper parts of the remaining tidal flats.

Further reading

Ashell, J., Duckworth, J., Smart, S., & Holder, C. In press. *Sand dune survey of Great Britain. Site report, Gronant Dunes and Talacre Warren.* Peterborough, Joint Nature Conservation Committee.

Ball, P.W., & Brown, K.G. 1970. A biosystematic and ecological study of *Salicornia* in the Dee Estuary. *Watsonia*, 8: 27-40.

Betteridge, C., *et al.* 1975. *A phytosociological investigation of the lower tidal reaches of the River Dee.* Report for the Central Water Planning Unit and Welsh National Water Development Authority, Liverpool University Botany Department.

Binnie & Partners. 1971. *Dee Estuary Scheme. Phase IIa.* London, HMSO.

Binnie & Partners. 1973. *Dee Estuary Scheme. Phase IIa. Supplementary Report.* London, HMSO.

British Trust for Ornithology. 1988. Ornithological significance of the Mostyn Docks area of the Dee Estuary to wildfowl and waders. *Nature Conservancy Council, CSD Report*, No. 96.

Burrows, E.M. 1960. The rate of successional change on a selected area of the Dee (Cheshire) saltmarsh. *Proceedings of the Botanical Society of the British Isles*, 3: 467.

Buxton, N., Gilham, R., & Pugh-Thomas, M. 1977. *The ecology of the Dee Estuary. Ecological studies on the Dee Estuary in relation to the proposed barrage scheme.* University of Salford, Department of Biology.

Clark, N.A., Donald, P.F., Mawdesley, T.M., & Waters, R.J. 1990. The day and night distributions of waterfowl on the Mersey and adjacent areas. *British Trust for Ornithology Research Report*, No. 66.

Clark, N.A., Donald, P.F., Mawdesley, T.M., & Waters, R.J. 1990. The impact of the Mersey oil spill of August 1989 on the populations and distributions of waterfowl. *British Trust for Ornithology Research Report*, No. 62.

Clark, N.A., Mawdesley, T.M., & Nobbs, J. 1990. Waterfowl migration and distribution in north-west estuaries. *British Trust for Ornithology Research Report*, No. 54.

Davis, P.E. 1982. *The Dee Estuary wader and* Spartina *survey 1981-82.* Unpublished report, Nature Conservancy Council Welsh Field Survey Unit.

Doarks, C., Holder, C., & Radley, G.P. 1990. Sand dune survey of Great Britain. Site report No. 88, Wirral, Merseyside. *Nature Conservancy Council, CSD Report*, No. 1,140.

Gall, A.A. 1987. Review of changes in the composition of saltmarsh vegetation over part of the Dee estuary. *Nature Conservancy Council, CSD Report*, No. 882.

Galliford, A.L. 1949. Some diatoms from the saltmarshes of the Dee near Neston, Cheshire. *Proceedings of the Liverpool Naturalist's Field Club*, 89: 14-15.

Galliford, A.L. 1956. Notes on the ecology of pools in the saltmarshes of the Dee Estuary. *Proceedings of the Liverpool Naturalist's Field Club*, 95: 15-19.

Garwood, P., & Foster-Smith, R. 1991. Intertidal survey from Rhos Point to New Brighton. (Contractor: Dove Marine Laboratory, Cullercoats.) *Nature Conservancy Council, CSD Report*, No. 1,194.

Gillham, R.M. 1978. *An ecological investigation of the intertidal benthic invertebrates of the Dee Estuary.* Ph.D. thesis, Salford University.

Henderson, M., & McMillan, N.F. 1955. Changes in the Dee marshes 1951-54. *Proceedings of the Liverpool Naturalist's Field Club*, 94: 20-21.

Hill, M. 1984. Population studies on the Dee. *In*: Spartina anglica *in Great Britain*, ed. by P. Doody. Peterborough, Nature Conservancy Council. (Focus on nature conservation, No. 5.)

Kirby, J.S. 1987. The ornithological significance of the Mostyn Docks area of the Dee Estuary to wildfowl and waders. *British Trust for Ornithology Research Report*, No. 24.

Kirby, J.S. 1987. The ornithological significance of Flint marshes and mudflats to wildfowl and waders. *British Trust for Ornithology Research Report*, No. 25.

Mitchell, J.R., Moser, M.E., & Kirby, J.S. 1988. Declines in midwinter counts of waders roosting on the Dee Estuary. *Bird Study*, 35: 191-198.

Morris, G.E. 1990. Recent increases in wintering black-tailed godwit, knot and dunlin in the Flint Sands/Oakenholt Marsh/Connah's Quay area of the Dee Estuary. *Clwyd Bird Report 1989*: 46-47.

Nature Conservancy Council North Wales Region. 1978. *Dee Estuary Research Review.* Blackwell, Nature Conservancy Council.

Perkins, E.J. 1956. The fauna of a sand bank in the mouth of the Dee Estuary. *Annals and Magazine of Natural History (Series 12)*, 9: 112-128.

Rehfisch, M.M., *et al.* 1991. Waterfowl distribution and diet on the Mersey estuary and adjacent areas. *British Trust for Ornithology Research Report*, No. 77.

Rice, K.A., & Putwain, P.D. 1990. *The Dee and Mersey Estuaries environmental background.* Shell U.K. Ltd.

Round, F.E. 1960. The diatom flora of a saltmarsh on the River Dee. *New Phytologist*, 59: 332-348.

Russell, G. 1972. Phytosociological studies on a two-zone shore. I. Basic patterns. *Journal of Animal Ecology*, 60: 539-545.

Russell, G. 1973. Phytosociological studies on a two-zone shore. II. Community structure. *Journal of Animal Ecology*, 61: 525-536.

Stopford, S.C.D. 1949. *A biological survey of the Dee Estuary.* M.Sc. thesis, Liverpool University.

Stopford, S.C.D. 1951. An ecological survey of the Cheshire foreshore of the Dee Estuary. *Journal of Animal Ecology*, 20: 103-122.

Taylor, M.C., & Burrows, E.M. 1968. Studies on the biology of *Spartina* in the Dee Estuary, Cheshire. *Journal of Ecology*, 55: 795-809.

White, D.A. 1982. *Dee Estuary vegetation monitoring 1971 to 1979.* Bangor, Nature Conservancy Council, Wales Field Unit.

Mersey Estuary

Centre grid: SJ4180
Counties: Merseyside, Cheshire

Districts: Liverpool, Sefton, Wirral, Ellesmere Port,
Halton, Vale Royal, Warrington
EN regions: North-west England, West Midlands

Review site location

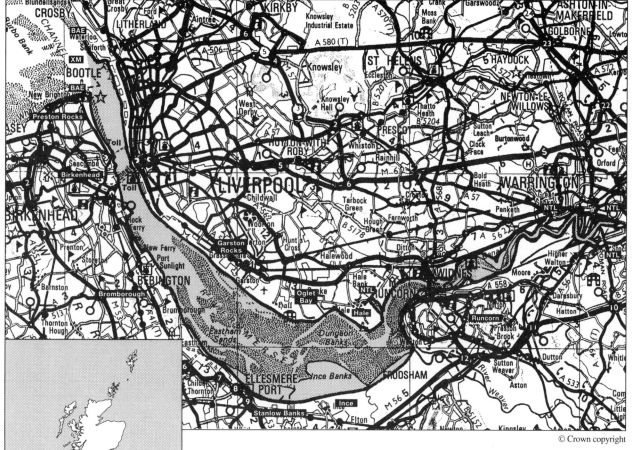

© Crown copyright

Total area (ha)	Intertidal area (ha)	Shore length (km)	Channel length (km)	Tidal range (m)	Geomorph. type	Human population
8,914	5,607	102.9	15.6	8.9	Coastal plain	834,000

NTL = Normal tidal limit

BAE = Between adjacent estuaries

XM = Across mouth

▨ = Core site

Description

The River Mersey has a large, sheltered estuary, flanked by the extensive conurbations of Runcorn, Birkenhead and Liverpool and with industrial complexes along much of its shoreline. Water quality of the estuary has been classified as grade C for most of its length, but upstream of Runcorn it has been classified as grade D.

A large proportion of the estuary is intertidal flats, which are sandy in the upper reaches and muddy downstream of Hale. The most extensive areas of intertidal flats are in the central, wider parts of the estuary and support a rich and abundant invertebrate fauna. On the northern shore of this central section there are generally narrow saltmarshes, and on the southern shore the Ince and Stanlow Banks form extensive areas of saltmarsh. At Oglet Bay on the northern shore the saltmarsh is accreting, while on the southern shore it is eroding as the river shifts course southwards. The continued migration of the deep-water channel is an important feature of the inner basin where

little mature saltmarsh is allowed to develop. Historically, large areas of saltmarsh have been claimed behind the Manchester Ship Canal, and these areas of coastal grasslands are now used by birds as feeding and roosting sites.

In addition some parts of the northern shore are formed of boulder clay cliffs, which have freshwater seepages and periodically sections are exposed by slumping. A number of unusual plants grow on these cliffs. The Mersey Estuary also has some areas of rocky shore at Garston Rocks, Bromborough, and on the southern side of the estuary mouth at Preston Rocks. Behind these latter rocks there is a narrow shingle beach.

The Mersey is of particular importance for wintering waterfowl, regularly supporting five internationally important populations and four nationally important populations.

Wildlife features

Coastal habitats

	Subtidal	Saltmarsh	Sandflats	Mudflats	Sand dunes	Rocky shores	Shingle	Lowland grassland	Lagoon	Other (cliffs)
	●	●	●	●		◉	◉	●		◉
Area (ha)	3,307	848	4,759							

● = major habitat   ◉ = minor habitat

Aquatic estuarine communities

Soft substrate

1	2	3	4	5	6	7	8	9	10	11	12	13	14	15	16
												●		●	

Hard substrate

17	18	19	20	21	22	23	24	25	26	27	28	29	30	31	32	33
			●													

Additional wildlife features

The invertebrate fauna recently recorded on the estuary includes two Notable species. Small numbers of grey seals are regularly recorded in the estuary.

Birds

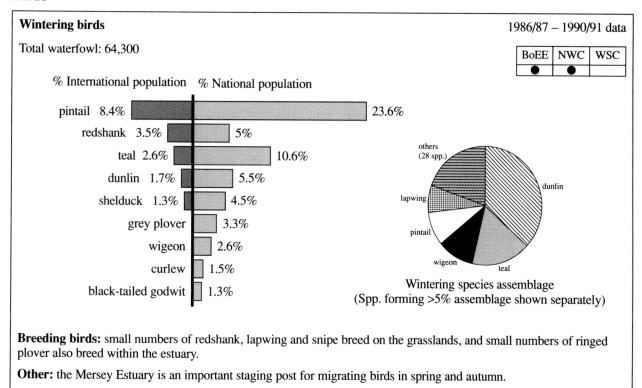

Wintering birds   1986/87 – 1990/91 data

Total waterfowl: 64,300

BoEE	NWC	WSC
●	●	

% International population   % National population

	% Int.	% Nat.
pintail	8.4%	23.6%
redshank	3.5%	5%
teal	2.6%	10.6%
dunlin	1.7%	5.5%
shelduck	1.3%	4.5%
grey plover		3.3%
wigeon		2.6%
curlew		1.5%
black-tailed godwit		1.3%

Wintering species assemblage
(Spp. forming >5% assemblage shown separately)

Breeding birds: small numbers of redshank, lapwing and snipe breed on the grasslands, and small numbers of ringed plover also breed within the estuary.

Other: the Mersey Estuary is an important staging post for migrating birds in spring and autumn.

Conservation status

● = designated   ◉ = proposed

	NCR	GCR	SSSI (B)	SSSI (G)	SSSI (M)	NNR	LNR	Ramsar	SPA	AONB	CWT	RSPB	ESA	NP	WWT	NT	NSA	HC	Other
	●		●					◉	◉		●								●
No.	1		1					1	1		2								9

A large proportion of the estuary is covered by the Mersey Estuary (6,700 ha) biological Site of Special Scientific Interest, which is also a Nature Conservation Review site. The Mersey Estuary is also a proposed Special Protection Area and Ramsar site.

There are two County Wildlife Trust reserves on the estuary, Hale Duck Decoy managed by the Cheshire Wildlife Trust and Seaforth Pools, a Lancashire Trust for Nature Conservation reserve. Manisty Bay is managed by the Merseyside Naturalist's Association, and there is a private reserve at Fiddler's Ferry power station.

In addition there are several areas that have been identified as Sites of Local Biological Interest, namely New Ferry, Seaforth Pools, Astmoor Saltmarsh, Fiddler's Ferry Saltmarsh, Speke to Clay Banks and Eastham Woods which is also a Country Park. A number of these sites are afforded protection under the Merseyside Structure Plan.

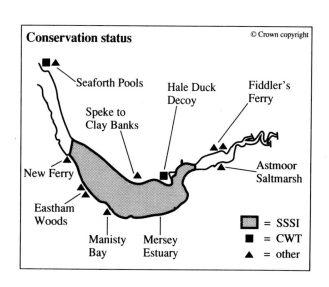

Conservation status   © Crown copyright

Seaforth Pools
Hale Duck Decoy
Fiddler's Ferry
Speke to Clay Banks
New Ferry
Astmoor Saltmarsh
Eastham Woods
Manisty Bay
Mersey Estuary

■ = SSSI
■ = CWT
▲ = other

Human activities

Coast protection & sea defences

Present	Proposed	Activity
●		Linear defences
●		Training walls
		Groynes
		Brushwood fences
		Spartina planting
		Marram grass planting

Barrage schemes

Present	Proposed	Activity
●		Weirs & barrages for river management
		Storm surge barrages
		Water storage barrages & bunds
	●	Leisure barrages
	●	Tidal power barrages

Power generation

Present	Proposed	Activity
●		Thermal power stations
●		Import/export jetties (power generation)
		Wind-power generation

Industrial, port & related development

Present	Proposed	Activity
●		Dock, port & harbour facilities
●		Manufacturing industries
●		Chemical industries
●		Ship & boat building
		Others

Extraction & processing of natural gas & oil

Present	Proposed	Activity
	●	Exploration
		Production
		Rig & platform construction
	●	Pipeline construction
	●	Pipeline installation
●		Import/export jetties & single-point moorings
●		Oil refineries
		Mothballing of rigs & tankers

Military activities

Present	Proposed	Activity
		Overflying by military aircraft
		Others

Waste discharge

Present	Proposed	Activity
●		Domestic waste disposal
●		Sewage discharge & outfalls
●	●	Sewage treatment works
●		Rubbish tips
●		Industrial & agricultural waste discharge
		Thermal discharges (power stations)
●		Dredge spoil
●		Accidental discharges
		Aerial crop spraying
		Waste incinerators
		Others

Sediment extraction

Present	Proposed	Activity
●		Capital dredging
●		Maintenance dredging
	●	Commercial estuarine aggregates extraction
		Commercial terrestrial aggregates extraction
		Non-commercial aggregates extraction
		Hard-rock quarrying

Transport & communications

Present	Proposed	Activity
●		Airports & helipads
●		Tunnels, bridges & aqueducts
	●	Causeways & fords
	●	Road schemes
●		Ferries
		Cables

Urbanisation

Present	Proposed	Activity
●		Land-claim for housing & car parks

Education & scientific research

Present	Proposed	Activity
●		Sampling, specimen collection & observation
●	●	Nature trails & interpretative facilities
		Seismic studies & geological test drilling
		Marine & terrestrial archaeology
		Fossil collecting

Tourism & recreation

Present	Proposed	Activity
		Infrastructure developments
●		Marinas
●		Non-marina moorings
●		Dinghy & boat parks
		Caravan parks & chalets
●		Leisure centres, complexes & piers
		Aquatic-based recreation
		Power-boating & water-skiing
		Jet-skiing
●		Sailing
		Sailboarding & wind-surfing
		SCUBA & snorkelling
		Canoeing
		Surfing
		Rowing
		Tourist boat trips/leisure barges
		Angling
		Other non-commercial fishing
		Bathing & general beach recreation
		Terrestrial & intertidal-based recreation
●		Walking, including dog walking
●		Bird-watching
		Sand-yachting
		4WD & trial-biking
●		Car sand-racing
		Horse-riding
		Rock-climbing
		Golf courses
		Clay-pigeon shooting
		Others
		Airborne recreation
●		Overflying by light aircraft
		Radio-controlled model aircraft
		Others

Wildfowling & hunting

Present	Proposed	Activity
●		Wildfowling
●		Other hunting-related activities

Bait-collecting

Present	Proposed	Activity
		Digging & pumping for lugworms & ragworms
		Hydraulic dredging for worms
		Others

Commercial fisheries

Present	Proposed	Activity
		Fish-netting & trawling
		Fyke-netting for eels
		Fish traps & other fixed devices & nets
		Crustacea
		Molluscs – Hand-gathering
		Dredging
		Hydraulic dredging

Cultivation of living resource

Present	Proposed	Activity
●		Saltmarsh grazing
		Sand dune grazing
		Agricultural land-claim
		Fish-farming
		Shellfish farming
		Bottom & tray cultivation
		Suspended cultivation
		Crustacea farming
		Reeds for roofing
		Salicornia picking
		Others

Management & killing of birds & mammals

Present	Proposed	Activity
		Killing of mammals
		Killing of birds
		Adult fish-eating birds
		Adult shellfish-eating birds
		Gulls
		Geese

Wildlife habitat management

Present	Proposed	Activity
●		*Spartina* control
		Habitat creation & restoration
		Marine
●		Intertidal
●		Terrestrial
		Habitat management

Present	Proposed	Activity
●		Others

Features of human use

The Mersey is a highly industrialised and urbanised estuary with strong communication links. The dock system is extensive and stretches from Seaforth to Dingle, and the southernmost of these docks are being redeveloped. There is a major oil import and export jetty at Tranmere. Industry is extensive along both the Wirral and Liverpool shores. From Runcorn Gap to Weaver there are a large number of chemical industries, many lying behind the docks, and at Ellesmere there is an extremely large industrial complex which includes an oil refinery and power station. There are further power stations at Fiddler's Ferry, Ince and Bromborough. Dredging to maintain the shipping channels is a major activity that produces large amounts of spoil.

Exploitation of the natural resources is limited, and includes saltmarsh grazing and wildfowling, the latter from Stanlow Point to Weaver on the south shore. Manisty Bay is a wildfowl refuge. Few leisure activities take place on the Mersey as access to the estuary is limited. Those pursuits that do occur include sailing in the central area of the estuary, and walking along the Mersey Way on the north shore.

In 1989 there were proposals for oil and gas exploration, a sewage treatment works and a tidal power barrage that would also be used for leisure. More recently there have been proposals for road crossings and expansion of the airport.

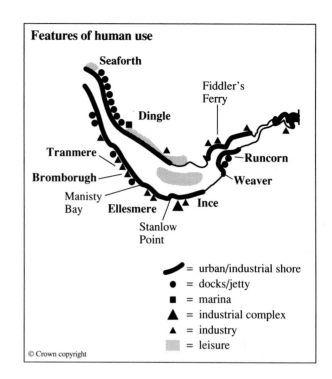

Categories of human use

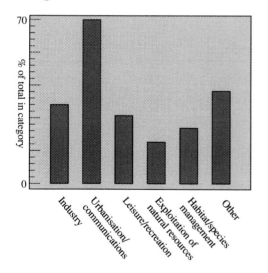

Further reading

Abdullah, M.I., & Royle, L.G. 1973. Chemical evidence for the dispersal of River Mersey run-off in Liverpool Bay. *Estuarine and Coastal Marine Science, 1*: 401-409.

Bamber, R.N. 1988. *A survey of the intertidal soft sediment fauna of the Mersey Estuary. March 1987.* Fawley, Central Electricity Research Laboratories. (Report No. RD/L/3338/R88)

Bassindale, R. 1938. The intertidal fauna of the Mersey Estuary. *Journal of the Marine Biological Association of the United Kingdom, 23*: 83-98.

Bull, K.R., Every, W.J., *et al.* 1983. Alkyl lead pollution and bird mortalities on the Mersey estuary, UK. 1979-1981. *Environmental Pollution, Series A, 31*: 239-259.

Burd, F. 1986. *Saltmarsh survey of Great Britain. County Report, Merseyside and Cheshire.* Unpublished, Nature Conservancy Council.

Buxton, N. 1978. *The wildlife importance of Stanlow and Ince banks.* Mersey Marshes Local Plan Technical Report No. 3, Cheshire County Council.

Carter, J.J. 1985. *The influence of environmental contamination on the fauna of the Mersey Estuary.* M.Sc. Thesis, Pollution Research Unit, University of Manchester.

Clark, N.A., Donald, P.F., Mawdesley, T.M., & Waters, R.J. 1990. The impact of the Mersey oil spill of August 1989 on the populations and distributions of waterfowl. *British Trust for Ornithology research report*, No. 62.

Clark, N.A., Donald, P.F., Mawdesley, T.M., & Waters, R.J. 1990. The day and night distributions of waterfowl on the Mersey and adjacent areas. *British Trust for Ornithology research report*, No. 66.

Corlett, J. 1948. Rates of settlement and growth of the "pile" fauna of the Mersey Estuary. *Proceedings and Transactions of the Liverpool Biological Society, 56*: 2-25.

Ghose, R.B. 1979. *An ecological investigation of the invertebrates of the Mersey Estuary.* Ph.D. Thesis, University of Salford.

Hall-Spencer, J. 1989. Pipeline leak into the Mersey. *Marine Pollution Bulletin, 20*: 480.

Herdmann, W.A., ed. 1886-1900. *Reports upon the fauna of Liverpool Bay and the neighbouring seas.* Longmans, Green & Co. (Vol. 1)/Liverpool Marine Biological Committee (Vols. 2-5).

Herdmann, W.A. 1920. Summary of the history and work of the Liverpool Marine Biological Committee. *Proceedings and Transactions of the Liverpool Biological Society, 34*: 23-74.

Lever, S.C. 1985. *The macrobenthos of the Mersey Estuary – a return to the 1930's?* Warrington, North-west Water Authority (Rivers Division).

Mills, D. J. L. 1991. Benthic marine ecosystems in Great Britain: a review of current knowledge. Cardigan Bay, North Wales, Liverpool Bay and the Solway (MNCR Coastal sectors 10 and 11). Nature Conservancy Council, CSD Report, No. 1,174. (Marine Nature Conservation Review Report, No. MNCR/OR/10)

Moore, D.M. 1978. Seasonal changes in distribution of intertidal macrofauna in the lower Mersey Estuary, UK. *Estuarine and Coastal Marine Science, 7*: 117-125.

Natural Environment Research Council. 1975. *Liverpool Bay: an assessment of present knowledge.* Unpublished, Natural Environment Research Council.

Porter, E. 1973. *Pollution in four industrial estuaries.* London, HMSO.

Pugh-Thomas, M. 1980. *The ecology of the Mersey Estuary.* University of Salford for the North-west Water Authority.

Rice, K.A., & Putwain, P.D. 1990. *The Dee and Mersey Estuaries environmental background.* Shell UK.

Rankin, S.C. 1986. *The ecology of the Mersey Estuary and likely effects of the proposed Mersey barrage, with special reference to the bird populations of the area.* M.Sc. Thesis, University of Manchester.

Rehfisch, M.M., *et al.* 1991. Waterfowl distribution and diet on the Mersey Estuary and adjacent estuaries. *British Trust for Ornithology Research Report,* No. 77.

Rothwell, P.I. 1984. *Spartina* in the Mersey. *In:* Spartina anglica *in Great Britain*, ed. by P. Doody. Peterborough, Nature Consevancy Council. (Focus on Nature Conservation, No. 5)

Williams, B. 1980. *Observations on the occurrence and distribution of invertebrates in part of the Mersey Estuary. November 1989.* Warrington, North-west Water Authority.

Alt Estuary

Centre grid: SD2903 District: Sefton
County: Merseyside EN region: North-west England

Review site location

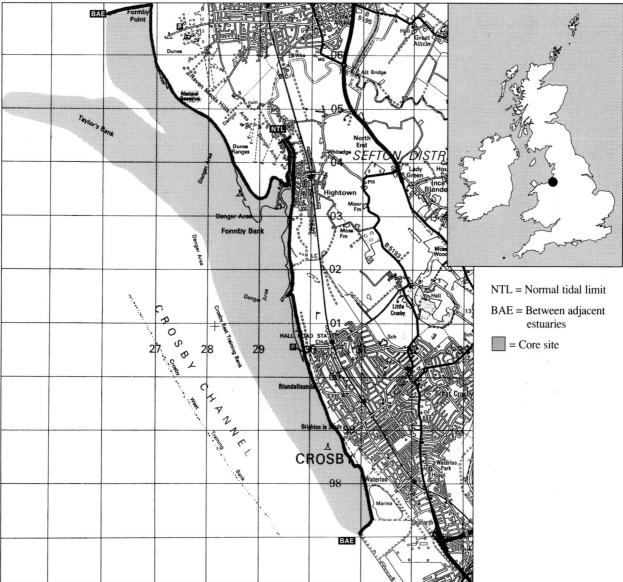

© Crown copyright

NTL = Normal tidal limit

BAE = Between adjacent estuaries

= Core site

Total area (ha)	Intertidal area (ha)	Shore length (km)	Channel length (km)	Tidal range (m)	Geomorph. type	Human population
1,413	1,413	14.0	5.2	8.0	Coastal plain	81,000

Description

The Alt Estuary is contiguous with two other review sites, the Ribble Estuary to the north and the Mersey Estuary to the south. The estuary receives a very limited freshwater input from the River Alt, and offshore the water flow is trained southwards by a stony invetment. The River Alt is heavily polluted, and the water quality of the estuary has been classified as grade D.

The sandflats are the most extensive feature of the estuary and are contiguous with those of the Ribble, where in the north they are predominantly sandy, with wet gullies and a thin layer of mud. The central flats of the Alt are also sandy but with a higher mud content, and the southern parts of the flats become muddy offshore. In addition there is a very small area of saltmarsh on the east bank of the Alt channel south of Hightown, which is largely dominated by *Spartina*.

Inshore the sandflats grade into sand dunes, and form an integral part of the calcareous dune system which extends northwards beyond the estuary to Southport. The Alt is an area of dune accretion, with extensive embryo, yellow and grey dunes up to 40 metres wide, and on the flatter land behind the dune ridges there are areas of dune pasture and wet slacks. The fauna here is varied and extremely rich in invertebrates, particularly butterflies, and the dunes are also home to natterjack toads and sand lizards.

The Alt Estuary regularly supports very large numbers of wintering waders, which are known to interchange between the Dee, Alt, Ribble and Mersey estuaries. The numbers of wintering waders have increased over recent years, which is thought to be due to disturbance and decline in roosting areas on the Dee Estuary. The Alt regularly supports internationally important populations of knot and bar-tailed godwit, and nationally important populations of grey plover, sanderling and redshank.

Wildlife features

Coastal habitats

	Subtidal	Saltmarsh	Sandflats	Mudflats	Sand dunes	Rocky shores	Shingle	Lowland grassland	Lagoon	Other (cliff)
	◍	◍	●	◍	●					
Area (ha)		1	1,412							

● = major habitat   ◍ = minor habitat

Aquatic estuarine communities

Soft substrate

1	2	3	4	5	6	7	8	9	10	11	12	13	14	15	16
●	●							●							

Hard substrate

17	18	19	20	21	22	23	24	25	26	27	28	29	30	31	32	33

Birds

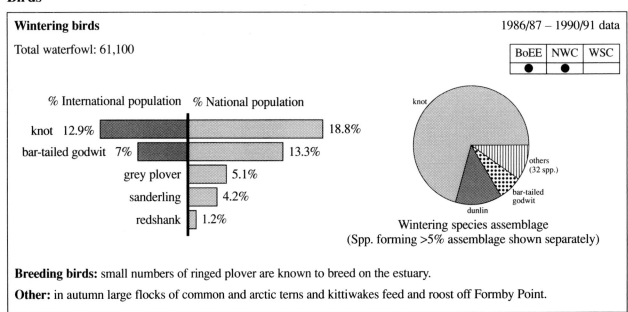

Wintering birds   1986/87 – 1990/91 data

Total waterfowl: 61,100

BoEE	NWC	WSC
●	●	

% International population   % National population

- knot 12.9% — 18.8%
- bar-tailed godwit 7% — 13.3%
- grey plover — 5.1%
- sanderling — 4.2%
- redshank — 1.2%

Wintering species assemblage
(Spp. forming >5% assemblage shown separately)

Breeding birds: small numbers of ringed plover are known to breed on the estuary.

Other: in autumn large flocks of common and arctic terns and kittiwakes feed and roost off Formby Point.

Additional wildlife features

The nationally rare Isle of Man cabbage *Rhynchosynapis monensis* grows within the estuary.

The invertebrate fauna of the dunes is extremely rich with several Red Data Book species recently recorded: the RDB 1 beetle *Aegialia rufa*, the RDB 2 beetle *Hypocaccus rugiceps*, the RDB 3 beetles *Dryocoetinus alni*, *Cicindela hybrida* and *Dryops griseus*, the RDB 3 bees *Colletes cunicularius* and *Stelis ornatula*, the RDB 3 wasps *Podalonia affinis* and *Psen littoralis*, and 55 Notable species.

The dunes also support a population of sand lizards *Lacerta agilis*, and up to 20% of the British breeding population of natterjack toad *Bufo calamita*.

Conservation status

● = designated   ◉ = proposed

	NCR	GCR	SSSI (B)	SSSI (G)	SSSI (M)	NNR	LNR	Ramsar	SPA	AONB	CWT	RSPB	ESA	NP	WWT	NT	NSA	HC	Other
	●		●			●	●	●	●										●
No.	1		2			1	1	1	1										2

Almost all of the estuary is covered by biological Sites of Special Scientific Interest, namely Formby Dunes and Foreshore (430 ha) and Altcar Sand Dunes and Foreshore (1,470 ha). Cabin Hills is a National Nature Reserve. Part of the estuary lies within the Sefton Coast Nature Conservation Review site.

Raven Meols is a Local Nature Reserve and has been identified as a Site of Local Biological Interest, and Hightown Sand Dunes is a proposed LNR and also a Site of Local Biological Interest. The Territorial Army Volunteer Reserves own large areas of land around the estuary.

The Alt has been designated as a Special Protection Area and Ramsar site, and lies within the proposed Ribble and Alt Estuaries SPA and Ramsar site.

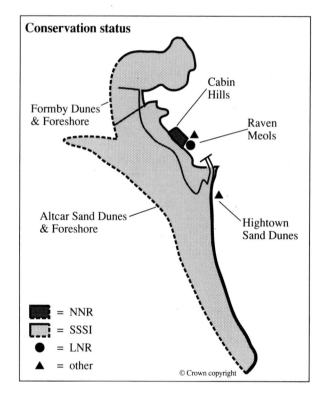

© Crown copyright

36.3

Human activities

Coast protection & sea defences

Present	Proposed	Activity
●		Linear defences
		Training walls
		Groynes
●		Brushwood fences
		Spartina planting
●		Marram grass planting

Barrage schemes

Present	Proposed	Activity
		Weirs & barrages for river management
		Storm surge barrages
		Water storage barrages & bunds
		Leisure barrages
		Tidal power barrages

Power generation

Present	Proposed	Activity
		Thermal power stations
		Import/export jetties (power generation)
		Wind-power generation

Industrial, port & related development

Present	Proposed	Activity
		Dock, port & harbour facilities
		Manufacturing industries
		Chemical industries
		Ship & boat building
		Others

Extraction & processing of natural gas & oil

Present	Proposed	Activity
	●	Exploration
		Production
		Rig & platform construction
		Pipeline construction
		Pipeline installation
		Import/export jetties & single-point moorings
		Oil refineries
		Mothballing of rigs & tankers

Military activities

Present	Proposed	Activity
●		Overflying by military aircraft
		Others

Waste discharge

Present	Proposed	Activity
		Domestic waste disposal
●		Sewage discharge & outfalls
		Sewage treatment works
●		Rubbish tips
		Industrial & agricultural waste discharge
		Thermal discharges (power stations)
		Dredge spoil
		Accidental discharges
		Aerial crop spraying
		Waste incinerators
		Others

Sediment extraction

Present	Proposed	Activity
		Capital dredging
		Maintenance dredging
		Commercial estuarine aggregates extraction
		Commercial terrestrial aggregates extraction
		Non-commercial aggregates extraction
		Hard-rock quarrying

Transport & communications

Present	Proposed	Activity
		Airports & helipads
●		Tunnels, bridges & aqueducts
		Causeways & fords
		Road schemes
		Ferries
		Cables

Urbanisation

Present	Proposed	Activity
●		Land-claim for housing & car parks

Education & scientific research

Present	Proposed	Activity
●		Sampling, specimen collection & observation
●		Nature trails & interpretative facilities
		Seismic studies & geological test drilling
		Marine & terrestrial archaeology
		Fossil collecting

Tourism & recreation

Present	Proposed	Activity
		Infrastructure developments
●		Marinas
		Non-marina moorings
●		Dinghy & boat parks
●		Caravan parks & chalets
		Leisure centres, complexes & piers
		Aquatic-based recreation
		Power-boating & water-skiing
		Jet-skiing
●		Sailing
		Sailboarding & wind-surfing
		SCUBA & snorkelling
		Canoeing
		Surfing
		Rowing
		Tourist boat trips/leisure barges
		Angling
		Other non-commercial fishing
●		Bathing & general beach recreation
		Terrestrial & intertidal-based recreation
●		Walking, including dog walking
●		Bird-watching
		Sand-yachting
		4WD & trial-biking
		Car sand-racing
		Horse-riding
		Rock-climbing
	●	Golf courses
		Clay-pigeon shooting
		Others
		Airborne recreation
		Overflying by light aircraft
		Radio-controlled model aircraft
		Others

Wildfowling & hunting

Present	Proposed	Activity
	●	Wildfowling
		Other hunting-related activities

Bait-collecting

Present	Proposed	Activity
		Digging & pumping for lugworms & ragworms
		Hydraulic dredging for worms
		Others

Commercial fisheries

Present	Proposed	Activity
		Fish-netting & trawling
		Fyke-netting for eels
		Fish traps & other fixed devices & nets
		Crustacea
		Molluscs – Hand-gathering
		Dredging
		Hydraulic dredging

Cultivation of living resource

Present	Proposed	Activity
		Saltmarsh grazing
●		Sand dune grazing
		Agricultural land-claim
		Fish-farming
		Shellfish farming
		Bottom & tray cultivation
		Suspended cultivation
		Crustacea farming
		Reeds for roofing
		Salicornia picking
		Others

Management & killing of birds & mammals

Present	Proposed	Activity
		Killing of mammals
		Killing of birds
		Adult fish-eating birds
		Adult shellfish-eating birds
		Gulls
		Geese

Wildlife habitat management

Present	Proposed	Activity
		Spartina control
		Habitat creation & restoration
		Marine
		Intertidal
●		Terrestrial
●		Habitat management

Others

Features of human use

Very few activities occur on the estuary and most are not intensive. Leisure pursuits include sailing, beach recreation on both north and south beaches, and walking mainly along the northern beach around Formby Point. There is also a marina isolated from the estuary in the south of the site.

Exploitation of the natural resources involves grazing the sand dunes at Cabin Hills, and there are nature trails within the Local Nature Reserve. Habitat management techniques include scrub clearance and marram grass planting on the dunes, and the clearance and creation of scrapes for natterjack toads.

In 1989 there were proposals for housing on the dunes, for a golf course which would surround the NNR, for wildfowlers to shoot on the Alt Estuary and for an exploratory oil well.

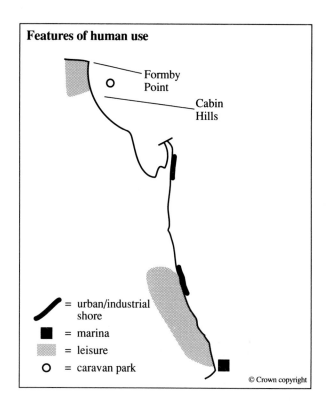

Categories of human use

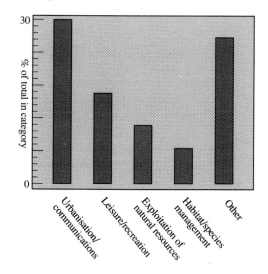

Further reading

Bamber, R.N. 1988. *A survey of the intertidal soft sediment fauna of the Mersey Estuary. March 1987.* Fawley, Central Electricity Research Laboratories. (Report No. RD/L/3338/R88)

Bassindale, R. 1938. The intertidal fauna of the Mersey Estuary. *Journal of the Marine Biological Association of the United Kingdom, 23*: 83-98.

Clark, N.A., Donald, P.F., Mawdesley, T.M., & Waters, R.J. 1990. The impact of the Mersey oil spill of August 1989 on the populations and distributions of waterfowl. *British Trust for Ornithology Research Report*, No. 62.

Clark, N.A., Donald, P.F., Mawdesley, T.M., & Waters, R.J. 1990. The day and night distributions of waterfowl on the Mersey and adjacent areas. *British Trust for Ornithology Research Report*, No. 66.

Clark, N.A., Mawdesley, T.M., & Nobbs, J. 1990. Waterfowl migration and distribution in north-west estuaries. *British Trust for Ornithology Research Report*, No. 54.

Davies, L.M. 1991. Littoral survey of the coast from Crosby to Fleetwood. *Nature Conservancy Council, CSD Report*, No. 1,217. (Marine Nature Conservation Review Report, No. MNCR/SR/17)

Edmondson, S.E., Gateley, P.S., & Nissenbaum, D.A. 1989. National sand dune vegetation survey. Sefton Coast, Merseyside. *Nature Conservancy Council, CSD Report*, No. 917.

Fawby, F.J. 1989. The spring migration of waders on the Ribble and Alt Estuaries. *Lancashire Bird Report 1988*: 49-55.

Kirby, J.S., Cross, S., Taylor, J.E., & Wolfenden, I.H. 1988. The distribution and abundance of waders wintering on the Alt Estuary, Merseyside, England. *Wader Study Group Bulletin, 54*: 23-28.

Mitchell, J.R., Moser, M.E., & Kirby, J.S. 1988. Declines in midwinter counts of waders roosting on the Dee Estuary. *Bird Study, 35*: 191-198.

Moore, D.M. 1978. Seasonal changes in distribution of intertidal macrofauna in the lower Mersey Estuary, U.K. *Estuarine and Coastal Marine Science, 7*: 117-125.

Natural Environment Research Council. 1975. *Liverpool Bay – An assessment of present knowledge.* Unpublished, Natural Environment Research Council.

Rehfisch, M.M. *et al.* 1991. Waterfowl distribution and diet on the Mersey Estuary and adjacent areas. *British Trust for Ornithology Research Report*, No. 77.

37 Ribble Estuary

Centre grid: SD3424
Counties: Merseyside, Lancashire

Districts: Fylde, Preston, South Ribble, West Lancashire
EN region: North-west England

Review site location

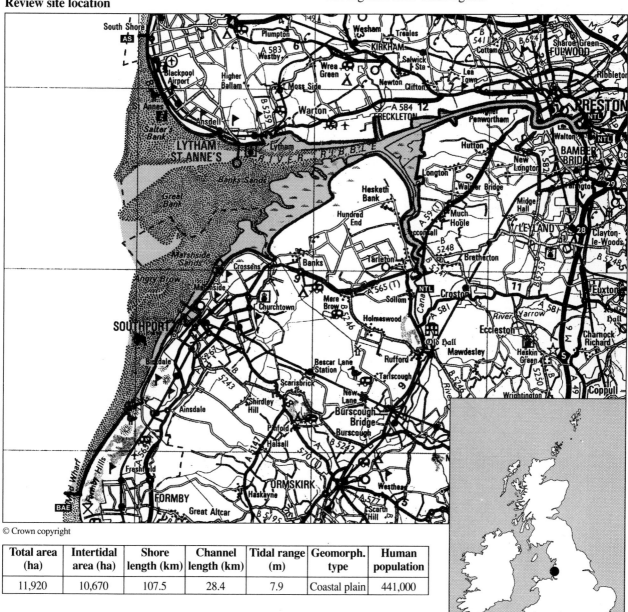

© Crown copyright

Total area (ha)	Intertidal area (ha)	Shore length (km)	Channel length (km)	Tidal range (m)	Geomorph. type	Human population
11,920	10,670	107.5	28.4	7.9	Coastal plain	441,000

NTL = Normal tidal limit

BAE = Between adjacent estuaries

AS = Along shore

▨ = Core site

Description

The Ribble is a large estuary on the north-west coast of England, adjacent to the Alt estuary review site which lies to the south. The normal tidal limit of the Ribble reaches as far inland as Preston, and the estuary flows past the towns of Lytham St Anne's and Southport. Water quality has been classified as grade B, apart from the upper tidal reaches of the River Douglas which are grade C.

The narrow upper tidal flats of the Ribble Estuary are a mixture of mud and sand, while the outer shores are sandy. The inner flats are fringed with saltmarshes, and the Ribble has one of the largest areas of unbroken saltmarsh in Britain. This consists mainly of a sward of mid-upper marsh vegetation with a belt of *Spartina* at the seaward edge. Historically, large areas of saltmarsh were embanked and much of this marsh has become freshwater with parts used for grazing. This unimproved grazing marsh is uncommon in North-west England and maintains a variety of saltmarsh plants in the more brackish parts near the sea and in the creeks. This area is of particular importance to waterfowl.

The calcareous dunes that extend northwards and southwards along the coast are an important feature of the Ribble. The southern dunes are eroding and to the north they are accreting with sediment from the tidal flats. The dunes show a complete succession from strandline vegetation through embryo, yellow and grey dunes, with numerous wet slacks that are extensive in places. Further inland the flora becomes more varied, and to the south of the site a layer of windblown sand covers peat of former peatbog. The sand here has leached unevenly, producing both acidic and neutral conditions and leading to the development of dune heath and dune pasture. This is the only surviving habitat of this kind which once extended along the inland side of Merseyside dune system.

The Ribble Estuary has a varied fauna, and the dunes are rich in invertebrates and home to the natterjack toad and sand lizard. The estuary regularly supports ten internationally important populations and ten nationally important wintering populations of waterfowl, and is the main centre in England for pink-footed geese.

Wildlife features

Coastal habitats

	Subtidal	Saltmarsh	Sandflats	Mudflats	Sand dunes	Rocky shores	Shingle	Lowland grassland	Lagoon	Other
	●	●	●	●	●			●		
Area (ha)	1,250	2,184	8,490							

● = major habitat   ◉ = minor habitat

Aquatic estuarine communities

Soft substrate

1	2	3	4	5	6	7	8	9	10	11	12	13	14	15	16
												●		●	

Hard substrate

17	18	19	20	21	22	23	24	25	26	27	28	29	30	31	32	33

Birds

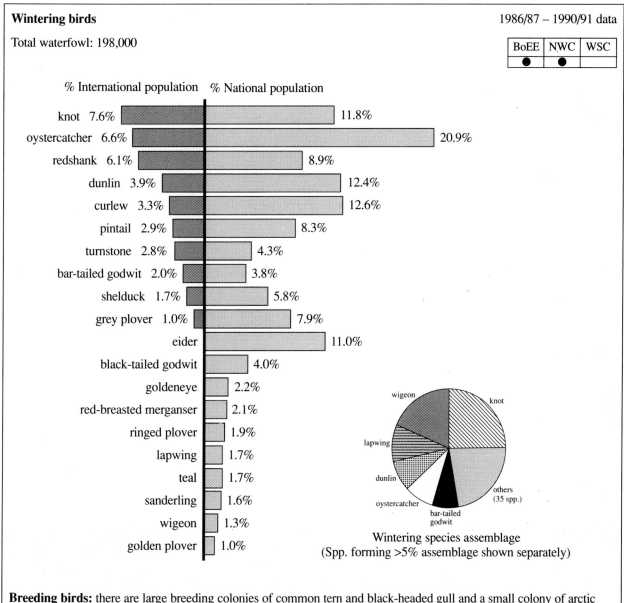

Wintering birds   1986/87 – 1990/91 data

Total waterfowl: 198,000

BoEE	NWC	WSC
●	●	

% International population   % National population

knot 7.6%		11.8%
oystercatcher 6.6%		20.9%
redshank 6.1%		8.9%
dunlin 3.9%		12.4%
curlew 3.3%		12.6%
pintail 2.9%		8.3%
turnstone 2.8%		4.3%
bar-tailed godwit 2.0%		3.8%
shelduck 1.7%		5.8%
grey plover 1.0%		7.9%
eider		11.0%
black-tailed godwit		4.0%
goldeneye		2.2%
red-breasted merganser		2.1%
ringed plover		1.9%
lapwing		1.7%
teal		1.7%
sanderling		1.6%
wigeon		1.3%
golden plover		1.0%

Wintering species assemblage
(Spp. forming >5% assemblage shown separately)

Breeding birds: there are large breeding colonies of common tern and black-headed gull and a small colony of arctic tern, and large numbers of redshank, moderate numbers of lapwing and oystercatcher and small numbers of ringed plover are known to breed on the estuary.

Other: from August to October the Ribble is an important site for moulting waders.

Additional wildlife features

The nationally rare plant dune helleborine *Epipactis dunensis* is found on the dunes adjacent to the estuary, and the invertebrate fauna recently recorded on the Ribble includes the proposed RDB 2 cranefly *Nephrotoma quadristriata* and thirteen Notable species.

Over 10% of the British population of natterjack toad *Bufo calamita* breed on the dunes at Ainsdale, which also support the most north-westerly population of the sand lizard *Lacerta agilis* in Europe.

Small numbers of grey seals regularly use the Ribble Estuary.

Conservation status

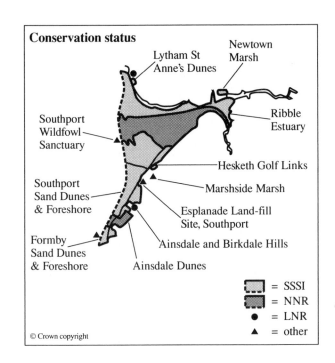

● = designated   ◉ = proposed

	NCR	GCR	SSSI (B)	SSSI (G)	SSSI (M)	NNR	LNR	Ramsar	SPA	AONB	CWT	RSPB	ESA	NP	WWT	NT	NSA	HC	Other
	●	●	●		●	●	●	◉	●							●			●
No.	2	2	6		1	2	2	1	1							1			3

There are several Sites of Special Scientific Interest within the Ribble Estuary. Formby Sand Dunes and Foreshore (428 ha), Southport Sand Dunes and Foreshore (1,680 ha), Lytham St Anne's Dunes (25 ha) and the Ribble Estuary (9,230 ha) are biological SSSIs, together with Newton Marsh (65 ha) and Hesketh Golf Links (15 ha) which are adjacent to the estuary.

Ainsdale Dunes (480 ha) is an SSSI for its biological and geomorphological interest and is a Geological Conservation Review site. Lytham St Anne's is also a GCR site.

The Ribble Estuary and Ainsdale Sand Dunes are National Nature Reserves, and the Ribble Estuary and Ainsdale Dunes are Nature Conservation Review sites. There are Local Nature Reserves at Ainsdale and Birkdale Hills and Lytham St Annes, and the estuary is a Special Protection Area and forms part of the proposed Ribble and Alt Estuaries SPA and Ramsar site.

In addition part of Formby Sand Dunes and Foreshore is National Trust land and part of the outer central area of the estuary forms Southport Wildfowl Sanctuary. Adjacent to the estuary Marshside Marsh and Esplanade Land-fill Site have been identified as Sites of Local Biological Interest under the Merseyside Structure Plan.

Conservation status

Lytham St Anne's Dunes · Newtown Marsh · Ribble Estuary · Southport Wildfowl Sanctuary · Hesketh Golf Links · Marshside Marsh · Southport Sand Dunes & Foreshore · Esplanade Land-fill Site, Southport · Formby Sand Dunes & Foreshore · Ainsdale and Birkdale Hills · Ainsdale Dunes

= SSSI
= NNR
● = LNR
▲ = other

© Crown copyright

Ribble Marshes National Nature Reserve. The Ribble Estuary regularly supports internationally important populations of wintering waterfowl. (Peter Wakely, English Nature)

Human activities

Present	Proposed	Activity
		Coast protection & sea defences
●		Linear defences
●		Training walls
		Groynes
●		Brushwood fences
		Spartina planting
●		Marram grass planting
		Barrage schemes
		Weirs & barrages for river management
		Storm surge barrages
		Water storage barrages & bunds
		Leisure barrages
		Tidal power barrages
		Power generation
		Thermal power stations
		Import/export jetties (power generation)
		Wind-power generation
		Industrial, port & related development
		Dock, port & harbour facilities
		Manufacturing industries
		Chemical industries
●		Ship & boat building
●		Others
		Extraction & processing of natural gas & oil
●	●	Exploration
		Production
		Rig & platform construction
●		Pipeline construction
		Pipeline installation
		Import/export jetties & single-point moorings
		Oil refineries
		Mothballing of rigs & tankers
		Military activities
●		Overflying by military aircraft
		Others
		Waste discharge
	●	Domestic waste disposal
●	●	Sewage discharge & outfalls
●		Sewage treatment works
●		Rubbish tips
●		Industrial & agricultural waste discharge
		Thermal discharges (power stations)
		Dredge spoil
		Accidental discharges
		Aerial crop spraying
		Waste incinerators
		Others
		Sediment extraction
		Capital dredging
		Maintenance dredging
●		Commercial estuarine aggregates extraction
		Commercial terrestrial aggregates extraction
		Non-commercial aggregates extraction
		Hard-rock quarrying
		Transport & communications
●		Airports & helipads
●		Tunnels, bridges & aqueducts
●		Causeways & fords
		Road schemes
●		Ferries
●		Cables
		Urbanisation
	●	Land-claim for housing & car parks
		Education & scientific research
●		Sampling, specimen collection & observation
●		Nature trails & interpretative facilities
		Seismic studies & geological test drilling
		Marine & terrestrial archaeology
		Fossil collecting

Present	Proposed	Activity
		Tourism & recreation
		Infrastructure developments
●	●	Marinas
●		Non-marina moorings
●		Dinghy & boat parks
		Caravan parks & chalets
●		Leisure centres, complexes & piers
		Aquatic-based recreation
		Power-boating & water-skiing
		Jet-skiing
		Sailing
		Sailboarding & wind-surfing
		SCUBA & snorkelling
		Canoeing
		Surfing
		Rowing
		Tourist boat trips/leisure barges
●		Angling
		Other non-commercial fishing
●		Bathing & general beach recreation
		Terrestrial & intertidal-based recreation
●		Walking, including dog walking
●		Bird-watching
●		Sand-yachting
●		4WD & trial-biking
●		Car sand-racing
●		Horse-riding
		Rock-climbing
●		Golf courses
		Clay-pigeon shooting
		Others
		Airborne recreation
●		Overflying by light aircraft
		Radio-controlled model aircraft
		Others
		Wildfowling & hunting
●		Wildfowling
●		Other hunting-related activities
		Bait-collecting
●		Digging & pumping for lugworms & ragworms
		Hydraulic dredging for worms
		Others
		Commercial fisheries
●		Fish-netting & trawling
●		Fyke-netting for eels
●		Fish traps & other fixed devices & nets
●		Crustacea
●		Molluscs – Hand-gathering
●		Dredging
		Hydraulic dredging
		Cultivation of living resource
●		Saltmarsh grazing
	●	Sand dune grazing
		Agricultural land-claim
		Fish-farming
		Shellfish farming
		Bottom & tray cultivation
		Suspended cultivation
		Crustacea farming
		Reeds for roofing
●		*Salicornia* picking
		Others
		Management & killing of birds & mammals
●		Killing of mammals
		Killing of birds
		Adult fish-eating birds
		Adult shellfish-eating birds
●		Gulls
		Geese
		Wildlife habitat management
●		*Spartina* control
		Habitat creation & restoration
		Marine
●		Intertidal
●		Terrestrial
●	●	Habitat management
●		**Others**

Features of human use

A large number of activities on the Ribble Estuary involve exploitation of the natural resources, including seine-netting, trawling and gill-netting for fish, fyke-netting for eels, shrimping, hand-gathering and dredging for mussels, and digging and dredging for cockles. Around 98% of the saltmarsh is grazed, and around 10 ha of saltmarsh are affected by *Salicornia* picking.

Leisure activities are fairly widespread and water-based pursuits are centred on the main river channel as the southern shores of the estuary are shallow. There is a marina at Preston Docks and moorings at Lytham, Becconsall on the River Douglas, and at Southport where there are also two sailing clubs and a dinghy park. Other activities, such as trial-biking, various forms of sand-racing and horse-riding, occur on the sand dunes and sandflats in the south of the estuary, and sand-yachting occurs at Lytham.

There is little industrial activity on the estuary apart from gas exploration, a gas pipeline which crosses the estuary and commercial sand extraction at Salters Bank and Horse Bank. There are also boatyards at Tarleton and Becconsall on the Douglas River. Species and habitat management activities include *Spartina* control, culling of foxes, rabbits, and gulls, and habitat management to protect the dunes and sandflats from various forms of recreation and to promote an increase in the natterjack toad population.

In 1989 there were proposals for a second gas/oil well, for sewage outfall construction, for marinas at Lytham and Southport and for an expansion of the existing marina at Preston and sand dune grazing at Ainsdale. There were also proposals for domestic waste disposal on Hesketh Out Marsh, and to move a clay-pigeon shoot closer to the estuary. More recently part of the sand dunes at Ainsdale have been grazed by sheep, jet-skiiers have been using the estuary and there is a major proposal to divert sewage outfalls at Southport to Crossens, which would involve constructing a tunnel under grazing marshes.

Categories of human use

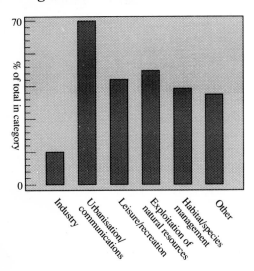

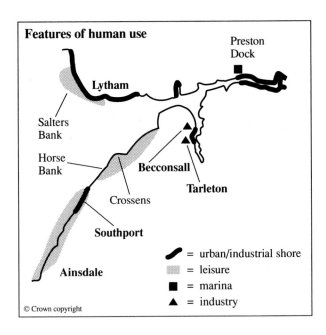

Land-claim

The map shows the areas of the Ribble Estuary lost to land-claim (predominantly for agriculture) in the last century, which amounts to around 1,960 ha. The effects of this land-claim have been disproportionate to a simple loss of saltmarsh, as the area of intertidal flats was reduced as new saltmarsh extended seawards. This process was amplified by the planting of *Spartina anglica* in 1932.

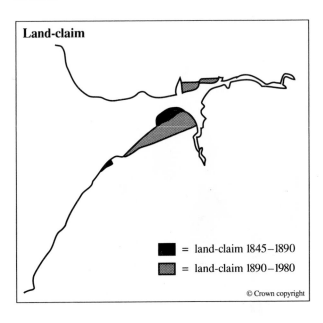

37.6

Further reading

Berry, L.A. 1977. *The saltmarshes of the Ribble Estuary.* B.Sc. dissertation, University of Liverpool.

Burd, F. 1986. *Saltmarsh survey of Great Britian. County report, Merseyside and Cheshire.* Unpublished, Nature Conservancy Council.

Conlan, K. 1987. *The hydrography and ecology of Preston docks and upper Ribble Estuary.* M.Sc. thesis, Department of Environmental Biology, University of Manchester.

Davies, L.M. 1991. Littoral survey of the coast from Crosby to Fleetwood. *Nature Conservancy Council, CSD Report,* No. 1,217. (MNCR/SR/017).

Davies, J. 1992. Littoral survey of the Ribble, Duddon and Ravenglass estuary systems. *Joint Nature Conservation Committee Report,* No. 37.

Dent, D. 1986. *A survey of the mussel beds on the Ribble Estuary at Lytham.* B.Sc. thesis, Department of Zoology, University of Manchester.

Greenhalgh, M.E. 1975. The breeding birds of the Ribble Estuary saltmarshes. *Nature in Lancashire,* 5: 11-19.

Marks, T.C., & Mullins, P. 1984. Population studies on the Ribble. *In:* Spartina anglica *in Great Britain,* ed. by P. Doody, 50-52. Peterborough, Nature Conservancy Council. (Focus on nature conservation, No. 5.)

Natural Environment Research Council. 1975. *Liverpool Bay, an assessment of present knowledge.* Unpublished, Natural Environment Research Council.

Priede, I.G., Solbe, J.F., Nott, J.E., O'Grady, K., & Cragg-Hine, D. 1988. Behaviour of adult atlantic salmon in the estuary of the River Ribble in relation to variations in dissolved oxygen and tidal flow. *Journal of Fish Biology, 33A*: 133-140.

Popham, E.J. 1966. The littoral fauna of the Ribble Estuary, Lancashire, England. *Oikos, 17*: 19-32.

Robinson, N.A. 1984. The history of *Spartina* in the Ribble Estuary. *In:* Spartina anglica *in Great Britain,* ed. by P. Doody, 27-29. Peterborough, Nature Conservancy Council. (Focus on nature conservation, No. 5.)

Smith, P.H., & Greenhalgh, M.E. 1977. A four-year census of wading birds on the Ribble Estuary, Lancashire/Merseyside. *Bird Study, 24*: 243-258.

38 Morecambe Bay

Centre grid: SD3668
Counties: Cumbria, Lancashire

Districts: Barrow-in-Furness, South Lakeland, Lancaster, Wyre
EN region: North-west England

Review site location

© Crown copyright

Total area (ha)	Intertidal area (ha)	Shore length (km)	Channel length (km)	Tidal range (m)	Geomorph. type	Human population
45,462	34,339	266.5	40.3	8.4	Embayment	117,000

NTL = Normal tidal limit
BAE = Between adjacent estuaries
AS = Along shore
■ = Core site

38.1

Description

Morecambe Bay is a very large estuary, adjacent to the Duddon Estuary review site to the north. Morecambe Bay is the joint estuary of five rivers, namely the Wyre, Lune, Keer, Kent and Leven. Water quality within the estuary has largely been classified as grade A, apart from Walney Channel and a stretch of water close to the shore from Grange-over-Sands to Humphrey Head, which were grade B.

At low water Morecambe Bay forms a vast expanse of intertidal sandflat, with only small areas of mudflat around Walney Island and the Lune channel. There are also exceptionally large mussel beds on the stony outcrops (scars or skeers) which are found off Heysham and Walney Island.

A large area of saltmarsh fringes the bay, which has phases of erosion and accretion. Many of the saltmarshes are dissected by creeks and channels, and as many are also heavily grazed the vegetation is dominated by low, dense swards. *Spartina* is spreading through the lower marsh, particularly along the shore from the River Lune to the River Wyre. On the River Wyre Burrows Marsh and Barnaby Sands Marsh are the only extensive areas of ungrazed saltmarsh, and show the full range of saltmarsh vegetation communities. These areas are unique in Lancashire in not having been influenced by sea defences or land-claim for agriculture. In addition, Morecambe Bay has a series of low limestone cliffs rising from the saltmarsh, with cliff-top grassland.

South Walney at the western extremity of the estuary is formed of sand and shingle ridges and bars, and has a rich shingle flora and a range of sand dunes of differing ages and varied vegetation. At its southern end, there is a series of artificial freshwater and brackish lagoons.

The fauna of Morecambe Bay is diverse, with a varied invertebrate population and a breeding population of natterjack toads. Morecambe Bay is also one of the most important British estuaries for wintering waterfowl, for it regularly supports over 200,000 birds and internationally important populations of ten species and nationally important populations of a further ten species. Morecambe Bay is one of the few sites in England where eider breed in large numbers.

Wildlife features

Coastal habitats

Subtidal	Saltmarsh	Sandflats	Mudflats	Sand dunes	Rocky shores	Shingle	Lowland grassland	Lagoon	Other
●	●	●	●	●	●	●	●	●	
Area (ha)	11,123	3,253	31,086						

● = major habitat   ◉ = minor habitat

Aquatic estuarine communities

Soft substrate

1	2	3	4	5	6	7	8	9	10	11	12	13	14	15	16
				●								●	●	●	

Hard substrate

17	18	19	20	21	22	23	24	25	26	27	28	29	30	31	32	33
				●												

Birds

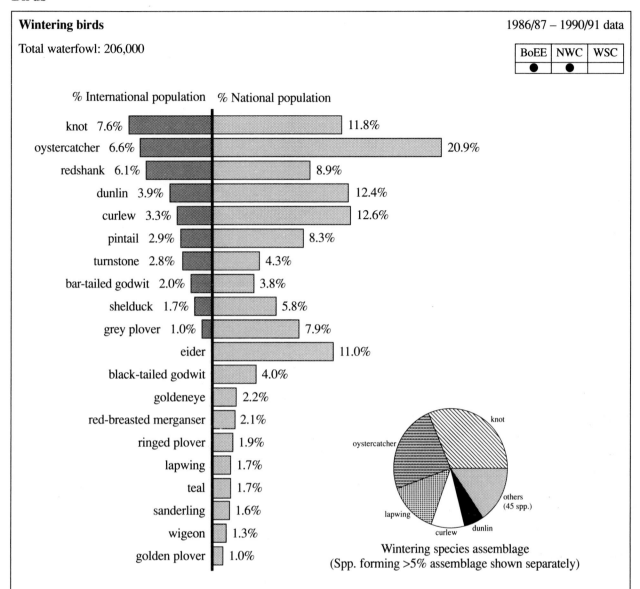

Wintering birds   1986/87 – 1990/91 data

Total waterfowl: 206,000

BoEE	NWC	WSC
●	●	

% International population   % National population

knot 7.6%		11.8%
oystercatcher 6.6%		20.9%
redshank 6.1%		8.9%
dunlin 3.9%		12.4%
curlew 3.3%		12.6%
pintail 2.9%		8.3%
turnstone 2.8%		4.3%
bar-tailed godwit 2.0%		3.8%
shelduck 1.7%		5.8%
grey plover 1.0%		7.9%
eider		11.0%
black-tailed godwit		4.0%
goldeneye		2.2%
red-breasted merganser		2.1%
ringed plover		1.9%
lapwing		1.7%
teal		1.7%
sanderling		1.6%
wigeon		1.3%
golden plover		1.0%

Wintering species assemblage
(Spp. forming >5% assemblage shown separately)

Breeding birds: there are large breeding colonies of black-headed gull, sandwich tern, common tern, herring gull and lesser black-backed gull, moderate sized colonies of little tern and arctic tern and small colonies of great black-backed gull and cormorant. High densities of redshank, moderate densities of oystercatcher and lapwing and low densities of curlew breed on the saltmarshes, and moderate numbers of oystercatcher and lapwing and small numbers of redshank, curlew, snipe and dunlin breed on the grasslands adjacent to the estuary. In addition there are moderate numbers of breeding ringed plover and eider and large numbers of breeding shelduck.

Other: Morecambe Bay is an important staging post for the spring and autumn passage of sanderling, and the spring passage of ringed plover and dunlin.

Additional wildlife features

The nationally rare plant Goldilocks *Aster linosyris* grows on the coastal grassland and the endemic nationally scarce Isle of Man cabbage *Rhyncosynapis monensis* can be found on the estuary. In addition the invertebrate fauna recently recorded on the estuary includes the RDB 2 high brown fritillary *Argynnis adippe*, the RDB 3 least minor moth *Photedes captiuncula*, the belted beauty moth *Lycia zonaria*, and fourteen Notable species.

Morecambe Bay is a major nursery for sea bass *Dicentrarchus labrax*, plaice *Pleuronectes platessa* and flounder *Platichthys flesus*. The dunes adjacent to the estuary support small numbers of the natterjack toad *Bufo calamita*.

Small numbers of grey seals regularly use the estuary.

Conservation status

● = designated   ◍ = proposed

	NCR	GCR	SSSI (B)	SSSI (G)	SSSI (M)	NNR	LNR	Ramsar	SPA	AONB	CWT	RSPB	ESA	NP	WWT	NT	NSA	HC	Other
	●	●	●	●	●	●		◍	◍	●	●	●		●		●			●
No.	1	5	8	1	4	1		1	1	1	4	1		1		1			3

There are several biological Sites of Special Scientific Interest on the estuary, namely Cockerham Marsh (10 ha), Lune Estuary (6,980 ha), Far Arnside (2 ha), Morecambe Bay (30,290 ha), Sea Wood (25 ha), Barnaby Sands and Marsh (67 ha) and Burrows Marsh (36 ha); and Roudsea Woods and Mosses (480 ha) adjacent to the estuary which is also a National Nature Reserve. Morecambe Bay is a Nature Conservation Review site.

South Walney and Piel Channel Flats (2,490 ha), Barker Scar (18 ha), Meathop Woods and Quarry (50 ha) and Humphrey Head (30 ha) are SSSIs for their biological, geological and geomorphological interest, and Skelwith Hill is a geological SSSI. Each of these SSSIs contain Geological Conservation Review sites.

Burrows Marsh and Barnaby Sands and Marsh are Lancashire Trust for Nature Conservation reserves, and South Haws and Walney Island are Cumbria Wildlife Trust reserves. Sea Wood is part of Bardsea Country Park, the National Trust have land at Jack Scout Land at Silverdale, and the Woodland Trust have a reserve at Crag Wood. The northernmost part of the estuary falls within the Lake District National Park, and part of the estuary lies within the Arnside and Silverdale Area of Outstanding Natural Beauty. The RSPB has a reserve north of Morecambe, and the estuary is subject to an Oystercatcher Order. Morecambe Bay is also proposed as a Special Protection Area and Ramsar site.

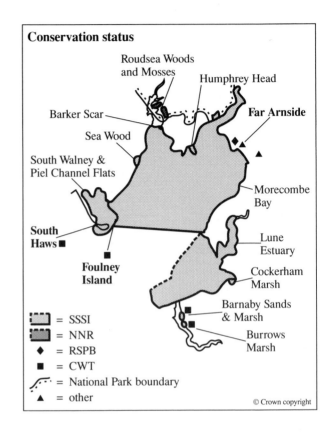

Conservation status

Roudsea Woods and Mosses
Humphrey Head
Barker Scar
Sea Wood
Far Arnside
South Walney & Piel Channel Flats
Morecombe Bay
South Haws ■
Lune Estuary
Cockerham Marsh
Foulney Island
Barnaby Sands & Marsh
Burrows Marsh

▨ = SSSI
▨ = NNR
◆ = RSPB
■ = CWT
⌒⋯ = National Park boundary
▲ = other

© Crown copyright

Morecambe Bay has the largest intertidal area of any estuary in Great Britain. (Peter Wakely, English Nature)

Human activities

Present	Proposed	Activity
		Coast protection & sea defences
●		Linear defences
●		Training walls
●		Groynes
		Brushwood fences
		Spartina planting
		Marram grass planting
		Barrage schemes
●		Weirs & barrages for river management
		Storm surge barrages
	●	Water storage barrages & bunds
	●	Leisure barrages
	●	Tidal power barrages
		Power generation
●		Thermal power stations
		Import/export jetties (power generation)
		Wind-power generation
		Industrial, port & related development
●		Dock, port & harbour facilities
		Manufacturing industries
●		Chemical industries
●		Ship & boat building
●		Others
		Extraction & processing of natural gas & oil
●		Exploration
●		Production
		Rig & platform construction
●		Pipeline construction
	●	Pipeline installation
●		Import/export jetties & single-point moorings
●		Oil refineries
		Mothballing of rigs & tankers
		Military activities
		Overflying by military aircraft
		Others
		Waste discharge
		Domestic waste disposal
●	●	Sewage discharge & outfalls
●		Sewage treatment works
●		Rubbish tips
●		Industrial & agricultural waste discharge
		Thermal discharges (power stations)
		Dredge spoil
●		Accidental discharges
		Aerial crop spraying
		Waste incinerators
		Others
		Sediment extraction
●		Capital dredging
●		Maintenance dredging
●		Commercial estuarine aggregates extraction
		Commercial terrestrial aggregates extraction
●		Non-commercial aggregates extraction
		Hard-rock quarrying
		Transport & communications
●		Airports & helipads
●	●	Tunnels, bridges & aqueducts
●		Causeways & fords
	●	Road schemes
●	●	Ferries
●		Cables
		Urbanisation
	●	Land-claim for housing & car parks
		Education & scientific research
●		Sampling, specimen collection & observation
●		Nature trails & interpretative facilities
●		Seismic studies & geological test drilling
		Marine & terrestrial archaeology
		Fossil collecting

Present	Proposed	Activity
		Tourism & recreation
		Infrastructure developments
	●	Marinas
●		Non-marina moorings
		Dinghy & boat parks
●		Caravan parks & chalets
●		Leisure centres, complexes & piers
		Aquatic-based recreation
●		Power-boating & water-skiing
		Jet-skiing
●		Sailing
●		Sailboarding & wind-surfing
		SCUBA & snorkelling
		Canoeing
		Surfing
		Rowing
		Tourist boat trips/leisure barges
●		Angling
●		Other non-commercial fishing
●		Bathing & general beach recreation
		Terrestrial & intertidal-based recreation
●		Walking, including dog walking
●		Bird-watching
		Sand-yachting
●		4WD & trial-biking
●		Car sand-racing
●		Horse-riding
●		Rock-climbing
●		Golf courses
		Clay-pigeon shooting
		Others
		Airborne recreation
●		Overflying by light aircraft
		Radio-controlled model aircraft
●		Others
		Wildfowling & hunting
●		Wildfowling
●		Other hunting-related activities
		Bait-collecting
●		Digging & pumping for lugworms & ragworms
		Hydraulic dredging for worms
●		Others
		Commercial fisheries
		Fish-netting & trawling
		Fyke-netting for eels
		Fish traps & other fixed devices & nets
●		Crustacea
●		Molluscs – Hand-gathering
●		Dredging
		Hydraulic dredging
		Cultivation of living resource
●		Saltmarsh grazing
●		Sand dune grazing
●		Agricultural land-claim
		Fish-farming
		Shellfish farming
●		Bottom & tray cultivation
		Suspended cultivation
		Crustacea farming
●		Reeds for roofing
●		*Salicornia* picking
		Others
		Management & killing of birds & mammals
●		Killing of mammals
		Killing of birds
		Adult fish-eating birds
●		Adult shellfish-eating birds
●		Gulls
		Geese
		Wildlife habitat management
●		*Spartina* control
		Habitat creation & restoration
		Marine
●		Intertidal
●		Terrestrial
●		Habitat management
		Others

Features of human use

Morecambe Bay is a very large estuary with many
on-going activities. There are several large industrial
complexes present which include a nuclear power station
at Heysham, chemical industries at Ulverston, Fleetwood
and Brine Wells, ship- and boat-building, a gas production
site and an oil refinery at Barrow-in-Furness. Sediment
extraction involves capital dredging along training walls,
maintenance of shipping channels and sand extraction
south of Barrow-in-Furness. There are also ports and
docks at Barrow, Heysham, Glasson and Fleetwood.

Leisure pursuits occur over most of the shoreline, with
moorings and water-based recreation centred around the
River Lune, the Walney Channel, Arnside, Morecambe
and Ulverston. Bathing and beach recreation occur at
Grange-over-Sands, Arnside, Morecambe, Bardsea, Knot
End-on-Sea and Heysham and angling is widespread.
4WD, trial-biking and sand-racing are centred on the
shore west of Pilling. Microlite aircraft also fly over the
southern parts of the River Lune.

Exploitation of the natural resources includes grazing over
most of the saltmarsh, sand dune grazing at Walney,
cultivation of shellfish, and dredging for mussels and
cockles. Three wildfowling clubs shoot over the estuary,
and in some areas land-claim for agriculture has recently
taken place such as between Pilling and Cockerham.
Habitat and species management activities include
restoration of shingle, management of the lagoons for
natterjack toads, and control of birds and mammals for
agricultural purposes.

In 1989 there were proposals for barrage schemes for
water storage, leisure and tidal power; a marina which
would include some land-claim for housing and car-
parking at Cavendish Dock, Barrow-in-Furness; an
extension to the existing docks for the nuclear power
station at Heysham; and an extension to the existing gas
pipeline.

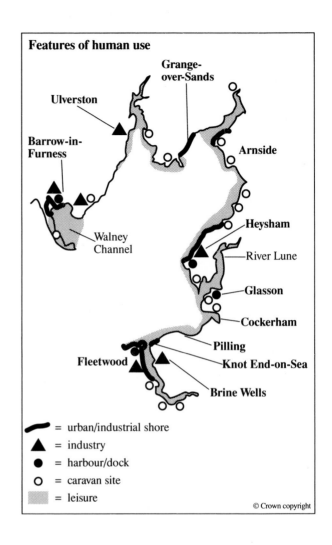

Features of human use

— = urban/industrial shore
▲ = industry
● = harbour/dock
○ = caravan site
▒ = leisure

© Crown copyright

Categories of human use

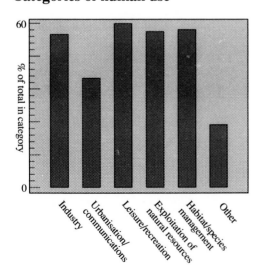

Further reading

Anderson, S.S. 1972. The ecology of Morecambe Bay. II. Intertidal invertebrates and factors affecting their distribution. *Journal of Applied Ecology, 9*: 161-178.

Clapham, C. 1978. The ringed plover populations of Morecambe Bay. *Bird Study, 25*: 175-180.

Corlett, J. 1970. *Morecambe Bay barrage feasibility study; report on biological aspects.* London, Natural Environment Research Council.

Corlett, J. 1972. The ecology of Morecambe Bay. I. Introduction. *Journal of Applied Ecology, 9*: 153-159.

Covey, R., & Davies, J. 1989. Littoral survey of South Cumbria (Barrow-in-Furness to St Bees Head). *Nature Conservancy Council, CSD report*, No. 985.

Elliott, J.M., & Corlett, J. 1972. The ecology of Morecambe Bay. IV. Invertebrate drift into and from the River Leven. *Journal of Applied Ecology, 9*: 195-205.

Energy Technology Support Unit. 1989. *Prospects for renewable energy in the NORWEB area.* Unpublished, North-west Electricity Board.

Gray, A.J. 1972. The ecology of Morecambe Bay. V. The saltmarshes of Morecambe Bay. *Journal of Applied Ecology, 9*: 207-220.

Gray, A.J., & Adam, P. 1974. The reclamation history of Morecambe Bay. *Nature in Lancashire, 4*: 13-20.

Gray, A.J., & Bunce, R.G.H. 1972. The ecology of Morecambe Bay. VI. Soils and vegetation of the saltmarshes: a multivariate analysis. *Journal of Applied Ecology, 9*: 221-234.

Gray, A.J., & Scott, R. 1977. The ecology of Morecambe Bay. VII. The distribution of *Puccinellia maritima*, *Festuca rubra* and *Agrostis stolonifera* in the saltmarshes. *Journal of Applied Ecology, 14*: 229-243.

Kestner, F.J.T. 1972. The effects of water conservation works on the regime of Morecambe Bay. *Geographical Journal, 138*: 178-208.

Mitchell, C. 1970. *Nature conservation in Morecambe Bay in relation to proposed water storage reservoirs in the intertidal zone.* Unpublished, Nature Conservancy Council, South-west England Region.

Pierce, T.G. 1988. Environmental survey, Roosecote Sands. (Contractor: Institute of Environmental and Biological Sciences, University of Lancaster.) *Nature Conservancy Council, CSD Report*, No. 845.

Prater, A.J. 1972. The ecology of Morecambe Bay. III. The food and feeding habits of knot *Calidris canutus* in Morecambe Bay. *Journal of Applied Ecology, 9*: 179-194.

Rankine, C.A. 1990. *The environmental impact of the proposed Wyre barrage, Lancashire, with special reference to birds.* M.Sc. Thesis, Lancaster University.

Robinson, N.A., & Pringle, A.W., eds. 1987. *Morecambe Bay: an assessment of present ecological knowledge.* Lancaster, Centre for North-west Regional Studies/Morecambe Bay Study Group.

Rostron, D. 1992. Sublittoral benthic sediment communities of Morecambe Bay. *Joint Nature Conservation Committee Report*, No. 47. (Marine Nature Conservation Review Report No. MNCR/SR/22)

Snowden, R.J. 1982. *The environmental impact of a heated effluent in the Walney Channel, Cumbria.* Ph.D. Thesis, University of Lancaster.

Whiteside, M. 1984. *Spartina* in Morecambe Bay. *In*: *Spartina anglica in Great Britain*, ed. by P. Doody, 30-33. Peterborough, Nature Conservancy Council. (Focus on Nature Conservation, No. 5.)

Woolfall, S.J. 1991. The importance of the Wyre estuary for bird populations in relation to the proposed barrage. *British Trust for Ornithology Research Report*, No. 73.

Duddon Estuary

Centre grid: SD1977
County: Cumbria

Districts: Copeland, South Lakeland,
Barrow-in-Furness
EN region: North-west England

Review site location

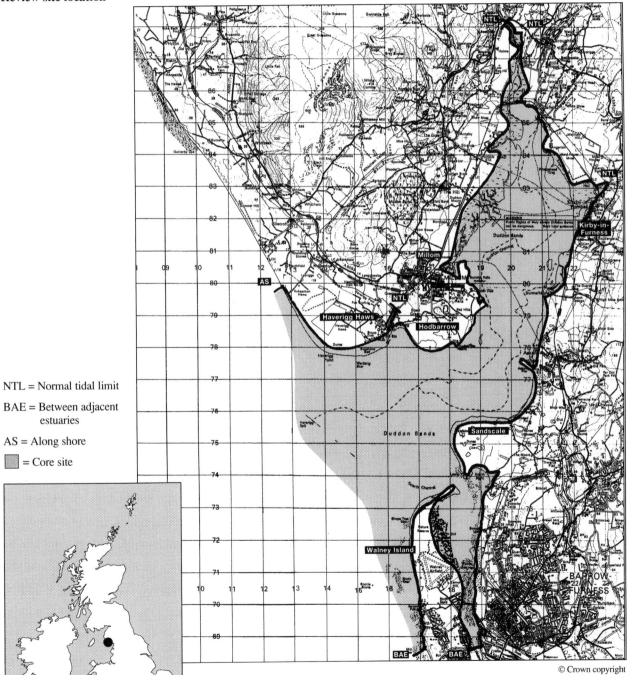

NTL = Normal tidal limit

BAE = Between adjacent
estuaries

AS = Along shore

= Core site

© Crown copyright

Total area (ha)	Intertidal area (ha)	Shore length (km)	Channel length (km)	Tidal range (m)	Geomorph. type	Human population
6,092	5,056	65.5	22.6	8.1	Coastal plain	56,000

Description

The Duddon is a large, sandy estuary adjacent to the Morecambe Bay review site to the south. Water quality in the Duddon Estuary has been classified as grade A. At low water the estuary is an extensive tract of sand and silt, dissected by narrow channels of water. The Duddon Estuary has extensive areas of saltmarsh particularly in its upper reaches north of Millom and Kirkby-in-Furness. There is much local variation in the saltmarshes, and at least twelve saltmarsh vegetation communities have been identified within them, including large areas of lower and upper marsh vegetation. In some areas, such as at Sandscale, the saltmarsh grades to sand dunes.

At Sandscale there is an extensive system of dunes which are quite wet and calcareous and rise sharply from underlying shingle. The vegetation includes saltmarsh, freshwater marsh, pools and wet grassland, and supports a wide range of plants and animals which includes a rich invertebrate fauna. At Haverigg Haws the dunes are drier, rising from sandflats, and become less mobile and more vegetated further inland progressing to maritime heath in the north-west. The dune system at Haverigg Haws is crescent-shaped due to the formation of a succession of shingle ridges, and supports a wide range of plant communities which include a transition from shingle to dunes.

The south-east corner of the estuary mouth is bounded by Walney Island, a barrier island unusual in that it is the product of erosion and reworking of glacial boulder clay rather than the result of coastal deposition. North Walney is a complex of habitats with dunes and dune slacks on a major shingle system, with both exposed and vegetated shingle. The flora is particularly rich with a number of locally rare species. In addition there is a large coastal lagoon at Hodbarrow, formed on the site of old mine workings and separated from the coast by a seawall. The lagoon is a focus for wintering, migrating and breeding birds.

The Duddon Estuary has a varied flora and fauna, which is rich in invertebrates with many scarce or rare species, and the dunes support a number of amphibians including large populations of the natterjack toad. Wintering bird populations are predominantly waders and include three species of international importance and eight species of national importance. There is also a breeding colony of little terns.

Wildlife features

Coastal habitats

	Subtidal	Saltmarsh	Sandflats	Mudflats	Sand dunes	Rocky shores	Shingle	Lowland grassland	Lagoon	Other
	●	●	●	◍	●		●	●	●	
Area (ha)	1,030	540	4,520							

● = major habitat   ◍ = minor habitat

Aquatic estuarine communities

Soft substrate

1	2	3	4	5	6	7	8	9	10	11	12	13	14	15	16
		●		●								●		●	

Hard substrate

17	18	19	20	21	22	23	24	25	26	27	28	29	30	31	32	33
	●						●									

Additional wildlife features

The nationally rare dune helleborine *Epipactis dunensis* and the endemic nationally scarce Isle of Man cabbage *Rhyncosynapis monensis* grow within the dunes.

The invertebrate fauna recently recorded on the estuary includes the RDB 3 mining bee *Colletes cunicularius* and 23 Notable species.

The estuary holds over 20% of the British breeding population of natterjack toad *Bufo calamita*, and is regularly used by small numbers of grey seals.

Birds

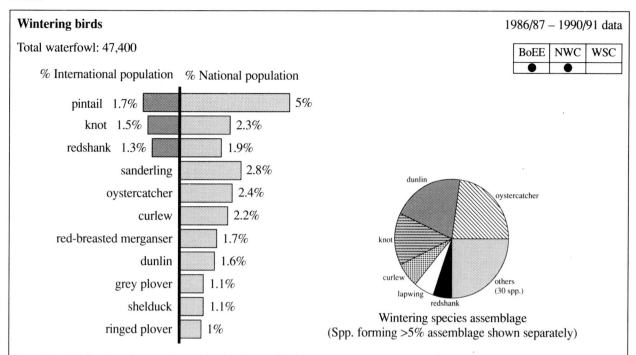

Wintering birds

1986/87 – 1990/91 data

BoEE	NWC	WSC
●	●	

Total waterfowl: 47,400

% International population   % National population

- pintail 1.7% 5%
- knot 1.5% 2.3%
- redshank 1.3% 1.9%
- sanderling 2.8%
- oystercatcher 2.4%
- curlew 2.2%
- red-breasted merganser 1.7%
- dunlin 1.6%
- grey plover 1.1%
- shelduck 1.1%
- ringed plover 1%

Wintering species assemblage
(Spp. forming >5% assemblage shown separately)

Breeding birds: there is a moderate-sized colony of little tern, and small colonies of lesser black-backed gull and black-headed gull. In addition moderate numbers of lapwing, redshank and oystercatcher and low numbers of curlew breed on the saltmarshes, and low numbers of lapwing and redshank breed on the grasslands adjacent to the estuary. Low numbers of ringed plover also breed within the Duddon Estuary.

Other: there is a large spring passage of sanderling through the estuary.

Conservation status

● = designated   ◉ = proposed

	NCR	GCR	SSSI (B)	SSSI (G)	SSSI (M)	NNR	LNR	Ramsar	SPA	AONB	CWT	RSPB	ESA	NP	WWT	NT	NSA	HC	Other
	●	●			●	●		◉	◉		●	●				●			
No.	2	1			1	1		1	1		1	1				1			

The Duddon Estuary formerly consisted of five Sites of Special Scentific Interest and was notified with extensions as a single SSSI (6,814ha) in 1991, for its biological and geomorphological interest. North Walney is also a National Nature Reserve and contains a Geological Conservation Review site. Walney and Sandscale Haws, and the Duddon Estuary are Nature Conservation Review sites.

Hodbarrow Lagoon is an RSPB reserve, and a large area of Sandscale Haws is owned by the National Trust. North Walney National Nature Reserve is managed by the Cumbria Wildlife Trust.

The Duddon Estuary is also a proposed Special Protection Area and Ramsar site.

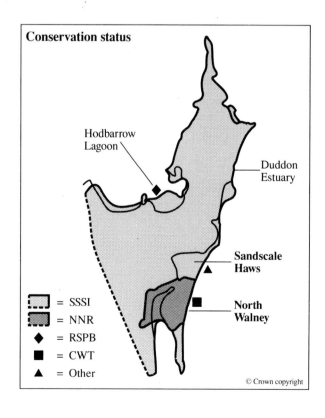

Conservation status

Hodbarrow Lagoon

Duddon Estuary

Sandscale Haws

North Walney

- ⬚ = SSSI
- ▨ = NNR
- ◆ = RSPB
- ■ = CWT
- ▲ = Other

© Crown copyright

Human activities

Present	Proposed	Activity
		Coast protection & sea defences
●	●	Linear defences
●		Training walls
		Groynes
		Brushwood fences
		Spartina planting
●		Marram grass planting
		Barrage schemes
		Weirs & barrages for river management
		Storm surge barrages
		Water storage barrages & bunds
	●	Leisure barrages
	●	Tidal power barrages
		Power generation
		Thermal power stations
		Import/export jetties (power generation)
		Wind-power generation
		Industrial, port & related development
●		Dock, port & harbour facilities
●		Manufacturing industries
●		Chemical industries
●		Ship & boat building
		Others
		Extraction & processing of natural gas & oil
		Exploration
		Production
		Rig & platform construction
		Pipeline construction
		Pipeline installation
		Import/export jetties & single-point moorings
		Oil refineries
		Mothballing of rigs & tankers
		Military activities
		Overflying by military aircraft
		Others
		Waste discharge
●		Domestic waste disposal
●		Sewage discharge & outfalls
●		Sewage treatment works
●		Rubbish tips
●		Industrial & agricultural waste discharge
		Thermal discharges (power stations)
		Dredge spoil
●		Accidental discharges
		Aerial crop spraying
		Waste incinerators
		Others
		Sediment extraction
	●	Capital dredging
		Maintenance dredging
		Commercial estuarine aggregates extraction
		Commercial terrestrial aggregates extraction
		Non-commercial aggregates extraction
		Hard-rock quarrying
		Transport & communications
●		Airports & helipads
●		Tunnels, bridges & aqueducts
		Causeways & fords
		Road schemes
		Ferries
●		Cables
		Urbanisation
●		Land-claim for housing & car parks
		Education & scientific research
●		Sampling, specimen collection & observation
●		Nature trails & interpretative facilities
		Seismic studies & geological test drilling
		Marine & terrestrial archaeology
●		Fossil collecting

Present	Proposed	Activity
		Tourism & recreation
		Infrastructure developments
●	●	Marinas
		Non-marina moorings
●		Dinghy & boat parks
		Caravan parks & chalets
		Leisure centres, complexes & piers
		Aquatic-based recreation
●		Power-boating & water-skiing
		Jet-skiing
		Sailing
●		Sailboarding & wind-surfing
		SCUBA & snorkelling
		Canoeing
		Surfing
		Rowing
●		Tourist boat trips/leisure barges
		Angling
●		Other non-commercial fishing
		Bathing & general beach recreation
		Terrestrial & intertidal-based recreation
●		Walking, including dog walking
●		Bird-watching
●		Sand-yachting
●		4WD & trial-biking
●		Car sand-racing
●		Horse-riding
		Rock-climbing
●	●	Golf courses
●		Clay-pigeon shooting
		Others
		Airborne recreation
●		Overflying by light aircraft
		Radio-controlled model aircraft
		Others
		Wildfowling & hunting
●		Wildfowling
●		Other hunting-related activities
		Bait-collecting
●		Digging & pumping for lugworms & ragworms
		Hydraulic dredging for worms
●		Others
		Commercial fisheries
		Fish-netting & trawling
		Fyke-netting for eels
		Fish traps & other fixed devices & nets
●		Crustacea
		Molluscs – Hand-gathering
		Dredging
		Hydraulic dredging
		Cultivation of living resource
●		Saltmarsh grazing
●		Sand dune grazing
		Agricultural land-claim
		Fish-farming
		Shellfish farming
		Bottom & tray cultivation
		Suspended cultivation
		Crustacea farming
		Reeds for roofing
		Salicornia picking
●		Others
		Management & killing of birds & mammals
●		Killing of mammals
		Killing of birds
		Adult fish-eating birds
		Adult shellfish-eating birds
		Gulls
		Geese
		Wildlife habitat management
●	●	*Spartina* control
		Habitat creation & restoration
●	●	Marine
●		Intertidal
●		Terrestrial
		Habitat management
		Others

Features of human use

Many industrial activities are present on the Duddon although the estuary is not extensively industrialised. There are docks at Barrow and Millom and chemical industries and a shipbuilding/repair yard at Barrow-in-Furness.

There are also a large number of leisure activities occuring on the estuary. Sailing occurs in the southern parts of the estuary and many activities (wind-surfing, 4WD, trial-biking) occur around Walney Island. Sandscale, Walney Island and Haverigg Haws are also popular areas for bathing and beach recreation, and horse-riders use Low Shaw, North Walney and Sandscale.

Exploitation of the natural resources is varied and includes digging for worms and mussel-collecting for bait, mussel-gathering and cockling near Walney, and turf-cutting on the southern shore. Most of the dunes are grazed by sheep and/or cattle apart from North Walney, and most of the saltmarshes are grazed by livestock. Two Wildfowl Association Clubs shoot over the estuary.

There is also a high number of habitat and species management with control of *Spartina* at Sandscale, and various habitat management techniques for the benefit of natterjack toads. Shingle banks are also managed for nesting terns.

Proposals in 1989 included a leisure and tidal power barrage, dredging to reopen Haverigg channel, a marina at Borwick Rails on the western shore, and a golf course.

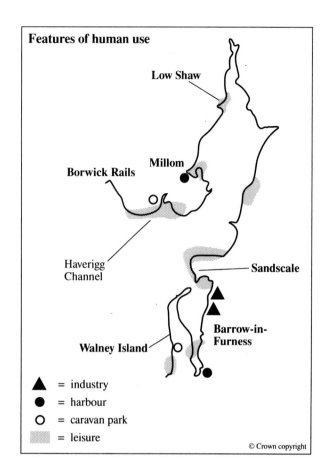

Categories of human use

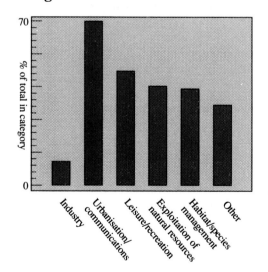

Further reading

Barrow-in Furness Borough Council. 1978. *The natural environment of North Walney and Sandscale Haws*. Unpublished, Barrow-in-Furness Borough Council.

British Lichen Society. 1984. Lichen habitats – lowland heath, dune and machair. A survey and assessment by the British Lichen Society. *Nature Conservancy Council, CSD Report*, No. 522.

Covey, R., & Davies, J. 1989. Littoral survey of South Cumbria (Barrow-in-Furness to St Bees Head). *Nature Conservancy Council, CSD Report*, No. 985. (MNCR review report No. MNCR/SR/007).

Crawford, I.C., & Waite, A.R. 1987. *National Sand Dune Vegetation Survey. Site report No. 1, Haverigg Haws, Cumbria*. Peterborough, Nature Conservancy Council. (Contract surveys, No. 10)

Crawford, I.C., & Waite, A.R. 1987. *National Sand Dune Vegetation Survey. Site report No. 2, Sandscale Haws, Cumbria*. Peterborough, Nature Conservancy Council. (Contract surveys, No. 11)

Dargie, T.C.D. 1971. *North Walney Island SSSI, Lancashire, botanical survey 1971*. Unpublished, Nature Conservancy Council North-west England Region.

Davies, J. 1992. Littoral survey of the Ribble, Duddon and Ravenglass estuary systems. *Joint Nature Conservation Committee Report*, No. 37.

Hill, A.S., Cameron, S., & Hawkings, S.J. 1987. Survey of saline lagoons on the Cumbrian coast. (Contractor: Department of Environmental Biology, University of Manchester.) *Nature Conservancy Council, CSD Report*, No. 726.

Lumb, C.M. 1988. *A marine biological survey of North Walney Lagoons, 9th August 1988*. Unpublished, Nature Conservancy Council North-west England Region.

Perkins, E.J., & May, D.J. 1981. *A preliminary account of the fauna of the Irish Sea coast of Cumbria, 1969-1980*. (Contractor: Marine Laboratory, University of Strathclyde.) Carlisle, Cumbria Sea Fisheries Committee. (CSFC Scientific Report 81/1.)

Radley, G.P. 1987. *National Sand Dune Vegetation Survey. Site Report No. 7, North Walney*. Peterborough, Nature Conservancy Council. (Contract surveys, No. 7)

Tonkin, J.M. 1985. Historical review of land-use at Haverigg Haws, Cumbria. *Nature Conservancy Council, CSD Contract (Interim) Report*.

Tonkin, J.M. 1989. Historical review of land-use at North Walney, Cumbria. *Nature Conservancy Council, CSD Report*, No. 934.

| 40 | Esk Estuary (Cumbria) |

Centre grid: SD0896 District: Copeland
County: Cumbria EN region: North-west England

Review site location

© Crown copyright

Total area (ha)	Intertidal area (ha)	Shore length (km)	Channel length (km)	Tidal range (m)	Geomorph. type	Human population
1,134	1,049	42.2	11.4	7.7	Bar built	< 5,000

NTL = Normal tidal limit

AS = Along shore

■ = Core site

Description

This estuary is the confluence of three rivers, the Irt, Mite and Esk, which discharge through a mouth that has been narrowed by large sand and shingle spits. The large expanse of sandflats and dunes of the estuary extend along the shore to Barn Scar in the north and Tarn Bay in the south. Water quality within the estuary has been classified as grade A.

At low tide a large area of intertidal flats are exposed, which are muddy in the Rivers Irt and Mite. The River Esk has a mixture of sandflats on the southern shore with vegetated shingle on both shores towards the mouth. There are areas of saltmarsh in all three river channels, with a broad range of saltmarsh communities. Towards the head of the rivers some areas of marsh show transition to freshwater communities including stands of reeds.

The sand dunes on either side of the estuary mouth are extensive and relatively undisturbed, with a range of sand dune vegetation that includes strandline, fixed and mobile dunes, dune slacks, and fixed dune grassland. The well-developed and extensive dune heath of northern Drigg is the largest example of this rare habitat on the English and Welsh coast. The dunes of Eskmeals and Ravenglass are considered to be of national importance for their lichen flora.

Within the estuary there is a diverse fauna, for invertebrates are well represented and include many scarce species, and several amphibians are to be found including great-crested newts and a large population of natterjack toads. Adders are also present. Wintering bird populations are dominated by waders.

Wildlife features

Coastal habitats

	Subtidal	Saltmarsh	Sandflats	Mudflats	Sand dunes	Rocky shores	Shingle	Lowland grassland	Lagoon	Other
	●	●	●	●	●		●			
Area (ha)	85	158	891							

● = major habitat ◉ = minor habitat

Birds

Wintering birds	1986/87 – 1990/91 data

Total waterfowl: 4,000

	BoEE	NWC	WSC
	●	●	

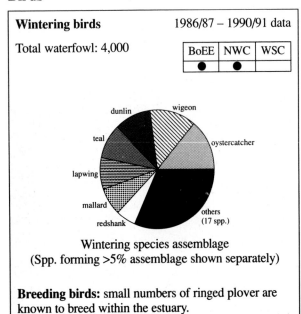

Wintering species assemblage
(Spp. forming >5% assemblage shown separately)

Breeding birds: small numbers of ringed plover are known to breed within the estuary.

Aquatic estuarine communities

Soft substrate

1	2	3	4	5	6	7	8	9	10	11	12	13	14	15	16
		●		●								●		●	

Hard substrate

17	18	19	20	21	22	23	24	25	26	27	28	29	30	31	32	33

Additional wildlife features

The nationally scarce endemic Isle of Man cabbage *Rhyncosinapis monensis* is found within the Esk estuary.

The terrestrial invertebrates recently recorded on the estuary include the RDB 2 beetle *Cicindela hybrida* and 38 Notable species.

Over 20% of the British population of natterjack toad *Bufo calamita* breeds within the dunes.

Conservation status

● = designated   ▓ = proposed

	NCR	GCR	SSSI (B)	SSSI (G)	SSSI (M)	NNR	LNR	Ramsar	SPA	AONB	CWT	RSPB	ESA	NP	WWT	NT	NSA	HC	Other
	●		●				●	▓			●			●					●
No.	1		1				1	1			1			1					1

Much of the northern parts of the estuary are covered by Drigg Coast biological Site of Special Scientific Interest (1,413 ha), which is also a Nature Conservation Review site. Drigg Dunes and Gullery is a Local Nature Reserve, and Eskmeals is a Cumbria Wildlife Trust reserve and MoD land. The Esk Estuary lies within the Lake District National Park, and Ravenglass is proposed as a Ramsar site.

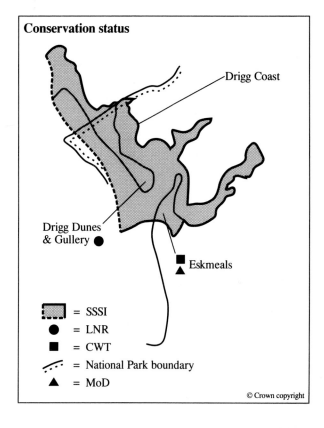

Conservation status

Drigg Coast

Drigg Dunes
& Gullery ●

■ Eskmeals
▲

▒▒▒ = SSSI
● = LNR
■ = CWT
⌒⌒ = National Park boundary
▲ = MoD

© Crown copyright

The Esk Estuary, showing both low- and high-level saltmarsh. (Pat Doody, JNCC)

Human activities

Coast protection & sea defences
- ● (Present)
- Linear defences
- Training walls
- Groynes
- Brushwood fences
- *Spartina* planting
- Marram grass planting

Barrage schemes
- Weirs & barrages for river management
- Storm surge barrages
- Water storage barrages & bunds
- Leisure barrages
- Tidal power barrages

Power generation
- Thermal power stations
- Import/export jetties (power generation)
- Wind-power generation

Industrial, port & related development
- Dock, port & harbour facilities
- Manufacturing industries
- Chemical industries
- Ship & boat building
- Others

Extraction & processing of natural gas & oil
- Exploration
- Production
- Rig & platform construction
- Pipeline construction
- Pipeline installation
- Import/export jetties & single-point moorings
  - Oil refineries
- Mothballing of rigs & tankers

Military activities
- ● (Present)
- Overflying by military aircraft
- Others

Waste discharge
- ● (Present)
- Domestic waste disposal
- Sewage discharge & outfalls
- Sewage treatment works
- ● ● (Present)
- Rubbish tips
- Industrial & agricultural waste discharge
- Thermal discharges (power stations)
- Dredge spoil
- Accidental discharges
- Aerial crop spraying
- Waste incinerators
- Others

Sediment extraction
- Capital dredging
- Maintenance dredging
- Commercial estuarine aggregates extraction
- Commercial terrestrial aggregates extraction
- Non-commercial aggregates extraction
- Hard-rock quarrying

Transport & communications
- Airports & helipads
- ● ● (Present)
- Tunnels, bridges & aqueducts
- Causeways & fords
- Road schemes
- Ferries
- ● (Present)
- Cables

Urbanisation
- Land-claim for housing & car parks

Education & scientific research
- ● ● (Present)
- Sampling, specimen collection & observation
- Nature trails & interpretative facilities
- Seismic studies & geological test drilling
- Marine & terrestrial archaeology
- Fossil collecting

Tourism & recreation
- Infrastructure developments
  - ● (Present)
  - Marinas
  - Non-marina moorings
  - Dinghy & boat parks
  - Caravan parks & chalets
  - Leisure centres, complexes & piers
- Aquatic-based recreation
  - Power-boating & water-skiing
  - Jet-skiing
  - ● (Present) Sailing
  - ● (Present) Sailboarding & wind-surfing
  - SCUBA & snorkelling
  - Canoeing
  - Surfing
  - Rowing
  - ● (Present) Tourist boat trips/leisure barges
  - Angling
  - Other non-commercial fishing
  - ● (Present) Bathing & general beach recreation
- Terrestrial & intertidal-based recreation
  - ● (Present) Walking, including dog walking
  - ● (Present) Bird-watching
  - Sand-yachting
  - 4WD & trial-biking
  - Car sand-racing
  - Horse-riding
  - Rock-climbing
  - Golf courses
  - Clay-pigeon shooting
  - Others
- Airborne recreation
  - Overflying by light aircraft
  - Radio-controlled model aircraft
  - Others

Wildfowling & hunting
- ● (Present)
- Wildfowling
- Other hunting-related activities

Bait-collecting
- ● (Present)
- Digging & pumping for lugworms & ragworms
- Hydraulic dredging for worms
- Others

Commercial fisheries
- Fish-netting & trawling
- Fyke-netting for eels
- Fish traps & other fixed devices & nets
- Crustacea
- Molluscs – Hand-gathering
  - Dredging
  - Hydraulic dredging

Cultivation of living resource
- ● (Present) Saltmarsh grazing
- ● (Present) Sand dune grazing
- Agricultural land-claim
- Fish-farming
- Shellfish farming
  - Bottom & tray cultivation
  - Suspended cultivation
- Crustacea farming
- Reeds for roofing
- *Salicornia* picking
- Others

Management & killing of birds & mammals
- ● (Present)
- Killing of mammals
- Killing of birds
- Adult fish-eating birds
- Adult shellfish-eating birds
- Gulls
- Geese

Wildlife habitat management
- *Spartina* control
- Habitat creation & restoration
  - Marine
  - Intertidal
  - Terrestrial
- ● ● (Present) Habitat management

Others

Features of human use

In 1989 there were few on-going activities on this estuary. Leisure activities are limited to the estuary mouth west of Ravenglass where there are small numbers of moorings. Such pursuits include sailing, wind-surfing, angling and bird-watching, but are not intensive.

Exploitation of the natural resources includes saltmarsh and sand dune grazing by livestock and some wildfowling on small areas of the saltmarsh. There are also a number of habitat and species management techniques used on the estuary with fox and deer culling, and habitat management and creation for the natterjack toad population.

There is no industrial activity present on the estuary, although low-level radioactive wastes are discharged from Drigg depot into the estuary.

More recently hand-gathering of molluscs and culling of adult fish-eating birds has occurred and seismic studies have been undertaken on the estuary.

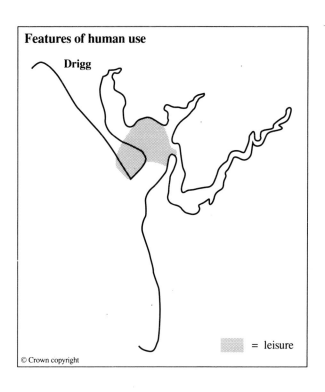

Features of human use

Drigg

= leisure

© Crown copyright

Categories of human use

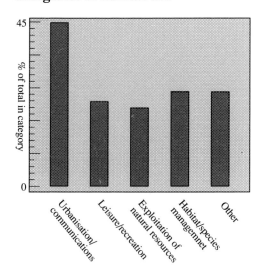

Further reading

British Lichen Society. 1984. Lichen habitats – lowland heath, dune and machair. A survey and assessment by the British Lichen Society. *Nature Conservancy Council, CSD Report*, No. 522.

Burd, F. 1986. *Saltmarsh survey of Great Britian. County report, Cumbria*. Unpublished, Nature Conservancy Council.

Covey, R., & Davies, J. 1989. Littoral survey of South Cumbria (Barrow-in-Furness to St Bees Head). *Nature Conservancy Council, CSD Report*, No. 985. (MNCR review report No. MNCR/SR/007.)

Dargie, T.C.D., & Dargie, M.M. 1971. *Ravenglass Local Nature Reserve: botanical survey 1971*. Carlisle, Cumbria County Council.

Dargie, T.C.D., & Dargie, M.M. 1976. *Ravenglass Local Nature Reserve: vegetation survey 1976*. Carlisle, Cumbria County Council.

Davies, J. 1992. Littoral survey of the Ribble, Duddon and Ravenglass estuary systems. *Joint Nature Conservation Committee Report*, No. 37.

Smith, R. 1977. *Monitoring vegetation changes at Ravenglass LNR*. Carlisle, Cumbria County Council.

Woolven, S.C., Radley, G.P., Crawford, I.C., & Waite, A.R. 1988. *National sand dune vegetation survey. Site report No. 9, Ravenglass*. Peterborough, Nature Conservancy Council. (Contract surveys, No. 26)

Woolven, S.C., & Radley, G.P. 1989. *National sand dune vegetation survey. Site report No. 19, Eskmeals dunes*. Peterborough, Nature Conservancy Council. (Contract surveys, No. 44)

Centre grid: NY2762
Counties: Cumbria, Dumfries & Galloway

Districts: Allerdale, Annandale & Eskdale, Carlisle, Nithsdale, Stewartry.
EN/SNH regions: North-west England, South-west Scotland

Review site location

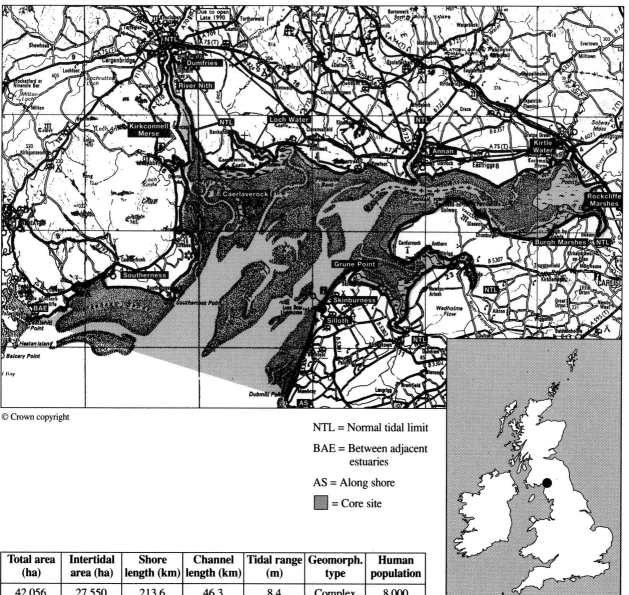

© Crown copyright

NTL = Normal tidal limit

BAE = Between adjacent estuaries

AS = Along shore

▨ = Core site

Total area (ha)	Intertidal area (ha)	Shore length (km)	Channel length (km)	Tidal range (m)	Geomorph. type	Human population
42,056	27,550	213.6	46.3	8.4	Complex	8,000

Description

The Solway Firth lies on the border between Scotland and England and is adjacent to Rough Firth and Auchencairn review site to the west. It is the joint estuary of the Rivers Nith, Annan, Esk, Eden, Waver, Wampool and Lochar Water, and water quality within the estuary has been classified as grade 1, except for Kirtle Water and Lochar Water which are grade 2.

The intertidal flats of the Solway form one of the largest continuous intertidal areas in Britain. The northern shores of the Solway are largely boulders and cobbles with occasional sand or shingle, while much of the southern shore is of mobile muddy fine sand. The inflowing rivers carry little suspended load and so the sediments within the estuary are derived mainly from the Irish Sea, and tend to be highly mobile particularly in the lower reaches of the estuary.

The aquatic estuarine communities of the Solway are predominantly soft substrate-based and include a *Spisula solida* variant of the gravel/shell gravel community and horse mussel beds. The hard substrate communities include an intertidal *Sabellaria* reef which is at the northern limit of its distribution, and a hydrozoan/bryozoan turf community.

There are extensive areas of saltmarsh along the shores of the Solway. The most extensive areas are Rockcliffe and Burgh Marshes on the innermost parts of the estuary, Caerlaverock and Kirkconnell Merses on the northern shores and Moricambe Bay on the southern shores.

The geomorphology of the marshes is outstanding with well-developed creek systems, saltmarsh cliffs up to 3 metres high caused by erosion, and marsh terraces formed by creek migration and isostatic uplift. The vegetation of the saltmarshes shows good transitions through to mature upper marsh and to brackish communities in the upper parts of the rivers, and in several areas there are tidal reed-beds, which are an uncommon feature in Scotland. The Solway marshes provide a link between northern and southern plant species and vegetation communities.

On the southern shore there are areas of sand and shingle and a sand-covered shingle spit at Grune Point which extends from Skinburness into the River Waver. There is also an extensive sand dune system that extends southwards from Silloth beyond the estuary, and these dunes have a wide range of soil pH over small distances which is reflected in clear zonation of the vegetation. The Solway has a further variation in habitat on the Southerness Coast, where there are cliffs rising up to 40 metres.

The Solway Firth supports a varied fauna which includes a large proportion of the British population of natterjack toads. The estuary regularly supports over 120,000 wintering waterfowl which include nine species of international importance and ten species of national importance. Of particular note is the entire Svalbard (Spitzbergen) breeding population of barnacle goose, which winters exclusively on the Solway.

Wildlife features

Coastal habitats

	Subtidal	Saltmarsh	Sandflats	Mudflats	Sand dunes	Rocky shores	Shingle	Lowland grassland	Lagoon	Other
	●	●	●	●	◉	●	◉	●		◉
Area (ha)	14,506	2,925	24,625							

● = major habitat   ◉ = minor habitat

Aquatic estuarine communities

Soft substrate

1	2	3	4	5	6	7	8	9	10	11	12	13	14	15	16
●	●				●						●	●		●	●

Hard substrate

17	18	19	20	21	22	23	24	25	26	27	28	29	30	31	32	33
						●				●						

Birds

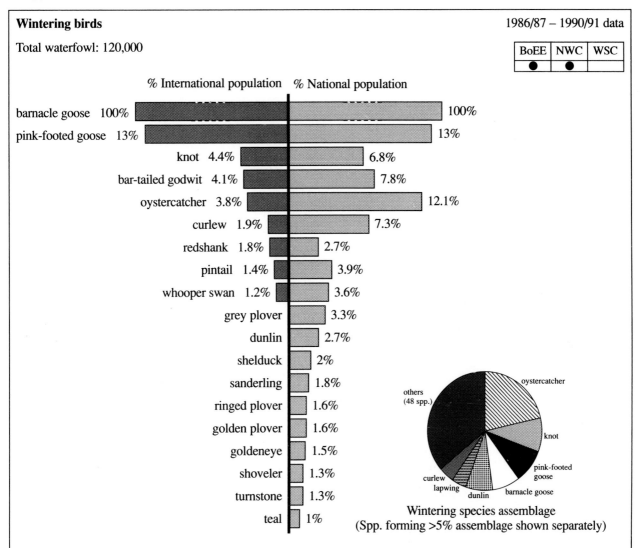

Wintering birds

Total waterfowl: 120,000

1986/87 – 1990/91 data

BoEE	NWC	WSC
●	●	

% International population   % National population

Species	% Int.	% Nat.
barnacle goose	100%	100%
pink-footed goose	13%	13%
knot	4.4%	6.8%
bar-tailed godwit	4.1%	7.8%
oystercatcher	3.8%	12.1%
curlew	1.9%	7.3%
redshank	1.8%	2.7%
pintail	1.4%	3.9%
whooper swan	1.2%	3.6%
grey plover		3.3%
dunlin		2.7%
shelduck		2%
sanderling		1.8%
ringed plover		1.6%
golden plover		1.6%
goldeneye		1.5%
shoveler		1.3%
turnstone		1.3%
teal		1%

Wintering species assemblage
(Spp. forming >5% assemblage shown separately)

Breeding birds: low numbers of redshank and curlew, moderate numbers of lapwing and high numbers of oystercatcher breed on the saltmarshes of the Solway, and low numbers of lapwing, curlew, snipe and dunlin, moderate numbers of redshank and high numbers of oystercatcher breed on the grasslands around the estuary. Moderate numbers of ringed plover are known to breed on the Solway, and there is a moderate-sized colony of common tern and a small colony of little tern on the estuary. In addition around 1% of the British population of cormorant (3.5% Scottish population) breed on the shores of the estuary.

Additional wildlife features

The nationally rare plants holy-grass *Hierochloe odorata* and sticky catchfly *Lychnis viscaria* and seven nationally scarce plants, including the endemic Isle of Man Cabbage *Rhyncosynapis monensis*, grow within the estuary. The invertebrate fauna recently recorded from the Inner Solway Firth includes three proposed Red Data Book species and 31 Notable species.

More than 10% of the British population of the natterjack toad *Bufo calamita* breeds in the extensive marsh and sand dune system, dispersed between several colonies. The Solway Firth is the northern limit of their range. Otters are also recorded on the estuary.

Conservation status

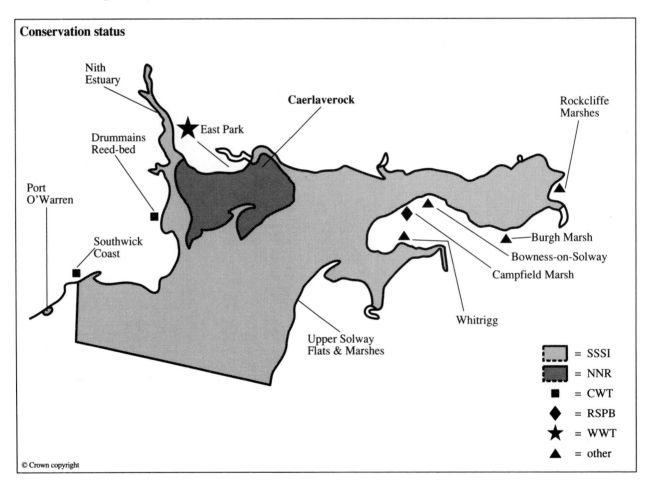

● = designated   ◉ = proposed

	NCR	GCR	SSSI (B)	SSSI (G)	SSSI (M)	NNR	LNR	Ramsar	SPA	AONB	CWT	RSPB	ESA	NP	WWT	NT	NSA	HC	Other
	●	●	●		●	●		●	●	●	●	●			●	●	●		●
No.	1	7	1		1	1		1	1	1	2	1			1	1	1		1

A large proportion of the Solway Firth is covered by Sites of Special Scientific Interest. The Upper Solway Flats and Marshes (29,950 ha) is an SSSI for its biological, geological and geomorphological interest and contains seven Geological Conservation Review blocks. There is a National Nature Reserve (5,500 ha) at Caerlaverock and the Upper Solway Flats and Marshes is a Nature Conservation Review Site. Port O'Warren is a biological SSSI (5.9 ha) and Allonby Bay, which extends to the south of the site, is proposed as an SSSI.

The Upper Solway Flats and Marshes are designated as a Ramsar site and Special Protection Area.

The Scottish Wildlife Trust has reserves at Drummains Reed-bed and Southwick Coast, and the Cumbria Wildlife Trust have a wardening agreement on Rockcliffe Marshes. The RSPB owns Campfield Marsh on the Cardurnock Peninsula and the Wildfowl and Wetlands Trust has a reserve at East Park.

The National Trust owns land at Whitrigg along the River Wampool and at Bowness-on-Solway, and leases an area at Burgh Marsh. In addition the Solway Coast is an Area of Outstanding Natural Beauty, and the Nith Estuary is a National Scenic Area.

Conservation status

Nith Estuary

Caerlaverock

Rockcliffe Marshes

East Park

Drummains Reed-bed

Port O'Warren

Burgh Marsh

Bowness-on-Solway

Southwick Coast

Campfield Marsh

Whitrigg

Upper Solway Flats & Marshes

= SSSI
= NNR
■ = CWT
♦ = RSPB
★ = WWT
▲ = other

© Crown copyright

Human activities

Present	Proposed	Activity
		Coast protection & sea defences
●		Linear defences
		Training walls
●		Groynes
●		Brushwood fences
		Spartina planting
		Marram grass planting
		Barrage schemes
●		Weirs & barrages for river management
		Storm surge barrages
		Water storage barrages & bunds
		Leisure barrages
	●	Tidal power barrages
		Power generation
●		Thermal power stations
		Import/export jetties (power generation)
		Wind-power generation
		Industrial, port & related development
●		Dock, port & harbour facilities
●		Manufacturing industries
●		Chemical industries
●		Ship & boat building
		Others
		Extraction & processing of natural gas & oil
		Exploration
		Production
		Rig & platform construction
		Pipeline construction
		Pipeline installation
		Import/export jetties & single-point moorings
		Oil refineries
		Mothballing of rigs & tankers
		Military activities
●		Overflying by military aircraft
		Others
		Waste discharge
		Domestic waste disposal
●		Sewage discharge & outfalls
●		Sewage treatment works
●		Rubbish tips
●		Industrial & agricultural waste discharge
		Thermal discharges (power stations)
		Dredge spoil
		Accidental discharges
		Aerial crop spraying
		Waste incinerators
		Others
		Sediment extraction
		Capital dredging
●		Maintenance dredging
		Commercial estuarine aggregates extraction
		Commercial terrestrial aggregates extraction
		Non-commercial aggregates extraction
		Hard-rock quarrying
		Transport & communications
		Airports & helipads
●		Tunnels, bridges & aqueducts
●		Causeways & fords
		Road schemes
		Ferries
●		Cables
		Urbanisation
●	●	Land-claim for housing & car parks
		Education & scientific research
●		Sampling, specimen collection & observation
●		Nature trails & interpretative facilities
●		Seismic studies & geological test drilling
		Marine & terrestrial archaeology
		Fossil collecting

Present	Proposed	Activity
		Tourism & recreation
		Infrastructure developments
●		Marinas
		Non-marina moorings
●		Dinghy & boat parks
●	●	Caravan parks & chalets
	●	Leisure centres, complexes & piers
		Aquatic-based recreation
	●	Power-boating & water-skiing
		Jet-skiing
●		Sailing
●		Sailboarding & wind-surfing
		SCUBA & snorkelling
		Canoeing
		Surfing
		Rowing
		Tourist boat trips/leisure barges
●		Angling
●		Other non-commercial fishing
●		Bathing & general beach recreation
		Terrestrial & intertidal-based recreation
●		Walking, including dog walking
●		Bird-watching
		Sand-yachting
		4WD & trial-biking
		Car sand-racing
		Horse-riding
		Rock-climbing
●		Golf courses
●		Clay-pigeon shooting
		Others
		Airborne recreation
●		Overflying by light aircraft
		Radio-controlled model aircraft
		Others
		Wildfowling & hunting
●		Wildfowling
●		Other hunting-related activities
		Bait-collecting
●		Digging & pumping for lugworms & ragworms
		Hydraulic dredging for worms
		Others
		Commercial fisheries
●		Fish-netting & trawling
		Fyke-netting for eels
●		Fish traps & other fixed devices & nets
●		Crustacea
●		Molluscs – Hand-gathering
●	●	Dredging
●	●	Hydraulic dredging
		Cultivation of living resource
●		Saltmarsh grazing
●		Sand dune grazing
	●	Agricultural land-claim
		Fish-farming
		Shellfish farming
		Bottom & tray cultivation
		Suspended cultivation
		Crustacea farming
		Reeds for roofing
		Salicornia picking
●		Others
		Management & killing of birds & mammals
●		Killing of mammals
		Killing of birds
●		Adult fish-eating birds
		Adult shellfish-eating birds
		Gulls
●		Geese
		Wildlife habitat management
		Spartina control
		Habitat creation & restoration
		Marine
		Intertidal
		Terrestrial
●	●	Habitat management
		Others

Features of human use

The towns of Dumfries, Silloth and Annan are the only urban areas around the estuary, and industrial activities are concentrated in these areas. At Annan there are metal and chemical industries, a boat-building and repair yard and a small fishing harbour, and at Silloth there is a small dock. North-east of Annan there is a power station that discharges into the estuary.

Leisure pursuits are not intensive and are confined to small areas. Beach recreation occurs at Southerness and Powfoot, which are also used by sailors and wind-surfers. 4WD occurs from Southerness to Mersehead Sands.

Exploitation of the natural resources is widespread and includes grazing over many of the saltmarshes, turf-cutting, fish-netting, shrimp trawling and bait-digging. Dredging for molluscs is widespread throughout the estuary. Two wildfowling clubs shoot over 90% of the saltmarsh and punt-gunning is also known to occur.

Species and habitat management also occurs on the estuary and includes culling of rabbits and birds, including geese, and habitat restoration and management. There is low-level flying by RAF jets, which from September to May observe an avoidance area.

In 1989 there were proposals for a tidal power barrage from Southerness to Grune Point; for interpretative facilities at Erskine Bridge; and for small areas of land-claim for housing and car parks. By 1992 there had been no action taken on the proposal for a tidal barrage or for a proposed leisure centre. By 1992 there were further proposals for linear sea defences, for two power stations that would involve thermal discharges into the estuary and an import/export jetty, and for exploration for natural gas.

Categories of human use

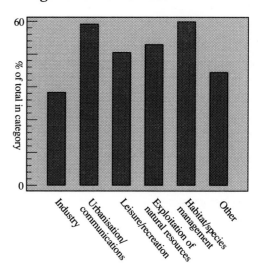

Features of human use

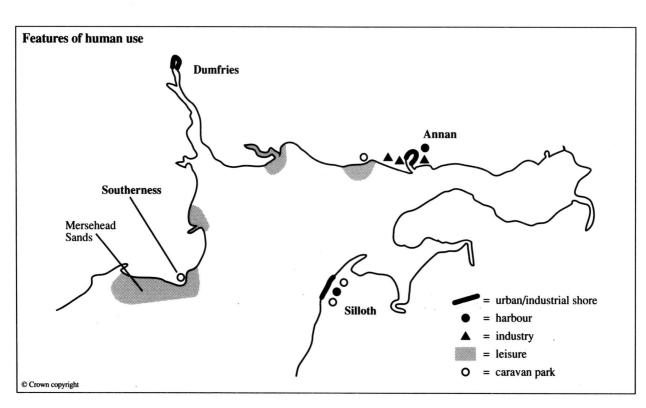

© Crown copyright

41.6

Further reading

Bridson, R.H. 1980. Saltmarsh, its accretion and erosion at Caerlaverock National Nature Reserve, Dumfries. *Transactions of the Dumfriesshire and Galloway Natural History and Antiquarian Society, 55*: 60-67.

Burd, F. 1986. *Saltmarsh survey of Great Britain. County report, Cumbria.* Unpublished, Nature Conservancy Council.

Clark, N.A., Turner, B.S., & Young, J.F. 1982. Spring passage of sanderlings *Calidris alba* on the Solway Firth. *Wader Study Group Bulletin*, 36: 10-11.

Covey, R., & Emblow, C.S. 1992. Littoral survey of the the Inner Solway Firth and additional sites in Dumfries and Galloway. *Joint Nature Conservation Committee Report*, No. 33.

Marshall, J.R. 1962. The morphology of the upper Solway saltmarshes. *Scottish Geographical Magazine*, 78: 81-99.

Marshall, J.R. 1962. The physiographic development of Caerlaverock merse. *Transactions of the Dumfriesshire and Galloway Natural History and Antiquarian Society, 39*: 102.

Doarks, C., & Holder, C. 1990. Sand dune survey of Great Britain. Site report No. 87, Grune Point, Cumbria. *Nature Conservancy Council, CSD Report*, No. 1,132.

Fojt, W. 1986. *Saltmarsh survey of Great Britain. Scottish regional report, South-west.* Unpublished, Nature Conservancy Council.

Kenwar, H.K. 1973. Hemiptera-Heteroptera from Caerlaverock National Nature Reserve, Dumfriesshire. *Entomologist's Monthly Magazine, 109*: 60.

Moser, M. 1984. *Solway Firth shorebird survey 1982-84.* British Trust for Ornithology Research Report, No. 14.

Moser, M., & Carrier, M. 1983. Patterns of population turnover in ringed plovers and turnstones during their spring passage through the Solway Firth in 1983. *Wader Study Group Bulletin*, 39: 37-41.

Nelson, J.M. 1980. The invertebrate fauna of a tidal marsh at Caerlaverock, Dumfriesshire. *Transactions of the Dumfriesshire & Galloway Natural History and Antiquarian Society, 55*: 68-76.

Perkins, E.J. 1973. The marine fauna and flora of the Solway Firth. *Transactions of the Dumfriesshire & Galloway Natural History and Antiquarian Society, 45*: 15.

Perkins, E.J. 1978. *The Solway Firth – its hydrology and biology.* Unpublished, Nature Conservancy Council, South-west Scotland Region.

Perkins, E.J. 1986. The ecology of scar grounds in the Solway Firth. *Transactions of Dumfriesshire and Galloway Natural History and Antiquarian Society, 61*: 4-19.

Phillips, A.M., & Maltby, A. 1978. *An investigation of the erosion and accretion regime on the saltmarshes of the upper Solway Firth from 1946-1975.* Peterborough, Nature Conservancy Council.

Radley, G.P., Waite, A.R., & Crawford, I.C. 1987. *National sand dune vegetation survey. Site report No. 3, Silloth to Maryport Dunes.* Peterborough, Nature Conservancy Council.

Rednall, D.A. 1992. *Biological and trace metal survey of Inner Solway Firth beaches.* Solway River Purification Board Biological Report, No. 9.

Rowe, S.M. 1978. An investigation of the erosion and accretion regime on the saltmarshes of the upper Solway Firth, from 1946 to 1975. *Nature Conservancy Council, CSD Report*, No. 147.

Rowe, S.M., Phillips, A.M., & Maltby, A. 1978. Investigation of erosion and accretion regime on saltmarshes of the Upper Solway Firth 1946-75. *Nature Conservancy Council, CSD Report*, No. 147.

Centre grid: NX8451 District: Stewartry
Region: Dumfries & Galloway SNH region: South-west Scotland

Review site location

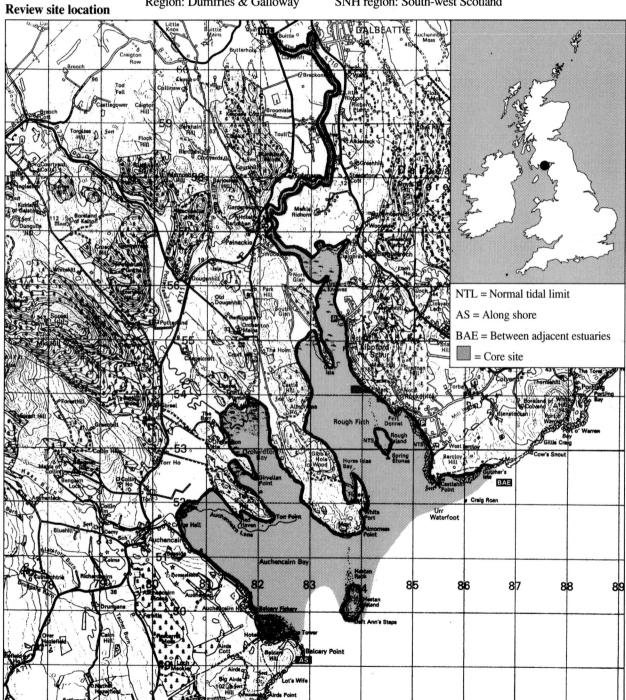

NTL = Normal tidal limit

AS = Along shore

BAE = Between adjacent estuaries

= Core site

© Crown copyright

Total area (ha)	Intertidal area (ha)	Shore length (km)	Channel length (km)	Tidal range (m)	Geomorph. type	Human population
1,290	1,289	44.4	14.4	6.7	Fjard	< 5,000

Description

The Rough Firth and Auchencairn Bay lies within a very broken coast and forms two shallow bays cut back into granite bed-rock. This estuary is adjacent to the Inner Solway Firth review site to the east, and the water quality within the Rough Firth and Auchencairn Bay has been classified as grade 1.

At low tide the estuary is an expanse of intertidal flats, with only a very small subtidal channel. The outermost flats of Auchencairn and Orchardton Bays are sandy, while the more sheltered inner flats of the Rough Firth are muddy. Beds of the eelgrass *Zostera* that were present in Auchencairn Bay have declined after cockle dredging was carried out in 1988.

Within the upper parts of the estuary there are areas of saltmarsh, which contain a number of plant species at the northern limit of their range and a variety of plant communities representing succession to alder carr. In Auchencairn and Orchardton Bays there has been a marked progressive colonisation by *Spartina*, which now accounts for 50% of the total saltmarsh area.

The coast on the south-western shore of Auchencairn Bay, which extends beyond the estuary, supports a large number of local and rare plant species on vegetated shingle, maritime grassland, swamps and flushes, hard cliffs and cliff crevices. There is also considerable invertebrate interest here that includes rare and local species, a rich fauna at the limit of its northern distribution.

The Rough Firth and Auchencairn Bay is frequented by wintering waders and wildfowl, and is of importance for its seabirds, for Almorness Point supports colonies of lesser black-headed gull and great black-headed gull.

Wildlife features

Coastal habitats

	Subtidal	Saltmarsh	Sandflats	Mudflats	Sand dunes	Rocky shores	Shingle	Lowland grassland	Lagoon	Other
	◉	●	●	●	◉	●	◉			
Area (ha)	1	135	1,154							

● = major habitat   ◉ = minor habitat

Birds

Wintering birds			1983/84 – 1987/88 data	
Total waterfowl: 5,220		BoEE	NWC	WSC
		●	●	

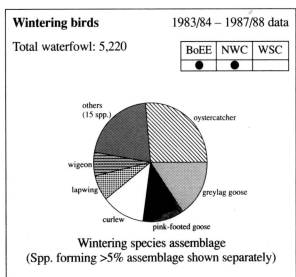

Wintering species assemblage
(Spp. forming >5% assemblage shown separately)

Breeding birds: there are moderate-sized colonies of lesser black-backed gull and herring gull, and a small number of common tern breeding on the estuary. Small numbers of ringed plover also breed within the Rough Firth and Auchencairn Bay.

Aquatic estuarine communities

Soft substrate

1	2	3	4	5	6	7	8	9	10	11	12	13	14	15	16
	●											●	●	●	●

Hard substrate

17	18	19	20	21	22	23	24	25	26	27	28	29	30	31	32	33
		●								●			●			

Additional wildlife features

The invertebrate fauna recently recorded on the estuary includes seven Notable species. Otters are also frequently recorded.

Conservation status

● = designated   ◉ = proposed

	NCR	GCR	SSSI (B)	SSSI (G)	SSSI (M)	NNR	LNR	Ramsar	SPA	AONB	CWT	RSPB	ESA	NP	WWT	NT	NSA	HC	Other
			●										●			●	●		
No.			2										1			3	1		

Small areas of the estuary are covered by biological Sites of Special Scientific Interest, namely Auchencairn and Orchardton Bays (442 ha) and Abbey Burn Foot to Balcony Point (531 ha), which extends beyond the westernmost boundary of the estuary. The National Trust for Scotland own land at Rough Island, Rockcliffe, and the Merse, Rockcliffe. In addition the estuary lies within the Stewartry Environmentally Sensitive Area and National Scenic Area.

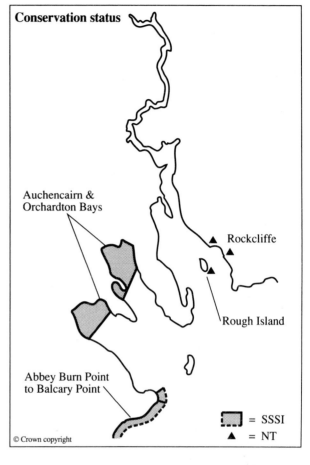

Conservation status

Auchencairn & Orchardton Bays

▲ Rockcliffe

Rough Island

Abbey Burn Point to Balcary Point

▦ = SSSI
▲ = NT

© Crown copyright

In Auchencairn Bay (above) and Orchardton Bay there has been a marked colonisation by the cordgrass *Spartina anglica*, which now accounts for 50% of the total saltmarsh area. (Pat Doody, JNCC)

Human activities

Present	Proposed	
●	●	**Coast protection & sea defences**
		Linear defences
		Training walls
		Groynes
		Brushwood fences
		Spartina planting
		Marram grass planting
		Barrage schemes
		Weirs & barrages for river management
		Storm surge barrages
		Water storage barrages & bunds
		Leisure barrages
		Tidal power barrages
		Power generation
		Thermal power stations
		Import/export jetties (power generation)
		Wind-power generation
●		**Industrial, port & related development**
		Dock, port & harbour facilities
		Manufacturing industries
		Chemical industries
		Ship & boat building
		Others
		Extraction & processing of natural gas & oil
		Exploration
		Production
		Rig & platform construction
		Pipeline construction
		Pipeline installation
		Import/export jetties & single-point moorings
		Oil refineries
		Mothballing of rigs & tankers
		Military activities
		Overflying by military aircraft
		Others
●		**Waste discharge**
		Domestic waste disposal
		Sewage discharge & outfalls
		Sewage treatment works
		Rubbish tips
		Industrial & agricultural waste discharge
		Thermal discharges (power stations)
		Dredge spoil
		Accidental discharges
		Aerial crop spraying
		Waste incinerators
		Others
		Sediment extraction
		Capital dredging
		Maintenance dredging
		Commercial estuarine aggregates extraction
		Commercial terrestrial aggregates extraction
		Non-commercial aggregates extraction
		Hard-rock quarrying
		Transport & communications
		Airports & helipads
		Tunnels, bridges & aqueducts
		Causeways & fords
		Road schemes
		Ferries
		Cables
		Urbanisation
		Land-claim for housing & car parks
●		**Education & scientific research**
		Sampling, specimen collection & observation
		Nature trails & interpretative facilities
		Seismic studies & geological test drilling
		Marine & terrestrial archaeology
		Fossil collecting

Present	Proposed	
		Tourism & recreation
		Infrastructure developments
●	●●	Marinas
		Non-marina moorings
		Dinghy & boat parks
		Caravan parks & chalets
		Leisure centres, complexes & piers
		Aquatic-based recreation
		Power-boating & water-skiing
		Jet-skiing
●		Sailing
		Sailboarding & wind-surfing
		SCUBA & snorkelling
		Canoeing
		Surfing
		Rowing
		Tourist boat trips/leisure barges
●		Angling
●		Other non-commercial fishing
●		Bathing & general beach recreation
		Terrestrial & intertidal-based recreation
●		Walking, including dog walking
		Bird-watching
		Sand-yachting
		4WD & trial-biking
		Car sand-racing
●		Horse-riding
		Rock-climbing
		Golf courses
		Clay-pigeon shooting
		Others
		Airborne recreation
		Overflying by light aircraft
		Radio-controlled model aircraft
●		Others
		Wildfowling & hunting
●		Wildfowling
●		Other hunting-related activities
		Bait-collecting
●		Digging & pumping for lugworms & ragworms
		Hydraulic dredging for worms
●		Others
		Commercial fisheries
		Fish-netting & trawling
		Fyke-netting for eels
●		Fish traps & other fixed devices & nets
		Crustacea
●		Molluscs – Hand-gathering
		Dredging
●		Hydraulic dredging
		Cultivation of living resource
●		Saltmarsh grazing
		Sand dune grazing
		Agricultural land-claim
		Fish-farming
		Shellfish farming
		Bottom & tray cultivation
		Suspended cultivation
		Crustacea farming
		Reeds for roofing
		Salicornia picking
		Others
		Management & killing of birds & mammals
		Killing of mammals
		Killing of birds
		Adult fish-eating birds
		Adult shellfish-eating birds
		Gulls
		Geese
		Wildlife habitat management
		Spartina control
		Habitat creation & restoration
		Marine
		Intertidal
●		Terrestrial
		Habitat management
●		**Others**

42.4

Features of human use

This estuary is largely unspoilt with little human activity. Those activities present are mainly low-level recreational pursuits, with sailing as the most intensive pursuit and centred around the moorings at Kippford. Walking and horse-riding occur over the sandier parts of the bays, i.e. in the lower reaches, and small numbers of people use the beach at Port Donnel.

Exploitation of the natural resources is varied but not intensive. Salmon nets are used south-west of Balcary, bait-collecting occurs in the south-west of Auchencairn Bay, and hydraulic dredging for cockles also occurs. Wildfowlers shoot from along the shores. At Palnackie there is a small harbour, which is used for landing cockles caught in the Solway Firth.

Other features of human use on the estuary include coastguard rescue exercises off Balcary Point.

In 1989 there were proposals in the Stewartry Local Plan to develop Kippford as a marina, which would include a number of floating moorings. By 1992 this were under construction.

Categories of human use

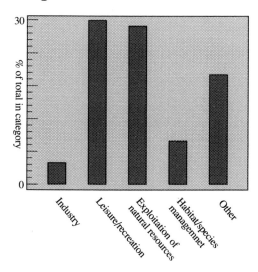

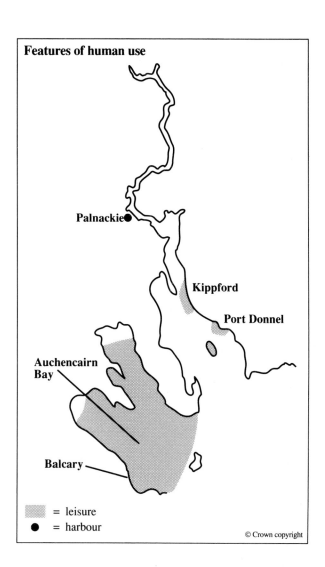

Further reading

Burd, F., & Fojt, W. 1987. *Saltmarsh survey of Great Britain. Scotland Regional report – South-west.* Unpublished, Nature Conservancy Council.

Covey, R. 1992. Sublittoral survey of the north coast of the outer Solway (Mull of Galloway to Auchencairn). *Nature Conservancy Council, CSD Report*, No. 1,193. (Marine Nature Conservation Review Report No. MNCR/SR/15)

Covey, R. , & Emblow, C. 1992. Littoral survey of the Inner Solway Firth and additional sites in Dumfries & Galloway. *Joint Nature Conservation Committee Report*, No. 33.

Perkins, E.J. 1988. *The impact of suction dredging upon the population of cockles*, Cerastoderma edulis, *in Auchencairn Bay, 1988.* Unpublished, Nature Conservancy Council, South-west Scotland Region.

Perkins, E.J. 1973. *The marine fauna and flora of the Solway Firth.* Dumfries, Dumfriesshire and Galloway Natural History and Antiquarian Society.

Wilkinson, M. 1973. Intertidal algae of some estuaries in Galloway. *The Western Naturalist, 4*: 42-50.

Dee Estuary
(Dumfries & Galloway)

Centre grid: NX6747
Region: Dumfries & Galloway

District: Stewartry
SNH region: South-west Scotland

Review site location

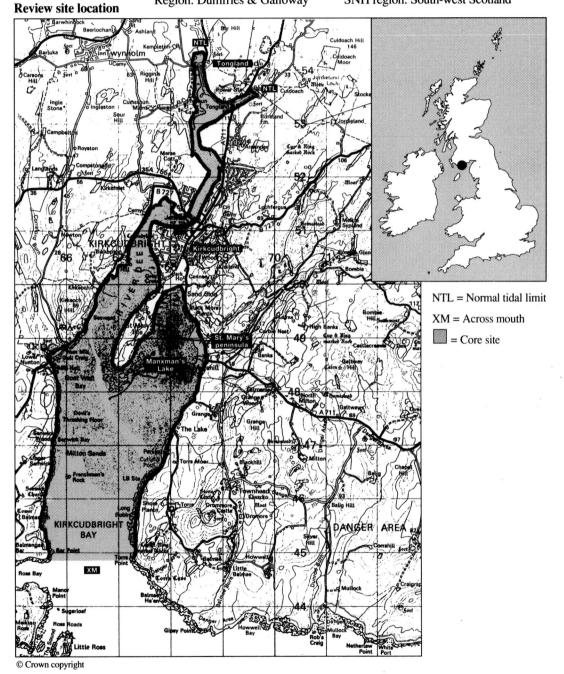

NTL = Normal tidal limit

XM = Across mouth

= Core site

© Crown copyright

Total area (ha)	Intertidal area (ha)	Shore length (km)	Channel length (km)	Tidal range (m)	Geomorph. type	Human population
1,144	825	28.6	11.7	6.7	Fjard	< 5,000

Description

This site is the estuary of the River Dee which flows past the town of Kirkcudbright and opens out into Kirkcudbright Bay. It includes Manxman's Lake which lies to the east of St Mary's Bay peninsula. Water quality in the Dee has been classified as grade 2 as far downstream as the tip of St Mary's peninsula, while the rest of the estuary is class 1.

At low tide the Dee is a narrow channel that flows across extensive mudflats, with a small freshwater input from the Buckland Burn that meanders across Manxman's Lake. The innermost flats are made of fine muddy silts, and at Manxman's Lake there are areas of the eelgrass *Zostera noltii*. Towards the mouth of the estuary the intertidal sediments become coarse-grained, and there are fringes of exposed shingle around St Mary's peninsula and the eastern shore.

Saltmarshes have developed in the upper reaches of the estuary and in the shelter of Manxman's Lake, with the largest continuous area of saltmarsh extending up the channel of the Dee towards Tongland. The vegetation here shows extensive transition from saline to freshwater communities, with reed-beds and freshwater-flushed communities.

Further downstream towards Kirkcudbright Bay and extending beyond the estuary boundaries there are long stretches of rocky shore which are interspersed with boulder-strewn shores, cliffs, grasslands, machair and maritime heath, and these areas are botanically highly varied.

Wildlife features

Coastal habitats

	Subtidal	Saltmarsh	Sandflats	Mudflats	Sand dunes	Rocky shores	Shingle	Lowland grassland	Lagoon	Other
	●	●	◉	●		●	◉			
Area (ha)	319	77	748							

● = major habitat ◉ = minor habitat

Birds

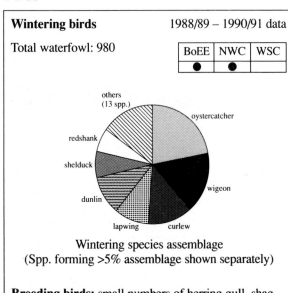

Wintering birds — 1988/89 – 1990/91 data

Total waterfowl: 980

BoEE	NWC	WSC
●	●	

others (13 spp.), oystercatcher, redshank, shelduck, dunlin, lapwing, curlew, wigeon

Wintering species assemblage
(Spp. forming >5% assemblage shown separately)

Breeding birds: small numbers of herring gull, shag and cormorant nest on the cliffs, and small numbers of ringed plover breed on the shores.

Other: the Dee Estuary is the only site for overwintering turnstone in Stewartry, and Canada geese use the estuary during their late summer moult.

Aquatic estuarine communities

Soft substrate

1	2	3	4	5	6	7	8	9	10	11	12	13	14	15	16
	●											●	●	●	●

Hard substrate

17	18	19	20	21	22	23	24	25	26	27	28	29	30	31	32	33
		●			●	●										

Additional wildlife features

Otters are regularly recorded on the estuary.

Conservation status

● = designated   ▒ = proposed

	NCR	GCR	SSSI (B)	SSSI (G)	SSSI (M)	NNR	LNR	Ramsar	SPA	AONB	CWT	RSPB	ESA	NP	WWT	NT	NSA	HC	Other
	●	●		●	●														●
No.	1	4		1	2														1

Only small areas of the estuary have been designated as Sites of Special Scientific Interest. Shoulder O'Craig (0.5 ha) is a geological SSSI, Borgue Coast (1,892 ha) and Torr's to Mason's Walk (168 ha) are SSSIs for their biological and geological interest, both of which extend along the coast beyond the estuary. There are also four Geological Conservation Review sites on the estuary, namely Torr's to Mason's Walk, Shoulder O'Craig, Borgue Coast and Meikle Ross.

In addition the western shore of the estuary lies within the Borgue Coast Nature Conservation Review site, and the Dee Estuary is recognised as having regional scenic significance within the Stewartry Local Plan.

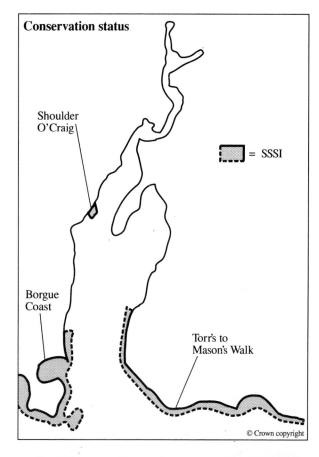

Conservation status

Shoulder O'Craig

▨ = SSSI

Borgue Coast

Torr's to Mason's Walk

© Crown copyright

The cliffs of the Dee Estuary and the Borgue Coast support a varied flora. (Pat Doody, JNCC)

Human activities

Present Proposed

●		**Coast protection & sea defences** Linear defences Training walls Groynes Brushwood fences *Spartina* planting Marram grass planting
		Barrage schemes Weirs & barrages for river management Storm surge barrages Water storage barrages & bunds Leisure barrages Tidal power barrages
		Power generation Thermal power stations Import/export jetties (power generation) Wind-power generation
●	●	**Industrial, port & related development** Dock, port & harbour facilities Manufacturing industries Chemical industries Ship & boat building Others
		Extraction & processing of natural gas & oil Exploration Production Rig & platform construction Pipeline construction Pipeline installation Import/export jetties & single-point moorings Oil refineries Mothballing of rigs & tankers
●		**Military activities** Overflying by military aircraft Others
● ●		**Waste discharge** Domestic waste disposal Sewage discharge & outfalls Sewage treatment works Rubbish tips Industrial & agricultural waste discharge Thermal discharges (power stations) Dredge spoil Accidental discharges Aerial crop spraying Waste incinerators Others
		Sediment extraction Capital dredging Maintenance dredging Commercial estuarine aggregates extraction Commercial terrestrial aggregates extraction Non-commercial aggregates extraction Hard-rock quarrying
● ●		**Transport & communications** Airports & helipads Tunnels, bridges & aqueducts Causeways & fords Road schemes Ferries Cables
		Urbanisation Land-claim for housing & car parks
		Education & scientific research Sampling, specimen collection & observation Nature trails & interpretative facilities Seismic studies & geological test drilling Marine & terrestrial archaeology Fossil collecting

Present Proposed

●
●
	●
	●
		Tourism & recreation
		Infrastructure developments
		   Marinas
		   Non-marina moorings
		   Dinghy & boat parks
		   Caravan parks & chalets
		   Leisure centres, complexes & piers
		Aquatic-based recreation
		   Power-boating & water-skiing
		   Jet-skiing
		   Sailing
		   Sailboarding & wind-surfing
		   SCUBA & snorkelling
		   Canoeing
		   Surfing
		   Rowing
		   Tourist boat trips/leisure barges
		   Angling
		   Other non-commercial fishing
		   Bathing & general beach recreation
		Terrestrial & intertidal-based recreation
		   Walking, including dog walking
		   Bird-watching
		   Sand-yachting
		   4WD & trial-biking
		   Car sand-racing
		   Horse-riding
		   Rock-climbing
		   Golf courses
		   Clay-pigeon shooting
		   Others
		Airborne recreation
		   Overflying by light aircraft
		   Radio-controlled model aircraft
		   Others

●		**Wildfowling & hunting** Wildfowling Other hunting-related activities
●		**Bait-collecting** Digging & pumping for lugworms & ragworms Hydraulic dredging for worms Others

		Commercial fisheries
		Fish-netting & trawling
		Fyke-netting for eels
		Fish traps & other fixed devices & nets
		Crustacea
		Molluscs – Hand-gathering
		       Dredging
		       Hydraulic dredging

●		**Cultivation of living resource**
		Saltmarsh grazing
		Sand dune grazing
		Agricultural land-claim
		Fish-farming
		Shellfish farming
		   Bottom & tray cultivation
		   Suspended cultivation
		Crustacea farming
		Reeds for roofing
		Salicornia picking
		Others

		Management & killing of birds & mammals Killing of mammals Killing of birds Adult fish-eating birds Adult shellfish-eating birds Gulls Geese

		Wildlife habitat management
		Spartina control
		Habitat creation & restoration
		     Marine
		     Intertidal
		     Terrestrial
		Habitat management

●		**Others**

Features of human use

Most activities present on the estuary are recreational. There are moorings and a dinghy and boat park at Kirkcudbright, and there is an active sailing club. Other leisure pursuits are not intensive and include occasional power-boating, canoeing and angling. A clay-pigeon shooting club shoots over an area on the south-eastern shore of the estuary.

The only industrial activity present is the small wharf at Kirkcudbright which is used primarily for fishing boats which operate outside the estuary, but it is also used as a landing point for coal, timber and oil.

In 1989 there were proposals for the construction of an industrial estate in the upper reaches of the estuary, and for a marina and moorings at Kirkcudbright to replace the existing jetty. By 1992 the marina was under construction, and there had been a more recent proposal for mineral exploitation within Kirkcudbright Bay.

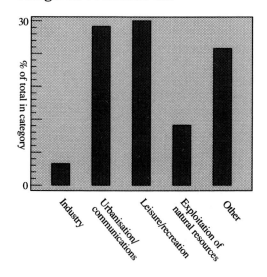

Categories of human use

Features of human use

Kirkcudbright

/ = urban/industrial shore
● = harbour
▨ = leisure

© Crown copyright

Further reading

Burd, F., & Fojt, W. 1987. *Saltmarsh survey of Great Britain. Scotland regional report, South-west.* Unpublished, Nature Conservancy Council.

Covey, R. 1990. Littoral survey of the north coast of the outer Solway (Mull of Galloway to Auchencairn). *Nature Conservancy Council, CSD Report,* No. 1,074. (Marine Conservation Review Report No. MNCR/SR/011.)

Covey, R. 1992. Sublittoral survey of the north coast of the outer Solway (Mull of Galloway to Auchencairn). *Nature Conservancy Council, CSD Report,* No. 1,193. (Marine Nature Conservation Review Report No. MNCR/SR/15.)

Covey, R., & Emblow, C.S. 1992. Littoral survey of the the Inner Solway Firth and additional sites in Dumfries and Galloway. *Joint Nature Conservation Committee Report,* No. 33. (Marine Nature Conservation Review Report No. MNCR/SR/20)

Perkins, E.J. 1973. *The marine fauna and flora of the Solway Firth.* Dumfries, Dumfriesshire and Galloway Natural History and Antiquarian Society.

Wilkinson, M. 1975. Intertidal algae of some estuaries in Galloway. *The Western Naturalist, 4*: 42-50.

44   Water of Fleet

Centre grid: NX5753   District: Stewartry

Region: Dumfries & Galloway   SNH region: South-west Scotland

Review site location

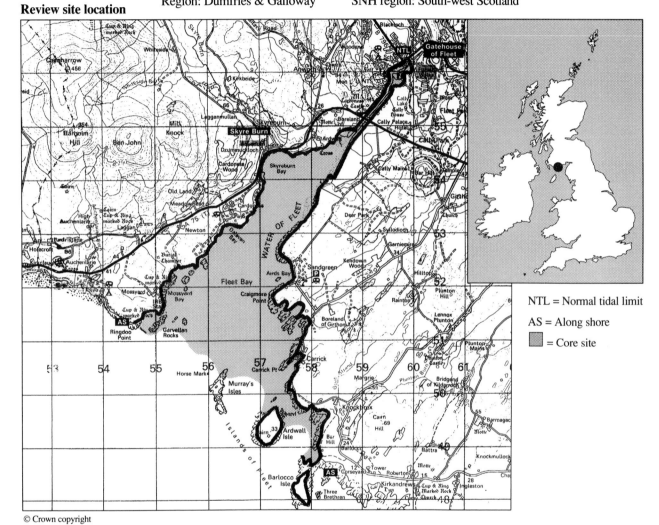

© Crown copyright

NTL = Normal tidal limit

AS = Along shore

▨ = Core site

Total area (ha)	Intertidal area (ha)	Shore length (km)	Channel length (km)	Tidal range (m)	Geomorph. type	Human population
790	790	19.9	7.2	6.7	Fjard	< 5,000

Description

The Water of Fleet flows through a sandy bay and into the south-east of Wigtown Bay. At low tide the freshwaters of the Water of Fleet and the Skyre Burn form very narrow channels which meander across the expanse of intertidal flats, and the estuary is shallow enough for the islands of Ardwall and Borlacco in the mouth of the site to be reached on foot. Water quality of the estuary has been classified as grade 1.

The lower parts of the bay are largely intertidal sandflats, which become more muddy in the upper parts of the estuary. In these upper, muddier reaches a small area of saltmarsh has developed. This is dominated by *Spartina* which forms approximately 50% of the saltmarsh vegetation.

Much of the western and northern shore is a raised beach which extends as far upstream as the Gatehouse of Fleet. The most seaward shores of the estuary are predominantly rocky, and the aquatic estuarine communities recorded on the estuary include a sheltered rocky shore community and a current-swept sand community. The rocky shores of the Borgue Coast extend eastwards from the estuary and have a varied flora associated with the pattern of soils, for basic outcrops occur within a generally acidic environment, with varying degrees of exposure. This vegetation includes maritime heath, machair and cliff species.

Wildlife features

Coastal habitats

	Subtidal	Saltmarsh	Sandflats	Mudflats	Sand dunes	Rocky shores	Shingle	Lowland grassland	Lagoon	Other
	◉	●	●	●		●				
Area (ha)		28	762							

● = major habitat   ◉ = minor habitat

Birds

Wintering birds   1986/87 – 1990/91 data

Total waterfowl: 110

BoEE	NWC	WSC
●	●	

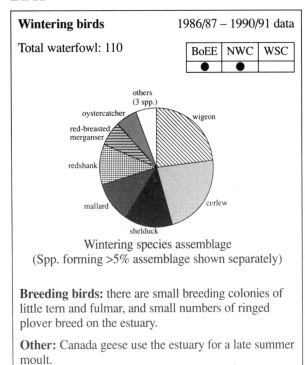

Wintering species assemblage
(Spp. forming >5% assemblage shown separately)

Breeding birds: there are small breeding colonies of little tern and fulmar, and small numbers of ringed plover breed on the estuary.

Other: Canada geese use the estuary for a late summer moult.

Aquatic estuarine communities

Soft substrate

1	2	3	4	5	6	7	8	9	10	11	12	13	14	15	16
								●							

Hard substrate

17	18	19	20	21	22	23	24	25	26	27	28	29	30	31	32	33
		●														

Additional wildlife features

Otters regularly use the estuary.

Conservation status

● = designated   ● = proposed

	NCR	GCR	SSSI (B)	SSSI (G)	SSSI (M)	NNR	LNR	Ramsar	SPA	AONB	CWT	RSPB	ESA	NP	WWT	NT	NSA	HC	Other
	●	●			●											●	●		
No.	1	2			1											1	1		

The south-eastern shores of the estuary are part of the Borgue Coast (1,892 ha) Site of Special Scientific Interest which is an SSSI for its biological and geological interest. The Borgue Coast and Barlocco Isle are Geological Conservation Review sites.

The National Trust have land in the upper reaches of the estuary at Cardoness, and the Water of Fleet is a National Scenic Area.

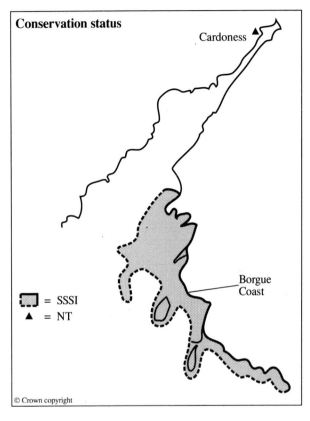

Conservation status

Cardoness

▭ = SSSI

▲ = NT

Borgue Coast

© Crown copyright

Carrick Shore, Water of Fleet. The seaward shores of the Water of Fleet are predominantly rocky. (Pat Doody, JNCC)

Human activities

Present	Proposed	
●		**Coast protection & sea defences** Linear defences Training walls Groynes Brushwood fences *Spartina* planting Marram grass planting
		Barrage schemes Weirs & barrages for river management Storm surge barrages Water storage barrages & bunds Leisure barrages Tidal power barrages
		Power generation Thermal power stations Import/export jetties (power generation) Wind-power generation
		Industrial, port & related development Dock, port & harbour facilities Manufacturing industries Chemical industries Ship & boat building Others
		Extraction & processing of natural gas & oil Exploration Production Rig & platform construction Pipeline construction Pipeline installation Import/export jetties & single-point moorings Oil refineries Mothballing of rigs & tankers
●		**Military activities** Overflying by military aircraft Others
● ●		**Waste discharge** Domestic waste disposal Sewage discharge & outfalls Sewage treatment works Rubbish tips Industrial & agricultural waste discharge Thermal discharges (power stations) Dredge spoil Accidental discharges Aerial crop spraying Waste incinerators Others
		Sediment extraction Capital dredging Maintenance dredging Commercial estuarine aggregates extraction Commercial terrestrial aggregates extraction Non-commercial aggregates extraction Hard-rock quarrying
● ●		**Transport & communications** Airports & helipads Tunnels, bridges & aqueducts Causeways & fords Road schemes Ferries Cables
		Urbanisation Land-claim for housing & car parks
		Education & scientific research Sampling, specimen collection & observation Nature trails & interpretative facilities Seismic studies & geological test drilling Marine & terrestrial archaeology Fossil collecting

Present	Proposed	

●
●
●
●
●
●
		Tourism & recreation
		Infrastructure developments
		  Marinas
		  Non-marina moorings
		  Dinghy & boat parks
		  Caravan parks & chalets
		  Leisure centres, complexes & piers
		Aquatic-based recreation
		  Power-boating & water-skiing
		  Jet-skiing
		  Sailing
		  Sailboarding & wind-surfing
		  SCUBA & snorkelling
		  Canoeing
		  Surfing
		  Rowing
		  Tourist boat trips/leisure barges
		  Angling
		  Other non-commercial fishing
		  Bathing & general beach recreation
		Terrestrial & intertidal-based recreation
		  Walking, including dog walking
		  Bird-watching
		  Sand-yachting
		  4WD & trial-biking
		  Car sand-racing
		  Horse-riding
		  Rock-climbing
		  Golf courses
		  Clay-pigeon shooting
		  Others
		Airborne recreation
		  Overflying by light aircraft
		  Radio-controlled model aircraft
		  Others

●		**Wildfowling & hunting** Wildfowling Other hunting-related activities
● ●		**Bait-collecting** Digging & pumping for lugworms & ragworms Hydraulic dredging for worms Others

●
●
		Commercial fisheries
		Fish-netting & trawling
		Fyke-netting for eels
		Fish traps & other fixed devices & nets
		Crustacea
		Molluscs – Hand-gathering
		    Dredging
		    Hydraulic dredging

●		**Cultivation of living resource**
		Saltmarsh grazing
		Sand dune grazing
		Agricultural land-claim
		Fish-farming
		Shellfish farming
		  Bottom & tray cultivation
		  Suspended cultivation
		Crustacea farming
		Reeds for roofing
		Salicornia picking
		Others

●		**Management & killing of birds & mammals** Killing of mammals Killing of birds Adult fish-eating birds Adult shellfish-eating birds Gulls Geese

		Wildlife habitat management
		Spartina control
		Habitat creation & restoration
		  Marine
		  Intertidal
		  Terrestrial
		Habitat management

		Others

Features of human use

Most activities on Water of Fleet are recreational and occur over most of the estuary as far upstream as Skyreburn Bay. At the height of the summer season there are up to 50 moorings in Mossyard Bay, Airds Bay and Carrick, and these areas are subject to pressure all year round from the launching of power-boats, sailboards and dinghies. Beach recreation is centred around the caravan sites and land-based pursuits are not intensive.

Exploitation of the natural resources includes fish-netting, saltmarsh grazing, bait-digging, collecting crabs, mussels and limpets for bait, and occasional wildfowling.

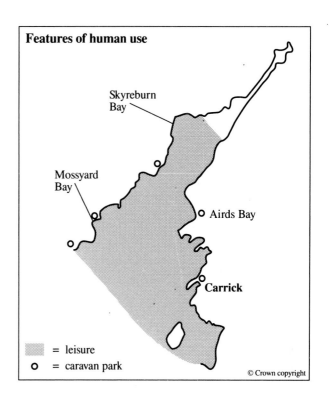

Features of human use

Categories of human use

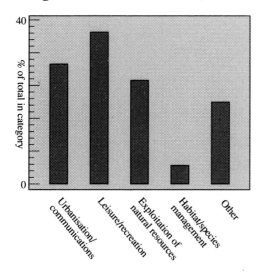

Further reading

Covey, R. 1990. Littoral survey of the north coast of the outer Solway (Mull of Galloway to Auchencairn). *Nature Conservancy Council, CSD Report*, No. 1,074. (Marine Nature Conservation Review Report MNCR/SR/011.)

Covey, R., & Emblow, C.S. 1992. Littoral survey of the the Inner Solway Firth and additional sites in Dumfries and Galloway. *Joint Nature Conservation Committee Report,* No. 33. (Marine Nature Conservation Review Report No. MNCR/SR/20)

Perkins, E.J. 1973. The marine fauna and flora of the Solway Firth. *Transactions of the Dumfriesshire and Galloway Natural History and Antiquarian Society,* 45: 15.

Wilkinson, M. 1975. Intertidal algae of some estuaries in Galloway. *The Western Naturalist, 4:* 42-50.

Wilkinson, M. 1980. The marine algae of Galloway. *British Phycological Journal, 85:* 265-273.

Cree Estuary

Centre grid: NX4655   District: Wigtown
Region: Dumfries & Galloway   SNH region: South-west Scotland

site location

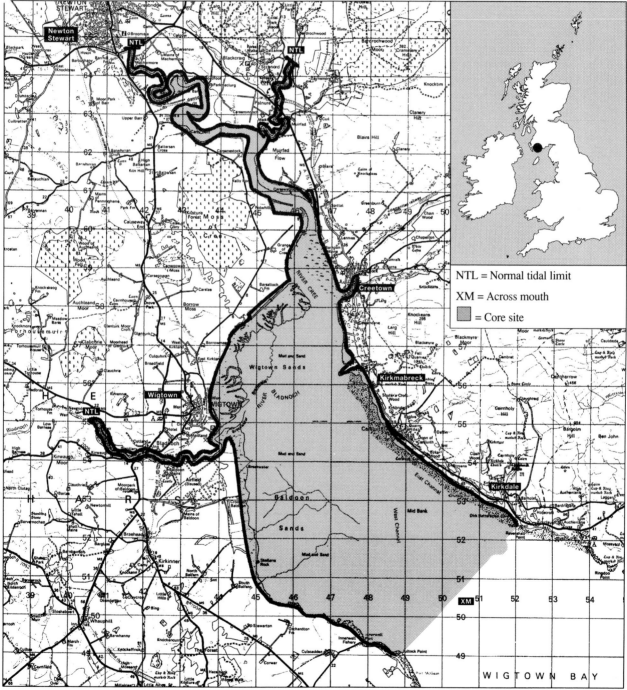

© Crown copyright

NTL = Normal tidal limit

XM = Across mouth

= Core site

Total area (ha)	Intertidal area (ha)	Shore length (km)	Channel length (km)	Tidal range (m)	Geomorph. type	Human population
4,728	3,340	24.3	63.2	6.7	Fjard	< 5,000

Description

This is one of the largest estuaries on the south-west coast of Scotland, with river inflows from the Rivers Cree and Bladnoch, and the Palnure Burn and Moneypool Burn. Water quality within the estuary has been classfied as grade 1, apart from the River Bladnoch which is grade 2.

At low tide the estuary is an extensive intertidal flat of mud and sand, rich in invertebrates. Much of the western shore is fringed with saltmarsh or merse, which is particularly extensive north of Wigtown. The vegetation is typical of closely grazed saltmarsh, and includes species that are locally rare or at the northern and western limit of their range. On the eastern shore there is a long ridge of sand and shingle, of which a narrow strip of shingle from Kirkmabreck and Kirkdale is vegetated.

On the east coast south of Creetown, a narrow belt of maritime oakwood extends southwards along the shore.

The strong influence of wind and salt-spray has produced stunted trees, and within the wood there is a specialised assemblage of lichens (including ten nationally scarce species) and invertebrates (including a large number of beetles). Closer to the shore there are also patches of strandline vegetation, maritime grassland and hard-cliff communities, and around spring lines there is willow carr and reedbed.

The Cree Estuary is one of the few estuaries on this part of the Scottish coast to support large numbers of wintering waterfowl. It regularly supports internationally important populations of pink-footed goose and nationally important populations of curlew, whooper swan and pintail. The Cree is also one of the few sites in Scotland where smelt (locally known as sparling), once a fairly common fish, are known to spawn.

Wildlife features

Coastal habitats

Subtidal	Saltmarsh	Sandflats	Mudflats	Sand dunes	Rocky shores	Shingle	Lowland grassland	Lagoon	Other
●	●	●	●		●	●			◉

Area (ha)	Subtidal	Saltmarsh	Sandflats	Mudflats
	1,388	445	2,895	

● = major habitat   ◉ = minor habitat

Aquatic estuarine communities

Soft substrate

1	2	3	4	5	6	7	8	9	10	11	12	13	14	15	16
												●		●	

Hard substrate

17	18	19	20	21	22	23	24	25	26	27	28	29	30	31	32	33
	●															

Birds

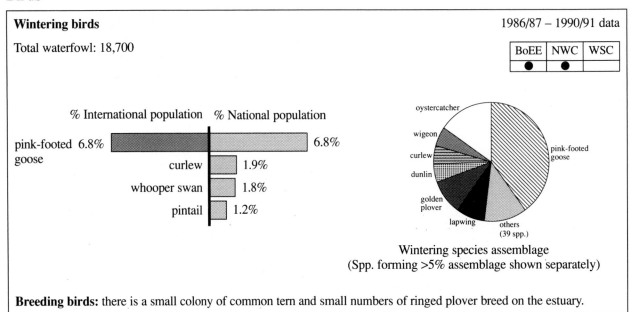

Wintering birds   1986/87 – 1990/91 data

Total waterfowl: 18,700

BoEE	NWC	WSC
●	●	

% International population   % National population

pink-footed goose 6.8% — 6.8%
curlew 1.9%
whooper swan 1.8%
pintail 1.2%

Wintering species assemblage
(Spp. forming >5% assemblage shown separately)

oystercatcher, wigeon, curlew, dunlin, golden plover, lapwing, others (39 spp.), pink-footed goose

Breeding birds: there is a small colony of common tern and small numbers of ringed plover breed on the estuary.

Additional wildlife features

The nationally rare plant holy-grass *Hierochloe odorata* has been found on the estuary. The invertebrate fauna recently recorded on the Cree Estuary includes seven Notable species.

The nationally rare fish smelt *Osmerus eperlanus* spawns in the estuary, here in one of only three locations in Scotland. Otters regularly use the estuary

Conservation status

● = designated   ◉ = proposed

	NCR	GCR	SSSI (B)	SSSI (G)	SSSI (M)	NNR	LNR	Ramsar	SPA	AONB	CWT	RSPB	ESA	NP	WWT	NT	NSA	HC	Other
	●		●				◉	◉	◉										
No.	2		2				1	1	1										

Two biological SSSIs encompass a large proportion of the estuary Site of Special Scientific Interest, the Cree Estuary (3,456 ha) and Ravenshall Wood (44 ha). Both are also Nature Conservation Review sites. There is a proposal to designate the Lower Cree estuary as an SSSI, and to designate Wigtown Bay as a Local Nature Reserve.

Wigtown Bay is proposed as both a Ramsar site and a Special Protection Area.

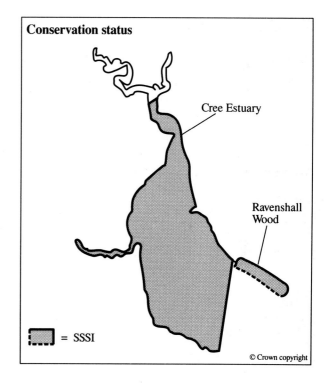

Conservation status

Cree Estuary

Ravenshall Wood

▦ = SSSI

© Crown copyright

Human activities

Present	Proposed	Coast protection & sea defences
●		Linear defences
		Training walls
●		Groynes
	●	Brushwood fences
		Spartina planting
		Marram grass planting

Present	Proposed	Barrage schemes
		Weirs & barrages for river management
		Storm surge barrages
		Water storage barrages & bunds
	●	Leisure barrages
		Tidal power barrages

Present	Proposed	Power generation
		Thermal power stations
		Import/export jetties (power generation)
		Wind-power generation

Present	Proposed	Industrial, port & related development
		Dock, port & harbour facilities
		Manufacturing industries
	●	Chemical industries
		Ship & boat building
		Others

Present	Proposed	Extraction & processing of natural gas & oil
		Exploration
		Production
		Rig & platform construction
		Pipeline construction
		Pipeline installation
		Import/export jetties & single-point moorings
		Oil refineries
		Mothballing of rigs & tankers

Present	Proposed	Military activities
●		Overflying by military aircraft
		Others

Present	Proposed	Waste discharge
		Domestic waste disposal
●		Sewage discharge & outfalls
		Sewage treatment works
		Rubbish tips
		Industrial & agricultural waste discharge
		Thermal discharges (power stations)
		Dredge spoil
		Accidental discharges
		Aerial crop spraying
		Waste incinerators
		Others

Present	Proposed	Sediment extraction
		Capital dredging
		Maintenance dredging
		Commercial estuarine aggregates extraction
		Commercial terrestrial aggregates extraction
●		Non-commercial aggregates extraction
		Hard-rock quarrying

Present	Proposed	Transport & communications
		Airports & helipads
		Tunnels, bridges & aqueducts
●		Causeways & fords
		Road schemes
		Ferries
●		Cables

Present	Proposed	Urbanisation
		Land-claim for housing & car parks

Present	Proposed	Education & scientific research
●		Sampling, specimen collection & observation
●		Nature trails & interpretative facilities
		Seismic studies & geological test drilling
		Marine & terrestrial archaeology
		Fossil collecting

Present	Proposed	Tourism & recreation
		Infrastructure developments
●		Marinas
		Non-marina moorings
●		Dinghy & boat parks
		Caravan parks & chalets
	●	Leisure centres, complexes & piers
		Aquatic-based recreation
		Power-boating & water-skiing
		Jet-skiing
●		Sailing
		Sailboarding & wind-surfing
		SCUBA & snorkelling
		Canoeing
		Surfing
		Rowing
		Tourist boat trips/leisure barges
●		Angling
		Other non-commercial fishing
		Bathing & general beach recreation
		Terrestrial & intertidal-based recreation
●		Walking, including dog walking
●		Bird-watching
		Sand-yachting
		4WD & trial-biking
		Car sand-racing
●		Horse-riding
		Rock-climbing
		Golf courses
		Clay-pigeon shooting
		Others
		Airborne recreation
		Overflying by light aircraft
		Radio-controlled model aircraft
		Others

Present	Proposed	Wildfowling & hunting
●		Wildfowling
●		Other hunting-related activities

Present	Proposed	Bait-collecting
●		Digging & pumping for lugworms & ragworms
		Hydraulic dredging for worms
		Others

Present	Proposed	Commercial fisheries
●		Fish-netting & trawling
		Fyke-netting for eels
●		Fish traps & other fixed devices & nets
●		Crustacea
●		Molluscs – Hand-gathering
		Dredging
		Hydraulic dredging

Present	Proposed	Cultivation of living resource
●		Saltmarsh grazing
		Sand dune grazing
		Agricultural land-claim
		Fish-farming
		Shellfish farming
		Bottom & tray cultivation
		Suspended cultivation
		Crustacea farming
		Reeds for roofing
		Salicornia picking
●		Others

Present	Proposed	Management & killing of birds & mammals
		Killing of mammals
		Killing of birds
		Adult fish-eating birds
		Adult shellfish-eating birds
		Gulls
	●	Geese

Present	Proposed	Wildlife habitat management
		Spartina control
		Habitat creation & restoration
		Marine
	●	Intertidal
		Terrestrial
		Habitat management

Present	Proposed	Others

Features of human use

Most activities involve exploitation of the natural resources. Commercial fishing includes seine-netting for salmon and sea trout, stake nets, lobster- and crab-potting, and mussel- and cockle-gathering. Bait-digging for worms takes place on Baldoon Sands, and wildfowling occurs throughout the estuary.

Leisure activities are widespread but not intensive. There are small numbers of moorings at Wigtown, Creetown and Innerwell Port which are used for fishing boats, and sailing is not intensive but occurs throughout the bay. Walking is centred around Wigtown and Creetown, and horse-riders use the southern parts of Baldoon Sands.

In 1989 there were proposals to build a cement works at Carty Port; for a leisure barrage and artificial island complex at Creetown; for the creation of grazing marsh at the mouth of the River Bladnoch with brushwood fences to enhance accretion; and for culling of geese for agricultural reasons. By 1992 goose culling was under way and hydraulic dredging for cockles was a large-scale activity within the estuary. The proposal for a leisure barrage had been dropped.

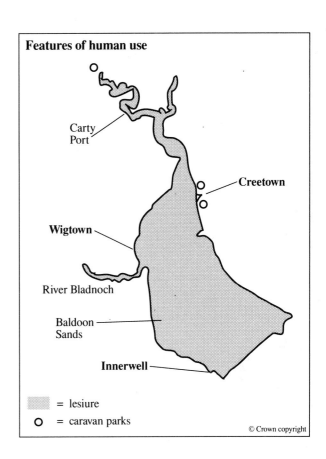

Features of human use

= lesiure

o = caravan parks

© Crown copyright

Categories of human use

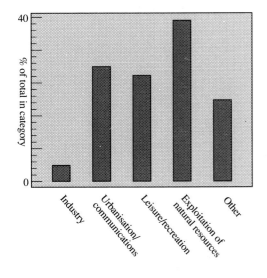

Further reading

Covey, R. 1990. Littoral survey of the north coast of the outer Solway (Mull of Galloway to Auchencairn). *Nature Conservancy Council, CSD Report*, No. 1,074. (Marine Nature Conservation Review Report No. MNCR/SR/011)

Covey, R., & Emblow, C.S. 1992. Littoral survey of the the Inner Solway Firth and additional sites in Dumfries and Galloway. *Joint Nature Conservation Committee Report*, No. 33. (Marine Nature Conservation Review Report No. MNCR/SR/20)

Perkins, E.J. 1973. *The marine fauna and flora of the Solway Firth*. Dumfries, Dumfriesshire and Galloway Natural History and Antiquarian Society.

Luce Bay

Centre grid: NX1855

District: Wigtown

Region: Dumfries & Galloway

SNH region: South-west Scotland

Review site location

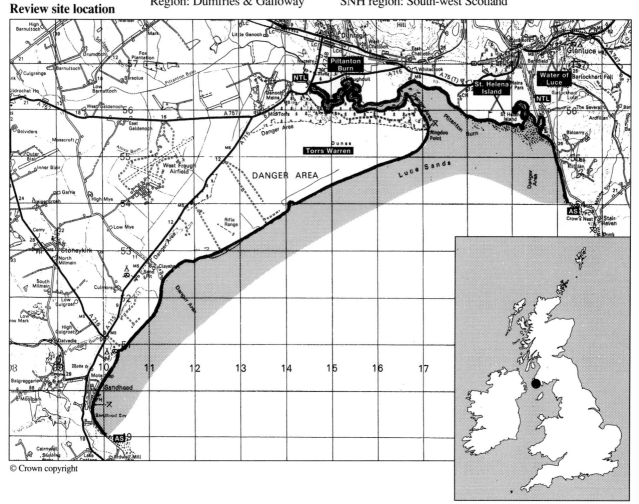

© Crown copyright

Total area (ha)	Intertidal area (ha)	Shore length (km)	Channel length (km)	Tidal range (m)	Geomorph. type	Human population
1,228	1,196	27.5	8.5	5.3	Linear shore	< 5,000

NTL = Normal tidal limit

AS = Along shore

▨ = Core site

Description

Luce Bay is a very shallow, sandy estuary on the south-west coast of Scotland. The two small inflows of freshwater stem from the Water of Luce and Piltanton Burn, which join near the eastern shore close to the sea. The water quality of the estuary has been graded as class 1, except for Piltanton Burn which was class 2.

There are two areas of saltmarsh within the estuary. The larger area stretches along Piltanton Burn and there is a smaller patch where the Water of Luce flows into the estuary. It is within the saltmarshes that the vegetation is most abundant, and the vegetation communities present show a transition to grassland.

At low water a large proportion of the estuary is an 800 metre wide sandflat which extends as far south-east as Sandhead Bay, and in the east of the estuary at St Helena Island the sand is interspersed with shingle. Behind this large sandflat lies the large and diverse sand dune system of Torrs Warren, the largest acidic dune system in western Scotland. The dunes extend for almost 10 km along the shore, and the system is well-supplied with sand sediments from offshore. There is a contrasting morphology within the site with low, parallel foredunes, high transverse dunes with recent erosion, older dunes on raised beach ridges, and well-developed dune slacks. Torrs Warren is considered to be of national importance for the undisturbed nature of the habitat and the diversity of plant communities and plant species present, for more than 200 higher plant species have been recorded here. The invertebrate fauna of the dunes is also diverse, with uncommon species of water beetles and grasshoppers.

Wildlife features

Coastal habitats

	Subtidal	Saltmarsh	Sandflats	Mudflats	Sand dunes	Rocky shores	Shingle	Lowland grassland	Lagoon	Other
	●	●	●	◍	●		◍			
Area (ha)	32	36	1160							

● = major habitat   ◍ = minor habitat

Birds

Wintering birds	1986/87 – 1990/91 data

Total waterfowl: 1,540

BoEE	NWC	WSC
●	●	

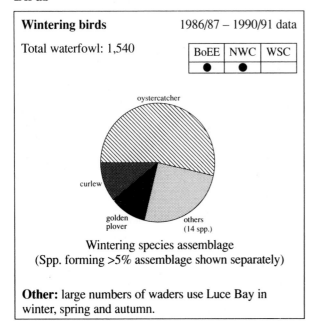

oystercatcher

curlew

golden plover

others (14 spp.)

Wintering species assemblage
(Spp. forming >5% assemblage shown separately)

Other: large numbers of waders use Luce Bay in winter, spring and autumn.

Aquatic estuarine communities

Soft substrate

1	2	3	4	5	6	7	8	9	10	11	12	13	14	15	16
	●											●			

Hard substrate

17	18	19	20	21	22	23	24	25	26	27	28	29	30	31	32	33
	●															

Additional wildlife features

The invertebrate fauna recently recorded on the estuary includes the RDB 3 beetle *Hydrochus brevis* and nine Notable species.

Otters are present on the estuary.

Conservation status

● = designated   ◉ = proposed

	NCR	GCR	SSSI (B)	SSSI (G)	SSSI (M)	NNR	LNR	Ramsar	SPA	AONB	CWT	RSPB	ESA	NP	WWT	NT	NSA	HC	Other
	●	●			●			◉	◉										●
No.	1	1			1			1	1										1

Much of the estuary lies within the Torrs Warren-Luce Sands Site of Special Scientific Interest (2,400 ha), which is an SSSI for its biological and geomorphological interest. Torrs Warren is a Nature Conservation Review site and Luce Sands is a Geological Conservation Review site, part of which is owned by the Ministry of Defence.

Lochinch and Torrs Warren are proposed as a Special Protection Area and Ramsar site.

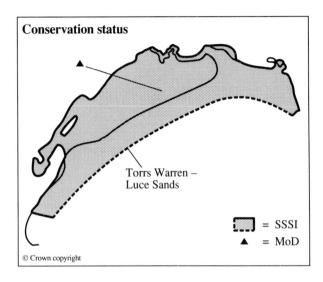

Conservation status

Torrs Warren – Luce Sands

▨ = SSSI
▲ = MoD

© Crown copyright

Torrs Warren, the largest acidic sand dune system in Scotland, extends for almost 10km along the shore. (Pat Doody, JNCC)

Human activities

Present / Proposed (left column)

Present	Proposed	Activity
		Coast protection & sea defences
		Linear defences
		Training walls
		Groynes
		Brushwood fences
		Spartina planting
		Marram grass planting
		Barrage schemes
●		Weirs & barrages for river management
		Storm surge barrages
		Water storage barrages & bunds
		Leisure barrages
		Tidal power barrages
		Power generation
		Thermal power stations
		Import/export jetties (power generation)
		Wind-power generation
		Industrial, port & related development
		Dock, port & harbour facilities
		Manufacturing industries
		Chemical industries
●		Ship & boat building
		Others
		Extraction & processing of natural gas & oil
		Exploration
		Production
		Rig & platform construction
		Pipeline construction
		Pipeline installation
		Import/export jetties & single-point moorings
		Oil refineries
		Mothballing of rigs & tankers
		Military activities
●		Overflying by military aircraft
●		Others
		Waste discharge
		Domestic waste disposal
●		Sewage discharge & outfalls
●		Sewage treatment works
		Rubbish tips
		Industrial & agricultural waste discharge
		Thermal discharges (power stations)
		Dredge spoil
●		Accidental discharges
		Aerial crop spraying
		Waste incinerators
		Others
		Sediment extraction
		Capital dredging
		Maintenance dredging
		Commercial estuarine aggregates extraction
●	●	Commercial terrestrial aggregates extraction
●		Non-commercial aggregates extraction
		Hard-rock quarrying
		Transport & communications
●		Airports & helipads
●		Tunnels, bridges & aqueducts
		Causeways & fords
●		Road schemes
		Ferries
		Cables
		Urbanisation
		Land-claim for housing & car parks
		Education & scientific research
●		Sampling, specimen collection & observation
		Nature trails & interpretative facilities
●		Seismic studies & geological test drilling
●		Marine & terrestrial archaeology
		Fossil collecting

Present / Proposed (right column)

Present	Proposed	Activity
		Tourism & recreation
		Infrastructure developments
		Marinas
		Non-marina moorings
		Dinghy & boat parks
●		Caravan parks & chalets
		Leisure centres, complexes & piers
		Aquatic-based recreation
		Power-boating & water-skiing
●		Jet-skiing
		Sailing
●		Sailboarding & wind-surfing
		SCUBA & snorkelling
		Canoeing
		Surfing
		Rowing
●		Tourist boat trips/leisure barges
		Angling
●		Other non-commercial fishing
		Bathing & general beach recreation
		Terrestrial & intertidal-based recreation
●		Walking, including dog walking
●		Bird-watching
		Sand-yachting
●		4WD & trial-biking
		Car sand-racing
●		Horse-riding
		Rock-climbing
		Golf courses
		Clay-pigeon shooting
		Others
		Airborne recreation
		Overflying by light aircraft
		Radio-controlled model aircraft
		Others
		Wildfowling & hunting
●		Wildfowling
		Other hunting-related activities
		Bait-collecting
●		Digging & pumping for lugworms & ragworms
		Hydraulic dredging for worms
●		Others
		Commercial fisheries
●		Fish-netting & trawling
		Fyke-netting for eels
		Fish traps & other fixed devices & nets
●		Crustacea
		Molluscs – Hand-gathering
		Dredging
		Hydraulic dredging
		Cultivation of living resource
		Saltmarsh grazing
		Sand dune grazing
		Agricultural land-claim
		Fish-farming
		Shellfish farming
		Bottom & tray cultivation
		Suspended cultivation
		Crustacea farming
		Reeds for roofing
		Salicornia picking
		Others
		Management & killing of birds & mammals
●		Killing of mammals
		Killing of birds
●		Adult fish-eating birds
		Adult shellfish-eating birds
		Gulls
		Geese
		Wildlife habitat management
		Spartina control
		Habitat creation & restoration
		Marine
		Intertidal
		Terrestrial
		Habitat management
		Others

Features of human use

On Luce Bay the human activities present are not intensive. Leisure pursuits are centred on Sandhead Bay in the south-east of the site and include sailing, horse-riding and beach recreation. An agreement exists that trial-biking occurs only within organised events.

Exploitation of the natural resources includes trawling for fish and Crustacea, lobster- and crab-potting, boulder turning for crabs for bait, and bait-digging on the shores of Sandhead Bay. Wildfowling occurs on the foreshore close to Piltanton Burn.

Other activities inlude the commercial extraction of sediments at the southern end of Torrs Warren, and military exercises.

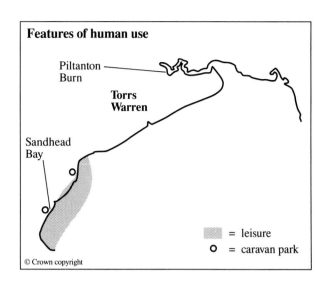

Categories of human use

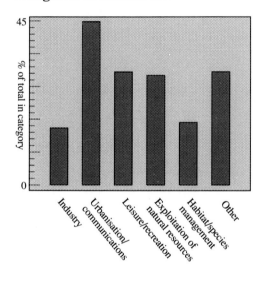

Further reading

Burd, F. 1986. *Saltmarsh survey of Great Britain. Regional report, South-west Scotland.* Unpublished, Nature Conservancy Council.

Covey, R. 1990. Littoral survey of the north coast of the outer Solway (Mull of Galloway to Auchencairn). *Nature Conservancy Council, CSD Report*, No. 1,074. (Marine Nature Conservation Review Report No. MNCR/SR/011.)

Covey, R., & Emblow, C.S. 1992. Littoral survey of the the Inner Solway Firth and additional sites in Dumfries and Galloway. *Joint Nature Conservation Committee Report*, No. 33. (Marine Nature Conservation Review Report No. MNCR/SR/20)

Doarks, C., Hedley, S.M., Radley, G.P., & Woolven, S.C. 1990. *Sand dune survey of Great Britain. Site report No. 94, Torrs Warren, Dumfries and Galloway.* Peterborough, Nature Conservancy Council. (Contract surveys, No. 201)

Idle, E.T., & Martin, J. 1974. The vegetation and land use of Torrs Warren, Wigtownshire. *Transactions of the Dumfries and Galloway Natural History and Antiquities Society, 51*: 1-10.

Nature Conservancy Council. 1974. *Torrs Warren - Site of Special Scientific Interest.* Balloch, Nature Conservancy Council Scotland (South-west Region).

Smith, J. 1891. The sand-hills of Torrs Warren, Wigtownshire. *Scottish Journal of Geology, 9*: 293-300.

Centre grid: NS3039   District: Cunninghame
Region: Strathclyde   SNH region: South-west Scotland

Review site location

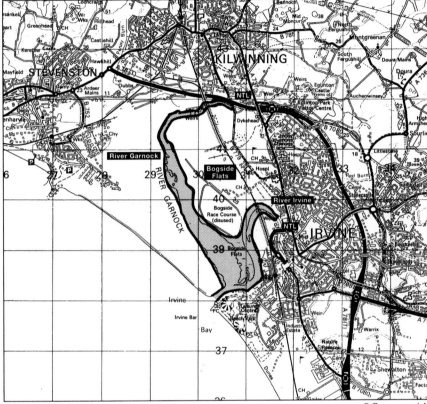

© Crown copyright

NTL = Normal tidal limit

XM = Across mouth

▨ = Core site

Total area (ha)	Intertidal area (ha)	Shore length (km)	Channel length (km)	Tidal range (m)	Geomorph. type	Human population
204	161	17.4	5.6	3.2	Bar built	49,000

Description

The Garnock is the common estuary of the Rivers Garnock and Irvine, and flows into the sea through a narrow mouth close to the town of Irvine. In the past this estuary has suffered severe industrial pollution from a chemical plant, lowering the pH to 2 and increasing organic nutrients, copper and zinc. Since the construction of a long sea outfall in 1981 pollution in the estuary has decreased, but although the algal flora has shown signs of improvement, the estuary has not yet fully recovered. Water quality within the estuary has been graded as class 2.

The Garnock Estuary has the only large expanse of saltmarsh or merse and mudflats between the Solway Firth and the Clyde Estuary, and is the best example of

this habitat in Ayrshire. The intertidal flats are predominantly muddy, apart from a small area of sandflat which fringes the shore at Irvine. The largest area of saltmarsh is at Bogside Flats, and narrow strips of saltmarsh extend along the eastern shores of the Rivers Garnock and Irvine. The saltmarsh vegetation present includes a variety of communities which represent different degrees of inundation, and shows a transition to grassland.

The intertidal mudflats, saltmarsh and adjoining pasture are used extensively as a feeding and roosting site by migrant and wintering waterfowl, and nationally important numbers of teal have recently been recorded in the estuary.

Wildlife features

Coastal habitats

	Subtidal	Saltmarsh	Sandflats	Mudflats	Sand dunes	Rocky shores	Shingle	Lowland grassland	Lagoon	Other
	●	●	◉	●						
Area (ha)	43	30	131							

● = major habitat ◉ = minor habitat

Birds

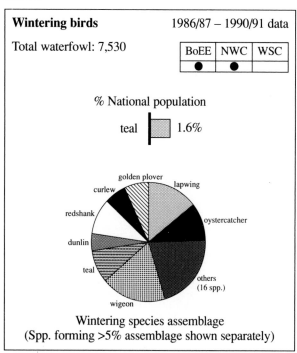

Wintering birds 1986/87 – 1990/91 data

Total waterfowl: 7,530

BoEE	NWC	WSC
●	●	

% National population

teal ▭ 1.6%

golden plover
curlew lapwing
redshank
dunlin oystercatcher
teal
wigeon others (16 spp.)

Wintering species assemblage
(Spp. forming >5% assemblage shown separately)

Aquatic estuarine communities

Information unavailable.

Additional wildlife features

The endemic nationally scarce plant Isle of Man Cabbage *Rhyncosynapis monensis* is found within the estuary.

Conservation status

● = designated ◉ = proposed

	NCR	GCR	SSSI (B)	SSSI (G)	SSSI (M)	NNR	LNR	Ramsar	SPA	AONB	CWT	RSPB	ESA	NP	WWT	NT	NSA	HC	Other
			●				◉												
No.			1				1												

Much of the estuary lies within the designated Bogside Flats biological Site of Special Scientific Interest (254 ha). There is also an informal proposal to designate the Garnock Estuary as a Local Nature Reserve.

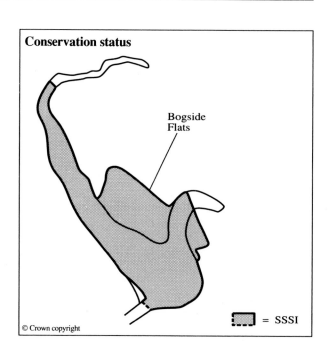

Conservation status

Bogside Flats

© Crown copyright

▭ = SSSI

Human activities

Coast protection & sea defences (Present ●)
Linear defences
Training walls
Groynes
Brushwood fences
Spartina planting
Marram grass planting

Barrage schemes (Present ●)
Weirs & barrages for river management
Storm surge barrages
Water storage barrages & bunds
Leisure barrages
Tidal power barrages

Power generation
Thermal power stations
Import/export jetties (power generation)
Wind-power generation

Industrial, port & related development (Present ● ● ●)
Dock, port & harbour facilities
Manufacturing industries
Chemical industries
Ship & boat building
Others

Extraction & processing of natural gas & oil
Exploration
Production
Rig & platform construction
Pipeline construction
Pipeline installation
Import/export jetties & single-point moorings
Oil refineries
Mothballing of rigs & tankers

Military activities
Overflying by military aircraft
Others

Waste discharge (Present ● ● ●)
Domestic waste disposal
Sewage discharge & outfalls
Sewage treatment works
Rubbish tips
Industrial & agricultural waste discharge
Thermal discharges (power stations)
Dredge spoil
Accidental discharges
Aerial crop spraying
Waste incinerators
Others

Sediment extraction (Present ●)
Capital dredging
Maintenance dredging
Commercial estuarine aggregates extraction
Commercial terrestrial aggregates extraction
Non-commercial aggregates extraction
Hard-rock quarrying

Transport & communications (Present ● ●)
Airports & helipads
Tunnels, bridges & aqueducts
Causeways & fords
Road schemes
Ferries
Cables

Urbanisation
Land-claim for housing & car parks

Education & scientific research (Present ●)
Sampling, specimen collection & observation
Nature trails & interpretative facilities
Seismic studies & geological test drilling
Marine & terrestrial archaeology
Fossil collecting

Tourism & recreation
Infrastructure developments (Present ●)
  Marinas
  Non-marina moorings
  Dinghy & boat parks
  Caravan parks & chalets
  Leisure centres, complexes & piers
Aquatic-based recreation (Present ● ●)
  Power-boating & water-skiing
  Jet-skiing
  Sailing
  Sailboarding & wind-surfing
  SCUBA & snorkelling
  Canoeing
  Surfing
  Rowing
  Tourist boat trips/leisure barges (Present ●)
  Angling
  Other non-commercial fishing
  Bathing & general beach recreation
Terrestrial & intertidal-based recreation (Present ● ●)
  Walking, including dog walking
  Bird-watching
  Sand-yachting
  4WD & trial-biking
  Car sand-racing (Present ●)
  Horse-riding
  Rock-climbing (Present ●)
  Golf courses
  Clay-pigeon shooting
  Others
Airborne recreation
  Overflying by light aircraft
  Radio-controlled model aircraft
  Others

Wildfowling & hunting (Present ●)
Wildfowling
Other hunting-related activities

Bait-collecting (Present ●)
Digging & pumping for lugworms & ragworms
Hydraulic dredging for worms
Others

Commercial fisheries
Fish-netting & trawling
Fyke-netting for eels
Fish traps & other fixed devices & nets
Crustacea
Molluscs – Hand-gathering
          Dredging
          Hydraulic dredging

Cultivation of living resource
Saltmarsh grazing
Sand dune grazing
Agricultural land-claim
Fish-farming
Shellfish farming
  Bottom & tray cultivation
  Suspended cultivation
Crustacea farming
Reeds for roofing
Salicornia picking
Others

Management & killing of birds & mammals
Killing of mammals
Killing of birds
Adult fish-eating birds
Adult shellfish-eating birds
Gulls
Geese

Wildlife habitat management
Spartina control
Habitat creation & restoration
  Marine
  Intertidal
  Terrestrial
Habitat management (Proposed ●)

Others

Features of human use

Most activities on the Garnock Estuary are generally not intensive. Leisure and recreational pursuits include sailing in the mouth of the estuary, angling, walking and horse-riding, and the south-eastern shore near the mouth of the estuary is devoted to leisure use.

Industrial activities include a major explosives industry that dominates the western side of the estuary mouth, covering an area of 270 ha of sand dune and saltmarsh. There is also a metal industry adjacent to the estuary at Irvine.

Exploitation of the natural resources is also not intensive, with bait-digging and wildfowling occurring on the Bogside Flats.

In 1989 there were proposals for habitat management of the area occupied by the explosives works. More recently jet-skiers have been using the estuary.

Features of human use

Bogside Flats

Irvine

⬧ = urban/industrial shore
▲ = large industrial complex
▲ = industry
● = harbour/dock facilities
░░ = leisure

© Crown copyright

Categories of human use

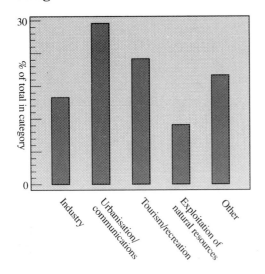

Further reading

Burd, F. 1986. *Saltmarsh survey of Great Britain. Regional report, South-west Scotland.* Unpublished, Nature Conservancy Council

Eleftherious, A., Robertson, M.R., & Murison, D.J. 1986. The benthic fauna of sandy bays, with particular reference to Irvine Bay. *Proceedings of the Royal Society of Edinburgh, 90B*: 317-327.

Hammerton, D., Newton, A.J., & Allcock, R. 1980. Determination of marine consent conditions. *Effluent and Water Treatment Journal, 11*: 215-223.

Lewis, R.E. 1986. The hydrography of Irvine Bay and its relation to the Clyde Sea area. *Proceedings of the Royal Society of Edinburgh, 90B*: 117-126.

Wilkinson, M., McLeod, L., & Fuller, I. 1980. A first account of estuarine algae under combined conditions of very low pH and metal enrichment. *Botanica Marina, 23*: 475-477.

Wilkinson, M., Fuller, I., & Rendall, D. 1986. The attached algae of the Clyde and Garnock estuaries. *Proceedings of the Royal Society of Edinburgh, 90B*: 143-150.

Hunterston Sands

Centre grid: NS1953
Region: Strathclyde

District: Cunninghame
SNH region: South-west Scotland

Review site location

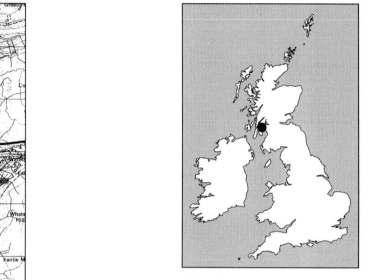

© Crown copyright

AS = Along shore

▨ = Core site

Total area (ha)	Intertidal area (ha)	Shore length (km)	Channel length (km)	Tidal range (m)	Geomorph. type	Human population
291	291	16.4	–	2.9	Linear shore	< 5,000

Description

This estuary, also known as Fairlie Flats, is the largest area of intertidal sand on the outer Firth of Clyde. The shore has been greatly modified by the development of industry, and it is estimated that 170 ha of intertidal area has been lost by land-claim since 1970 (37% of the former estuary), with the establishment of the ore terminal, oil rig construction and power stations.

The estuary is a narrow band of intertidal flats stretching from Largs in the north to Hunterston in the south. North of Fairlie the narrow flats are a mixture of sand and

shingle, which become broader and sandier further south. In the shelter of the construction yard at Hunterston, the intertidal flats of Gulls Walk are more muddy. In the extreme south of the site Hunterston Sands is bounded by a small sand and shingle spit.

The estuary regularly supports wintering waders and wildfowl, which feed on the Southannan and Hunterston Sands and often use the pool known as Dorothy's Lagoon as a roosting site.

Wildlife features

Coastal habitats

	Subtidal	Saltmarsh	Sandflats	Mudflats	Sand dunes	Rocky shores	Shingle	Lowland grassland	Lagoon	Other
			●	●		◉	◉			
Area (ha)			290							

● = major habitat   ◉ = minor habitat

Birds

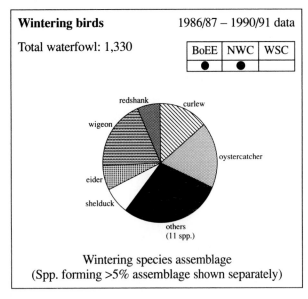

Wintering birds   1986/87 – 1990/91 data

Total waterfowl: 1,330

BoEE	NWC	WSC
●	●	

redshank, curlew, wigeon, oystercatcher, eider, shelduck, others (11 spp.)

Wintering species assemblage
(Spp. forming >5% assemblage shown separately)

Aquatic estuarine communities

Information unavailable.

Conservation status

● = designated   ◉ = proposed

	NCR	GCR	SSSI (B)	SSSI (G)	SSSI (M)	NNR	LNR	Ramsar	SPA	AONB	CWT	RSPB	ESA	NP	WWT	NT	NSA	HC	Other
			●																●
No.			1																2

Portencross – Southannan Sands Site of Special Scientific Interest is awaiting renotification as an SSSI for its biological interest.

The Ministry of Defence own land at Fairlie, and Hunterston Sands falls within Strathclyde Regional Council's Renfrew Hills Regional Scenic Area. Offshore from the estuary the Great and Little Cumbrae Islands are a Marine Consultation Area.

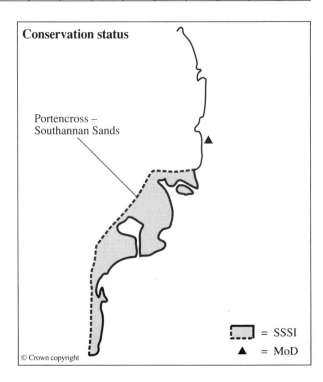

Conservation status

Portencross – Southannan Sands

▦ = SSSI
▲ = MoD

© Crown copyright

Human activities

Present	Proposed	Activity
		Coast protection & sea defences
●	●	Linear defences
		Training walls
		Groynes
		Brushwood fences
		Spartina planting
		Marram grass planting
		Barrage schemes
		Weirs & barrages for river management
		Storm surge barrages
		Water storage barrages & bunds
		Leisure barrages
		Tidal power barrages
		Power generation
●		Thermal power stations
		Import/export jetties (power generation)
		Wind-power generation
		Industrial, port & related development
●	●	Dock, port & harbour facilities
●		Manufacturing industries
		Chemical industries
●		Ship & boat building
		Others
		Extraction & processing of natural gas & oil
		Exploration
		Production
●		Rig & platform construction
		Pipeline construction
		Pipeline installation
		Import/export jetties & single-point moorings
		Oil refineries
		Mothballing of rigs & tankers
		Military activities
		Overflying by military aircraft
●		Others
		Waste discharge
		Domestic waste disposal
●		Sewage discharge & outfalls
		Sewage treatment works
		Rubbish tips
		Industrial & agricultural waste discharge
●		Thermal discharges (power stations)
		Dredge spoil
		Accidental discharges
		Aerial crop spraying
		Waste incinerators
●		Others
		Sediment extraction
		Capital dredging
		Maintenance dredging
		Commercial estuarine aggregates extraction
		Commercial terrestrial aggregates extraction
		Non-commercial aggregates extraction
		Hard-rock quarrying
		Transport & communications
		Airports & helipads
		Tunnels, bridges & aqueducts
●		Causeways & fords
		Road schemes
		Ferries
		Cables
		Urbanisation
		Land-claim for housing & car parks
		Education & scientific research
		Sampling, specimen collection & observation
		Nature trails & interpretative facilities
		Seismic studies & geological test drilling
●		Marine & terrestrial archaeology
		Fossil collecting

Present	Proposed	Activity
		Tourism & recreation
		Infrastructure developments
●		Marinas
		Non-marina moorings
●		Dinghy & boat parks
		Caravan parks & chalets
		Leisure centres, complexes & piers
		Aquatic-based recreation
●		Power-boating & water-skiing
		Jet-skiing
●		Sailing
●		Sailboarding & wind-surfing
		SCUBA & snorkelling
		Canoeing
		Surfing
		Rowing
		Tourist boat trips/leisure barges
		Angling
		Other non-commercial fishing
●		Bathing & general beach recreation
		Terrestrial & intertidal-based recreation
●		Walking, including dog walking
●		Bird-watching
		Sand-yachting
		4WD & trial-biking
		Car sand-racing
●		Horse-riding
		Rock-climbing
		Golf courses
		Clay-pigeon shooting
		Others
		Airborne recreation
		Overflying by light aircraft
		Radio-controlled model aircraft
		Others
		Wildfowling & hunting
		Wildfowling
		Other hunting-related activities
		Bait-collecting
		Digging & pumping for lugworms & ragworms
		Hydraulic dredging for worms
		Others
		Commercial fisheries
		Fish-netting & trawling
		Fyke-netting for eels
		Fish traps & other fixed devices & nets
		Crustacea
		Molluscs – Hand-gathering
		Dredging
		Hydraulic dredging
		Cultivation of living resource
		Saltmarsh grazing
		Sand dune grazing
		Agricultural land-claim
●		Fish-farming
		Shellfish farming
●	●	Bottom & tray cultivation
		Suspended cultivation
		Crustacea farming
		Reeds for roofing
		Salicornia picking
		Others
		Management & killing of birds & mammals
		Killing of mammals
		Killing of birds
		Adult fish-eating birds
		Adult shellfish-eating birds
		Gulls
		Geese
		Wildlife habitat management
		Spartina control
		Habitat creation & restoration
		Marine
		Intertidal
		Terrestrial
		Habitat management
		Others

Features of human use

Hunterston Sands is dominated by industry, with a large
ore terminal, oil rig construction and a steel metal
stripping yard extending along the shore. In addition there
are two small boat repair yards at Largs and Fairlie, and at
the south end of the site Hunterston A and B power
stations emit thermal discharges into the estuary.

Leisure pursuits are not extensive, with wind-surfing
focused around the marinas at Fairlie and Largs. Sailing
occurs mostly offshore, from the marinas and from the
sports centre outside the estuary on Cumbrae Island.
Exploitation of the natural resources is not extensive, but
includes an established and well-contained turbot fish
farm and shellfish cultivation.

In 1989 there were proposals to extend the facilities at the
ore terminal and oil rig construction yard, and for mollusc
cultivation.

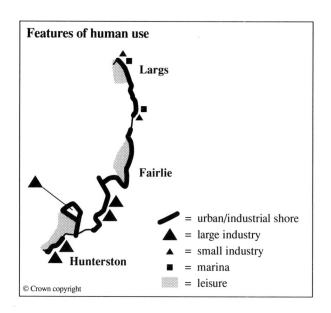

Categories of human use

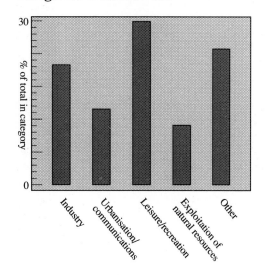

Further reading

Barnett, P.R.O., & Watson, J. 1986. Long-term changes in
   some benthic species in the Firth of Clyde with
   particular reference to *Tellina tenuis* (da Costa).
   Proceedings of the Royal Society of Edinburgh, 90B:
   287-302.

Centre grid: NS3675
Region: Strathclyde

Districts: Clydebank, Dumbarton, Glasgow, Inverclyde, Renfrew.
SNH region: South-west Scotland

Review site location

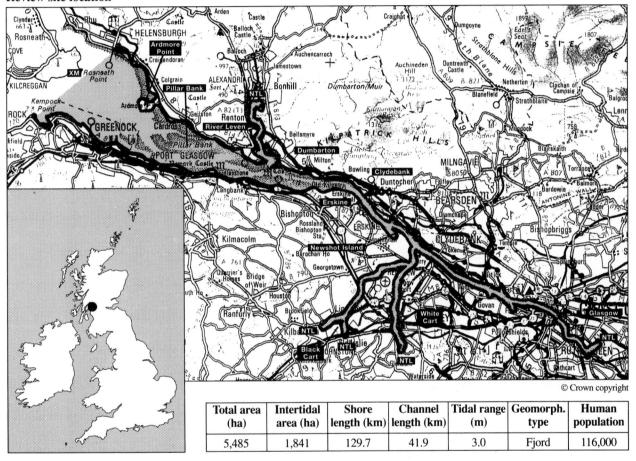

© Crown copyright

Total area (ha)	Intertidal area (ha)	Shore length (km)	Channel length (km)	Tidal range (m)	Geomorph. type	Human population
5,485	1,841	129.7	41.9	3.0	Fjord	116,000

NTL = Normal tidal limit

XM = Across mouth

= Core site

Description

The River Clyde flows through the centre of the city of Glasgow, and is fed from the freshwaters of the White Cart, Black Cart and the River Leven tributaries. The Clyde has suffered from industrial pollution for many years and in parts the estuary is still heavily polluted, with particularly high levels of chromium, lead and organic matter. Water quality within the estuary varies considerably, for the upper limits from Glasgow to Clydebank have been graded as class 4, from Clydebank to Dumbarton as class 3, and the lower estuary as class 2. The water quality of the estuary is beginning to show signs of improvement.

From its upper tidal limit down to Erskine, an urban and industrial shore dominates the narrow canalised river of the Clyde Estuary. Below Erskine the estuary widens, the salinity becomes more stable and at low tide banks of mud and sand are obvious on both north and south shores. The aquatic estuarine communities include beds of the eelgrass *Zostera* and a large bed of common mussels at Pillar Bank.

Only a relatively small proportion of the Clyde is saltmarshes, which lie largely in the upper reaches of the estuary at Newshot Island, west of Dumbarton on the northern shore and east of Erskine on the southern shore. There is also a small patch of saltmarsh at Ardmore Point. The vegetation contains a variety of typical saltmarsh communities with some plant species that are uncommon in Scotland. However the saltmarshes are of particular significance for, despite historical land-claim of intertidal areas for industrial development which usually results in loss of upper saltmarsh, a large proportion of the remaining saltmarshes show transition to freshwater swamps and grassland.

The Clyde Estuary is also known to regularly support almost 20,000 wintering waterfowl, which include nationally important numbers of five species and internationally significant numbers of redshank.

Wildlife features

Coastal habitats

	Subtidal	Saltmarsh	Sandflats	Mudflats	Sand dunes	Rocky shores	Shingle	Lowland grassland	Lagoon	Other
	●	●	●	●		◉	◉	◉		
Area (ha)	3,644	76	1,774							

● = major habitat   ◉ = minor habitat

Aquatic estuarine communities

Soft substrate

1	2	3	4	5	6	7	8	9	10	11	12	13	14	15	16
				●									●	●	

Hard substrate

17	18	19	20	21	22	23	24	25	26	27	28	29	30	31	32	33

Birds

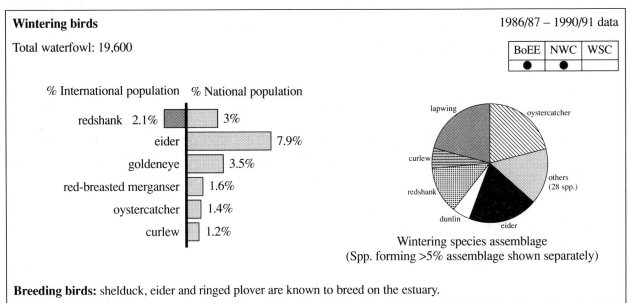

Wintering birds   1986/87 – 1990/91 data

Total waterfowl: 19,600

BoEE	NWC	WSC
●	●	

% International population   % National population

redshank 2.1% — 3%
eider — 7.9%
goldeneye — 3.5%
red-breasted merganser — 1.6%
oystercatcher — 1.4%
curlew — 1.2%

Wintering species assemblage
(Spp. forming >5% assemblage shown separately)

Breeding birds: shelduck, eider and ringed plover are known to breed on the estuary.

Conservation status

● = designated　　● = proposed

	NCR	GCR	SSSI (B)	SSSI (G)	SSSI (M)	NNR	LNR	Ramsar	SPA	AONB	CWT	RSPB	ESA	NP	WWT	NT	NSA	HC	Other
		●	●	●	●			●	●			●							
No.		2	2	1	1			1	1			2							

The central parts of the estuary are covered by Sites of Special Scientific Interest. Dumbuck Foreshore to Pillar Bank (820 ha) and Erskine to Langbank (545 ha) are biological SSSIs and parts are also RSPB reserves. Dumbarton Rock (4 ha) is a geological SSSI, Ardmore Point (134 ha) is an SSSI for its biological and geological interest, and both are also Geological Conservation Review sites.

The Inner Clyde is proposed as a Special Protection Area and Ramsar site.

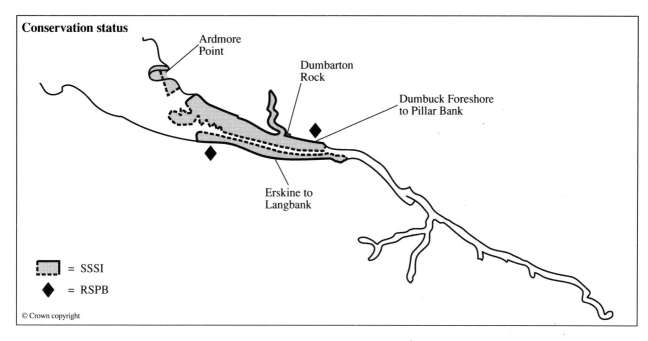

Conservation status

Ardmore Point

Dumbarton Rock

Dumbuck Foreshore to Pillar Bank

Erskine to Langbank

▰ = SSSI

◆ = RSPB

© Crown copyright

An oil terminal on the shores of the Clyde. The Clyde Estuary is dominated by industry and urban Glasgow. (Pat Doody, JNCC)

Human activities

Present	Proposed	Activity
		Coast protection & sea defences
●	●	Linear defences
		Training walls
●		Groynes
		Brushwood fences
		Spartina planting
		Marram grass planting
		Barrage schemes
		Weirs & barrages for river management
		Storm surge barrages
		Water storage barrages & bunds
		Leisure barrages
		Tidal power barrages
		Power generation
		Thermal power stations
		Import/export jetties (power generation)
		Wind-power generation
		Industrial, port & related development
●		Dock, port & harbour facilities
●		Manufacturing industries
●		Chemical industries
●		Ship & boat building
		Others
		Extraction & processing of natural gas & oil
		Exploration
		Production
		Rig & platform construction
		Pipeline construction
		Pipeline installation
●		Import/export jetties & single-point moorings
●		Oil refineries
		Mothballing of rigs & tankers
		Military activities
		Overflying by military aircraft
		Others
		Waste discharge
		Domestic waste disposal
●		Sewage discharge & outfalls
●		Sewage treatment works
		Rubbish tips
●		Industrial & agricultural waste discharge
		Thermal discharges (power stations)
		Dredge spoil
		Accidental discharges
		Aerial crop spraying
		Waste incinerators
		Others
		Sediment extraction
	●	Capital dredging
●		Maintenance dredging
●		Commercial estuarine aggregates extraction
		Commercial terrestrial aggregates extraction
		Non-commercial aggregates extraction
		Hard-rock quarrying
		Transport & communications
		Airports & helipads
●		Tunnels, bridges & aqueducts
		Causeways & fords
		Road schemes
●		Ferries
		Cables
		Urbanisation
	●	Land-claim for housing & car parks
		Education & scientific research
●		Sampling, specimen collection & observation
●	●	Nature trails & interpretative facilities
		Seismic studies & geological test drilling
		Marine & terrestrial archaeology
		Fossil collecting

Present	Proposed	Activity
		Tourism & recreation
		Infrastructure developments
	●	Marinas
●		Non-marina moorings
●		Dinghy & boat parks
		Caravan parks & chalets
		Leisure centres, complexes & piers
		Aquatic-based recreation
●		Power-boating & water-skiing
		Jet-skiing
●		Sailing
		Sailboarding & wind-surfing
		SCUBA & snorkelling
●		Canoeing
		Surfing
		Rowing
●		Tourist boat trips/leisure barges
●		Angling
		Other non-commercial fishing
		Bathing & general beach recreation
		Terrestrial & intertidal-based recreation
●	●	Walking, including dog walking
●		Bird-watching
		Sand-yachting
●		4WD & trial-biking
		Car sand-racing
●		Horse-riding
		Rock-climbing
●		Golf courses
●		Clay-pigeon shooting
		Others
		Airborne recreation
		Overflying by light aircraft
		Radio-controlled model aircraft
		Others
		Wildfowling & hunting
●		Wildfowling
		Other hunting-related activities
		Bait-collecting
●		Digging & pumping for lugworms & ragworms
		Hydraulic dredging for worms
		Others
		Commercial fisheries
		Fish-netting & trawling
		Fyke-netting for eels
		Fish traps & other fixed devices & nets
		Crustacea
		Molluscs – Hand-gathering
		Dredging
		Hydraulic dredging
		Cultivation of living resource
		Saltmarsh grazing
		Sand dune grazing
		Agricultural land-claim
		Fish-farming
		Shellfish farming
		Bottom & tray cultivation
		Suspended cultivation
		Crustacea farming
		Reeds for roofing
		Salicornia picking
		Others
		Management & killing of birds & mammals
		Killing of mammals
		Killing of birds
		Adult fish-eating birds
		Adult shellfish-eating birds
		Gulls
		Geese
		Wildlife habitat management
		Spartina control
		Habitat creation & restoration
		Marine
		Intertidal
		Terrestrial
		Habitat management
		Others

Features of human use

The shores of the Clyde Estuary are dominated by industry with large ports at Greenock and various metal industries in Glasgow, Greenock, Port Glasgow and Clydebank. There are also ship-building yards at Glasgow and oil terminals at Bowling and Mountblow.

Leisure pursuits are numerous but generally not intensive, and most activities take place close to the estuary mouth. There are moorings on the Rivers Leven and Cart and at Gourock (just outside the estuary mouth) which are a focus for sailing; bird-watching is centred around Ardmore; and 4WD and horse-riding are known to occur occasionally on the north shore around the Pillar Bank and Dumbarton area.

There is little exploitation of the natural resources within the estuary. Bait-digging and wildfowling are known to occur but these are not intensive.

In 1989 there were proposals for capital dredging, a large marina at Bowling, and an interpretative centre at Erskine Bridge. Since that time there have been proposals to improve access to the estuary foreshore, which by 1992 had gone ahead, in part, at Dumbarton. There was also another more recent proposal for the development of light industry at Parklea, which would involve some land-claim.

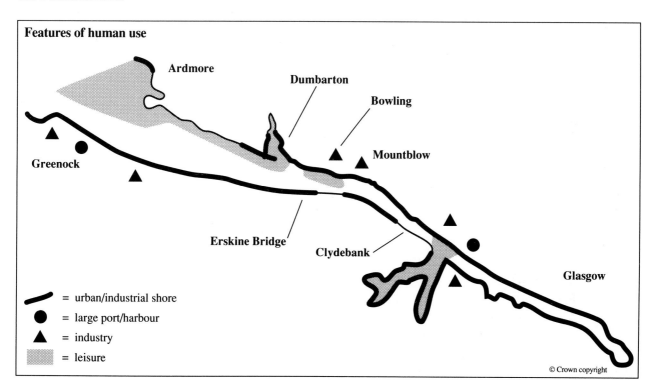

Categories of human use

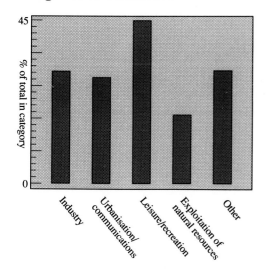

49.5

Further reading

Allen, J.A., Barnett, P.R.O., Boyd, J.M., Kirkwood, R.C., Mackay, D.W., & Smyth, J.C. (eds). 1986. The environment of the estuary and Firth of Clyde. *Proceedings of the Royal Society of Edinburgh, 90B.*

Barnett, P.R.O., & Watson, J. 1986. Long term changes in some benthic species in the Firth of Clyde. *Proceedings of the Royal Society of Edinburgh, 90B: 287-302.*

Connor, D.W. 1991. Benthic marine ecosystems in Great Britain: a review of current knowledge. Clyde Sea, west Scotland, Outer Hebrides and north-west Scotland (MNCR Coastal sectors 12 to 15). *Nature Conservancy Council, CSD Report,* No. 1,175. (Marine Nature Conservation Review Report, No. MNCR/OR/11)

Curtis, D.J., Gibson, I., Smyth, J.C., & Wilkinson, M. 1974. Intertidal organisms of an industrialised estuary. *Marine Pollution Bulletin, 5:* 189-190.

Haig, A.J.N. 1986. Use of the Clyde Estuary and Firth for the disposal of effluents. *Proceedings of the Royal Society of Edinburgh, 90B:* 383-405.

Haig, A.J.N., & Miller, B.S. 1984. Chemistry of the Firth of Clyde. *Analytical Proceedings, 21.*

Halliday, J.B. 1978. *The feeding distribution of birds on the Clyde estuary tidal flats 1976-77.* Paisley College of Technology, unpublished report to the Nature Conservancy Council.

Halliday, J.B., Curtis, D.J., Thompson, D.B.A., Bignal, E.M., & Smyth, J.C. 1982. The abundance and feeding distribution of Clyde Estuary shore birds. *Scottish Birds, 12:* 65-72.

Halliday, J.B., & Smyth, J.C. 1978. Feeding distribution of birds on the Clyde Estuary tidal flats. *In: Nature conservation interests in the Clyde Estuary,* ed. by J.C. Smyth. Nature Conservancy Council, South-west Scotland region.

Henderson, A.R. 1984. Long term monitoring of the macrobenthos of the upper Clyde Estuary. *Water Science and Technology, 16.*

Laurie, I.G., & Robertson, S.B. 1979. *Report on sampling of eight sites in the Clyde Estuary, March 1979.* Paisley College of Technology, unpublished report to the Nature Conservancy Council.

Mackay, D.W., Taylor, W.K., & Henderson, A.R. 1978. The recovery of the polluted Clyde Estuary. *Proceedings of the Royal Society of Edinburgh, 76B.*

Minto, M.W., Scott, D.J., & Wilkinson, M. 1974. *The distribution of intertidal mudflat invertebrates in the Clyde Estuary – summer 1973.* Paisley College of Technology, unpublished report to the Nature Conservancy Council.

Natural Environment Research Council. 1974. The Clyde Estuary and Firth. An assessment of present knowledge. *NERC Publications Series C,* No. 11.

Shiells, G.M., Curtis, D.J., Gray, H., & Smyth, J.C. 1976. *Particle size and numbers of macrofauna at certain sites on the Clyde mudflats.* Paisley, Paisley College.

Smyth, J.C. *et al.* 1977. Birds and invertebrates of the Clyde Estuary tidal flats. *Western Naturalist, 6:* 73-102.

Stobie, R., Curtis, D.J., Gray, H., & Smyth, J.C. 1976. *Intertidal invertebrates of the Clyde Estuary mudflats 1974/75 survey.* Paisley College of Technology, unpublished report to the Nature Conservancy Council.

Thompson, D.B.A. 1981. The feeding behaviour of wintering shelduck on the Clyde Estuary. *Wildfowl, 32:* 88-98.

Thompson, D.B.A. 1982. The abundance and distribution of intertidal invertebrates and an estimation of their selection by shelduck. *Wildfowl, 33:* 151-158.

Thompson, D.B.A., Curtis, D.J., & Smyth, J.C. 1986. Patterns of association betweeen birds and invertebrates in the Clyde Estuary. *Proceedings of the Royal Society of Edinburgh, 90B:* 185-201.

Walker, C.R. 1979. *An investigation of the fish population of the Clyde Estuary.* Paisley, Paisley College.

West, J.W. 1972. *A survey of the invertebrate fauna of the upper Clyde estuary.* Paisley College, unpublished report to the Nature Conservancy Council.

Wilkinson, M. 1973. A preliminary survey of the intertidal benthic algae of the Clyde Estuary. *Western Naturalist, 2:* 59-69.

<table>
<tr><td>**50**</td><td># Ruel Estuary</td></tr>
</table>

Ruel Estuary

a.k.a. Loch Riddon

Centre grid: NS0079   District: Argyll & Bute
Region: Strathclyde   SNH region: South-west Scotland

Review site location

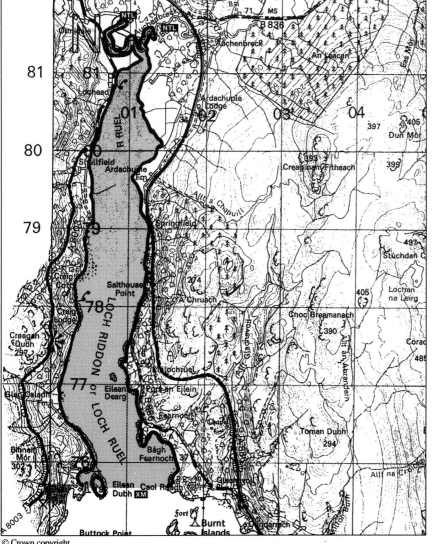

© Crown copyright

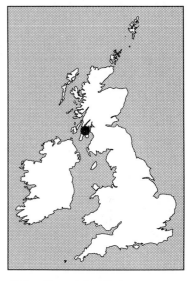

NTL = Normal tidal limit

XM = Across mouth

= Core site

Total area (ha)	Intertidal area (ha)	Shore length (km)	Channel length (km)	Tidal range (m)	Geomorph. type	Human population
426	184	15.4	6.7	3.0	Fjord	< 5,000

Description

The estuary of the River Ruel is also known as Loch Riddon, and lies at the northern end of the Kyles of Bute. The upper parts of the estuary are shallow, and at low tide broad silt and sandflats are exposed which overlie shingle deposits. Along both western and eastern shores there are narrow strips of bare shingle. Extensive intertidal flats are a relatively scarce habitat in the west of Scotland, and the very sheltered intertidal flats at the head of the Ruel Estuary are known to support a wide diversity of invertebrates.

At the head of the estuary is a small area of saltmarsh showing transition from saltmarsh to woodland, which is very rare in Great Britain. It is regarded as the most important saltmarsh in the Firth of Clyde. Close to the tidal limit of the estuary, the vegetation shows gradation from salt to freshwater marsh, and transitions through marsh to woodland, where oak, ash and alder growing on the estuarine silt are subject to occasional flooding with tidal water. The saltmarsh vegetation also displays interesting contrasts due to variations in grazing intensity, for the majority of the saltmarsh on the western shore is heavily grazed, while that on the eastern shore is virtually ungrazed.

In addition there are stretches of rocky shore in the lower parts of Loch Ruel, and much of the estuary is surrounded by woodland on steep slopes.

Wildlife features

Coastal habitats

	Subtidal	Saltmarsh	Sandflats	Mudflats	Sand dunes	Rocky shores	Shingle	Lowland grassland	Lagoon	Other
	●	●	◉	●		●	◉			◉
Area (ha)	242	7	177							

● = major habitat   ◉ = minor habitat

Birds

The Ruel Estuary is not a regularly counted site. Casual records indicate that the saltmarsh at the north end of the estuary acts as a small high tide roost, where gulls, shelduck and red-breasted merganser are often seen.

Additional wildlife features

Otters are known to use the estuary.

Aquatic estuarine communities

Soft substrate

1	2	3	4	5	6	7	8	9	10	11	12	13	14	15	16
				●								●		●	

Hard substrate

17	18	19	20	21	22	23	24	25	26	27	28	29	30	31	32	33
				●												

Conservation status

● = designated   ◉ = proposed

	NCR	GCR	SSSI (B)	SSSI (G)	SSSI (M)	NNR	LNR	Ramsar	SPA	AONB	CWT	RSPB	ESA	NP	WWT	NT	NSA	HC	Other
	●		●														●		●
No.	1		1														1		2

The northern parts of the estuary have been designated as the Ruel Estuary (342 ha) biological Site of Special Scientific Interest, and it is also a Nature Conservation Review site. The estuary forms part of the Kyles of Bute National Scenic Area, and is recognised as a Coastal Conservation Zone.

The estuary has been designated by the EC as a shellfish rearing area.

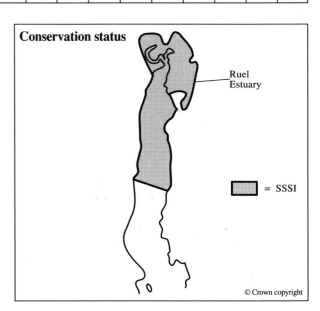

Conservation status

Ruel Estuary

▨ = SSSI

© Crown copyright

Human activities

Coast protection & sea defences
Linear defences
Training walls
Groynes
Brushwood fences
Spartina planting
Marram grass planting

Barrage schemes
Weirs & barrages for river management
Storm surge barrages
Water storage barrages & bunds
Leisure barrages
Tidal power barrages

Power generation
Thermal power stations
Import/export jetties (power generation)
Wind-power generation

Industrial, port & related development
Dock, port & harbour facilities
Manufacturing industries
Chemical industries
Ship & boat building
Others

Extraction & processing of natural gas & oil
Exploration
Production
Rig & platform construction
Pipeline construction
Pipeline installation
Import/export jetties & single-point moorings
Oil refineries
Mothballing of rigs & tankers

Military activities
Overflying by military aircraft
Others

Waste discharge
Domestic waste disposal
● Sewage discharge & outfalls
Sewage treatment works
Rubbish tips
Industrial & agricultural waste discharge
Thermal discharges (power stations)
Dredge spoil
Accidental discharges
Aerial crop spraying
Waste incinerators
Others

Sediment extraction
Capital dredging
Maintenance dredging
Commercial estuarine aggregates extraction
Commercial terrestrial aggregates extraction
Non-commercial aggregates extraction
Hard-rock quarrying

Transport & communications
Airports & helipads
Tunnels, bridges & aqueducts
Causeways & fords
Road schemes
Ferries
Cables

Urbanisation
Land-claim for housing & car parks

Education & scientific research
Sampling, specimen collection & observation
Nature trails & interpretative facilities
Seismic studies & geological test drilling
Marine & terrestrial archaeology
Fossil collecting

Tourism & recreation
Infrastructure developments
● Marinas
Non-marina moorings
Dinghy & boat parks
○ Caravan parks & chalets
Leisure centres, complexes & piers
Aquatic-based recreation
Power-boating & water-skiing
● Jet-skiing
Sailing
Sailboarding & wind-surfing
● SCUBA & snorkelling
Canoeing
Surfing
Rowing
● Tourist boat trips/leisure barges
Angling
Other non-commercial fishing
Bathing & general beach recreation
Terrestrial & intertidal-based recreation
● Walking, including dog walking
● Bird-watching
Sand-yachting
4WD & trial-biking
Car sand-racing
Horse-riding
Rock-climbing
Golf courses
Clay-pigeon shooting
Others
Airborne recreation
Overflying by light aircraft
Radio-controlled model aircraft
Others

Wildfowling & hunting
Wildfowling
Other hunting-related activities

Bait-collecting
Digging & pumping for lugworms & ragworms
Hydraulic dredging for worms
Others

Commercial fisheries
Fish-netting & trawling
Fyke-netting for eels
Fish traps & other fixed devices & nets
Crustacea
Molluscs – Hand-gathering
Dredging
Hydraulic dredging

Cultivation of living resource
● Saltmarsh grazing
Sand dune grazing
Agricultural land-claim
● Fish-farming
Shellfish farming
Bottom & tray cultivation
Suspended cultivation
Crustacea farming
Reeds for roofing
Salicornia picking
Others

Management & killing of birds & mammals
Killing of mammals
Killing of birds
Adult fish-eating birds
Adult shellfish-eating birds
Gulls
Geese

Wildlife habitat management
Spartina control
Habitat creation & restoration
Marine
Intertidal
Terrestrial
Habitat management

● **Others**

50.3

Features of human use

In 1989 there were very few human activities present on the Ruel Estuary. Leisure pursuits include canoeing and sailing which are not intensive, and there were a small number of moorings at Eilean Dubh. Anglers fish for salmon and sea trout in the upper reaches of the estuary. Exploitation of the natural resources included intensive grazing over 70% of the saltmarsh, and there was also a rainbow trout fish farm within the estuary.

In 1989 there had been a recent proposal for chalets close to the south-west shore of the site and for a small marina. By 1992 these had both been dropped.

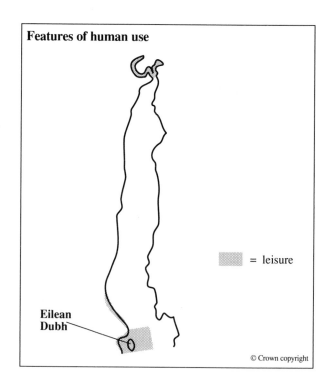

Features of human use

Eilean Dubh

= leisure

© Crown copyright

Further reading

Doody, P. 1986. The saltmarshes of the Firth of Clyde. *Proceedings of the Royal Society of Edinburgh, 90B*: 519-536.

Holt, R., & Davies, M. 1991. Surveys of Scottish sealochs – sealochs in the northern Firth of Clyde. (Contractor: University Marine Biological Station, Millport.) *Nature Conservancy Council, CSD Report*, No. 1,147.

Hunter, R. 1983. *An investigation into the distribution of the macrobenthos of Loch Riddon*. B.Sc. Thesis, University of Stirling.

Kerr, A.K. 1981. *Aspects of the biology of* Lutraria lutraria *(L) Bivalvia, Mactracea*. Ph.D. Thesis, University of Glasgow.

McLusky, D., & Hunter, R. 1985. Loch Riddon revisited – the intertidal of the sealoch resurveyed after fifty-three years. *Glasgow Naturalist, 21*: 53-62.

Stephen, A.C. 1930. Studies on the Scottish marine fauna. Additional observations on the fauna of the sandy and muddy areas of the tidal zone. *Transactions of the Royal Society of Edinburgh, 56*: 521-535.

Loch Gilp

Centre grid: NS8687   District: Argyll and Bute
Region: Strathclyde   SNH region: South-west Scotland

Review site location

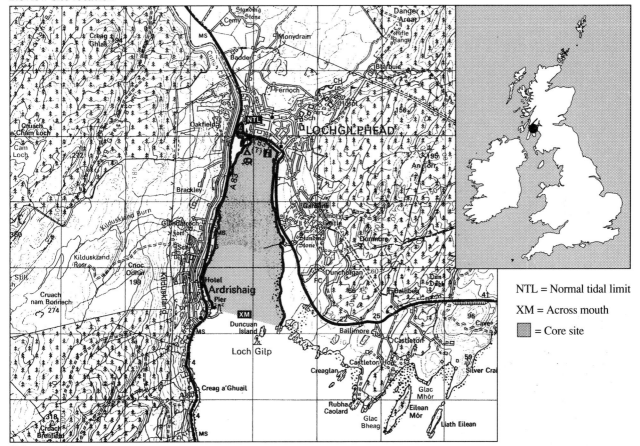

© Crown copyright

Total area (ha)	Intertidal area (ha)	Shore length (km)	Channel length (km)	Tidal range (m)	Geomorph. type	Human population
245	143	6.8	3.4	3.1	Fjord	< 5,000

NTL = Normal tidal limit

XM = Across mouth

= Core site

Description

Loch Gilp lies at the southern end of the geological fault that runs between Crinan and Lochgilphead. It is a shallow estuary at the head of a small tidal sea loch, which deepens gently into Loch Fyne. The estuary receives freshwater inflow from the Bishopston Burn, which runs through the town of Lochgilphead.

At low tide a large proportion of the estuary is exposed as an intertidal flat of fine sands, which generally become finer towards the head of the estuary. The aquatic estuarine communities within Loch Gilp include the normal/variable muddy sand community, the variable/reduced salinity mud community and beds of the eelgrass *Zostera* in the upper parts of the estuary. On the western shore of the Loch there is strip of shingle, and on the eastern shore there is a stretch of sand and shingle.

Wildlife features

Coastal habitats

	Subtidal	Saltmarsh	Sandflats	Mudflats	Sand dunes	Rocky shores	Shingle	Lowland grassland	Lagoon	Other
	●		●	●			●			
Area (ha)	110		140							

● = major habitat   ◉ = minor habitat

Birds

Wintering birds   1988/89 – 1990/91 data

Total waterfowl: 645

	BoEE	NWC	WSC
	●		

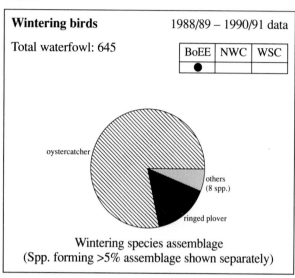

Wintering species assemblage
(Spp. forming >5% assemblage shown separately)

Aquatic estuarine communities

Soft substrate

1	2	3	4	5	6	7	8	9	10	11	12	13	14	15	16
												●	●	●	

Hard substrate

17	18	19	20	21	22	23	24	25	26	27	28	29	30	31	32	33

Additional wildlife features

Otters are present on the estuary.

Conservation status

● = designated   ◉ = proposed

	NCR	GCR	SSSI (B)	SSSI (G)	SSSI (M)	NNR	LNR	Ramsar	SPA	AONB	CWT	RSPB	ESA	NP	WWT	NT	NSA	HC	Other
																			●
No.																			2

There are no statutory designations on the estuary, but
Loch Gilp forms part of Mid Argyll Local Plan, which
includes policies and proposals for the mudflats, and Loch
Gilp is recognised as a preferred Coastal Preservation
Zone.

Human activities

Present Proposed

●		**Coast protection & sea defences** Linear defences Training walls Groynes Brushwood fences *Spartina* planting Marram grass planting
	●	**Barrage schemes** Weirs & barrages for river management Storm surge barrages Water storage barrages & bunds Leisure barrages Tidal power barrages
		Power generation Thermal power stations Import/export jetties (power generation) Wind-power generation
● ● ●		**Industrial, port & related development** Dock, port & harbour facilities Manufacturing industries Chemical industries Ship & boat building Others
		Extraction & processing of natural gas & oil Exploration Production Rig & platform construction Pipeline construction Pipeline installation Import/export jetties & single-point moorings Oil refineries Mothballing of rigs & tankers
		Military activities Overflying by military aircraft Others
● ● ●		**Waste discharge** Domestic waste disposal Sewage discharge & outfalls Sewage treatment works Rubbish tips Industrial & agricultural waste discharge Thermal discharges (power stations) Dredge spoil Accidental discharges Aerial crop spraying Waste incinerators Others
		Sediment extraction Capital dredging Maintenance dredging Commercial estuarine aggregates extraction Commercial terrestrial aggregates extraction Non-commercial aggregates extraction Hard-rock quarrying
●		**Transport & communications** Airports & helipads Tunnels, bridges & aqueducts Causeways & fords Road schemes Ferries Cables
	●	**Urbanisation** Land-claim for housing & car parks
		Education & scientific research Sampling, specimen collection & observation Nature trails & interpretative facilities Seismic studies & geological test drilling Marine & terrestrial archaeology Fossil collecting

Present Proposed

●
●
	●	**Tourism & recreation**
		Infrastructure developments
		   Marinas
		   Non-marina moorings
		   Dinghy & boat parks
		   Caravan parks & chalets
		   Leisure centres, complexes & piers

●
●
●
●
	●	Aquatic-based recreation
		   Power-boating & water-skiing
		   Jet-skiing
		   Sailing
		   Sailboarding & wind-surfing
		   SCUBA & snorkelling
		   Canoeing
		   Surfing
		   Rowing
		   Tourist boat trips/leisure barges

● ●		Angling Other non-commercial fishing Bathing & general beach recreation

●
●
●
		Terrestrial & intertidal-based recreation
		   Walking, including dog walking
		   Bird-watching
		   Sand-yachting
		   4WD & trial-biking
		   Car sand-racing
		   Horse-riding
		   Rock-climbing
		   Golf courses
		   Clay-pigeon shooting
		   Others

●	●	

		Airborne recreation
		   Overflying by light aircraft
		   Radio-controlled model aircraft
		   Others

		Wildfowling & hunting Wildfowling Other hunting-related activities
●		**Bait-collecting** Digging & pumping for lugworms & ragworms Hydraulic dredging for worms Others

		Commercial fisheries
		Fish-netting & trawling
		Fyke-netting for eels
		Fish traps & other fixed devices & nets
		Crustacea
		Molluscs – Hand-gathering
		            Dredging
		            Hydraulic dredging

●		**Cultivation of living resource**
		Saltmarsh grazing
		Sand dune grazing
		Agricultural land-claim
		Fish-farming
		Shellfish farming
		   Bottom & tray cultivation
		   Suspended cultivation
		Crustacea farming
		Reeds for roofing
		Salicornia picking
		Others

		Management & killing of birds & mammals Killing of mammals Killing of birds Adult fish-eating birds Adult shellfish-eating birds Gulls Geese

		Wildlife habitat management
		Spartina control
		Habitat creation & restoration
		            Marine
		            Intertidal
		            Terrestrial
		Habitat management

		Others

Features of human use

Leisure activities are numerous but are not intensive, and water-based sports are focused on the western shore at Ardrishaig, where there are a few moorings and a sailing club. Beach recreation and bird-watching occur at Lochgilphead.

Industrial activities include harbour facilities and a boat repair yard at Ardrishaig, and there is a pottery and acrylic works at Lochgilphead. Exploitation of the natural resources includes bait-digging and goats grazing on the marsh at Carron.

In 1989 there was a proposal for a leisure barrage with housing and marina development, which would involve some land-claim for housing and cause an increase in sailing. By 1992 the proposal for a marina had been dropped.

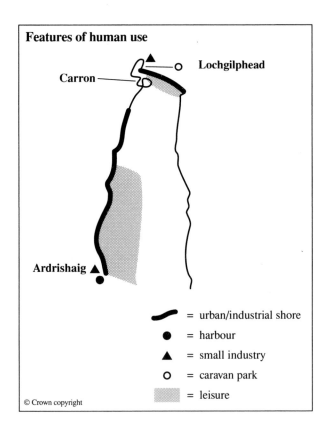

Categories of human use

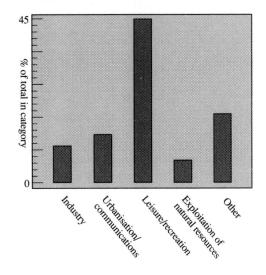

Further reading

McLusky, D. 1986. The intertidal ecology of three west of Scotland estuaries (Loch Crinan, Loch Gilp and West Loch Tarbert). *Bulletin of the Estuarine and Brackish Water Sciences Association*, 43: 15-25.

Patterson, D.W. 1984. *An investigation into the distribution of the macrobenthos of Loch Gilp, with a detailed study of the bivalve mollusc* Cardium edule. B.Sc. thesis, University of Stirling.

Stephens, A.C. 1930. Studies on the Scottish marine fauna. Additional observations on the fauna of the sandy and muddy areas of the tidal zone. *Transactions of the Royal Society of Edinburgh*, 56: 521-535.

52 Traigh Cill-a-Rubha

a.k.a. Bridgend Flats

Centre grid: NR3362 District: Argylle & Bute
Region: Strathclyde SNH region: South-west Scotland

Review site location

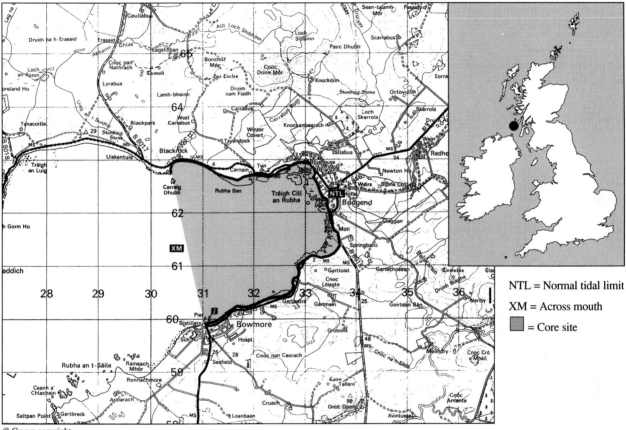

© Crown copyright

NTL = Normal tidal limit
XM = Across mouth
■ = Core site

Total area (ha)	Intertidal area (ha)	Shore length (km)	Channel length (km)	Tidal range (m)	Geomorph. type	Human population
639	288	8.6	3.0	1.5	Embayment	< 5,000

Description

Traigh Cill-a-Rubha is the shallow, sandy estuary of the River Sorn which lies sheltered at the head of Loch Indaal on the south-west coast of Islay.

The estuary lies within the Loch Indaal Marine Consultation Area (MCA), which includes subtidal communities which are unusual within both Islay and the west coast of Scotland. The aquatic estuarine communities within the estuary include a normal/variable salinity muddy sand community, a variable/reduced salinity mud community, and beds of the eelgrass *Zostera*. Within Loch Indaal the algal communities growing with or attached to *Zostera* beds are known to include species rarely encountered elsewhere.

The intertidal flats of Traigh Cill-a-Rubha are made up of sand and silt, and include extensive beds of the lugworm *Arenicola marina*. In the upper parts of the estuary the intertidal flats grade into saltmarsh, which although not extensive is one of the largest areas of saltmarsh in this part of Scotland.

Together the flats and saltmarsh are part of a network of roosting and feeding sites on Islay that forms an area of international importance for both wintering waders and geese. Large numbers of Greenland barnacle geese roost and feed on the estuarine sites, but tend to feed more extensively on the agricultural land within Islay.

52.1

Wildlife features

Coastal habitats

	Subtidal	Saltmarsh	Sandflats	Mudflats	Sand dunes	Rocky shores	Shingle	Lowland grassland	Lagoon	Other
	●	●	●			◉	◉			
Area (ha)	351	40	248							

● = major habitat   ◉ = minor habitat

Birds

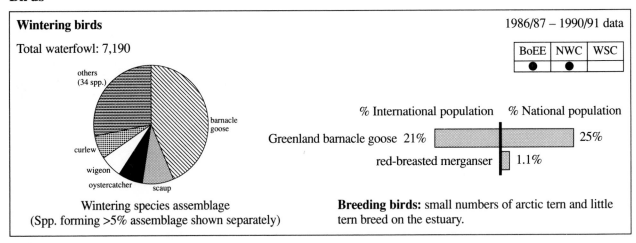

Wintering birds   1986/87 – 1990/91 data

Total waterfowl: 7,190

BoEE	NWC	WSC
●	●	

others (34 spp.)
barnacle goose
curlew
wigeon
oystercatcher
scaup

Wintering species assemblage
(Spp. forming >5% assemblage shown separately)

% International population   % National population

Greenland barnacle goose 21%   25%

red-breasted merganser   1.1%

Breeding birds: small numbers of arctic tern and little tern breed on the estuary.

Aquatic estuarine communities

Soft substrate

1	2	3	4	5	6	7	8	9	10	11	12	13	14	15	16
												●	●	●	

Hard substrate

17	18	19	20	21	22	23	24	25	26	27	28	29	30	31	32	33

Additional wildlife features

Otters are present on this estuary.

Conservation status

● = designated   ◉ = proposed

	NCR	GCR	SSSI (B)	SSSI (G)	SSSI (M)	NNR	LNR	Ramsar	SPA	AONB	CWT	RSPB	ESA	NP	WWT	NT	NSA	HC	Other
	●		●					●	●										●
No.	1		1					1	1										3

Much of the estuary lies within Bridgend Flats (331 ha) biological Site of Special Scientific Interest, and forms part of the Loch Indaal Nature Conservation Review site. Loch Indaal is also a Marine Consultation Area.

Bridgend Flats have been designated as both a Special Protection Area and a Ramsar site.

The estuary has been designated by the District Council as being of Local Landscape Importance, and over part of the site a formal agreement exists with local farmers for the Islay Goose Sanctuary.

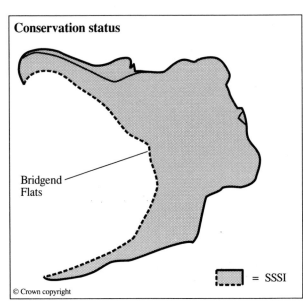

Conservation status

Bridgend Flats

© Crown copyright

▨ = SSSI

Human activities

Present	Proposed	Activity
		Coast protection & sea defences
		Linear defences
		Training walls
		Groynes
		Brushwood fences
		Spartina planting
		Marram grass planting
		Barrage schemes
		Weirs & barrages for river management
		Storm surge barrages
		Water storage barrages & bunds
		Leisure barrages
		Tidal power barrages
		Power generation
		Thermal power stations
		Import/export jetties (power generation)
		Wind-power generation
●		**Industrial, port & related development**
		Dock, port & harbour facilities
		Manufacturing industries
		Chemical industries
		Ship & boat building
		Others
		Extraction & processing of natural gas & oil
		Exploration
		Production
		Rig & platform construction
		Pipeline construction
		Pipeline installation
		Import/export jetties & single-point moorings
		Oil refineries
		Mothballing of rigs & tankers
		Military activities
		Overflying by military aircraft
		Others
		Waste discharge
		Domestic waste disposal
●		Sewage discharge & outfalls
		Sewage treatment works
		Rubbish tips
●		Industrial & agricultural waste discharge
		Thermal discharges (power stations)
		Dredge spoil
		Accidental discharges
		Aerial crop spraying
		Waste incinerators
		Others
		Sediment extraction
		Capital dredging
		Maintenance dredging
		Commercial estuarine aggregates extraction
		Commercial terrestrial aggregates extraction
		Non-commercial aggregates extraction
		Hard-rock quarrying
		Transport & communications
		Airports & helipads
		Tunnels, bridges & aqueducts
		Causeways & fords
	●	Road schemes
		Ferries
		Cables
		Urbanisation
		Land-claim for housing & car parks
		Education & scientific research
●	●	Sampling, specimen collection & observation
		Nature trails & interpretative facilities
		Seismic studies & geological test drilling
		Marine & terrestrial archaeology
		Fossil collecting

Present	Proposed	Activity
		Tourism & recreation
		Infrastructure developments
		Marinas
		Non-marina moorings
		Dinghy & boat parks
		Caravan parks & chalets
		Leisure centres, complexes & piers
		Aquatic-based recreation
		Power-boating & water-skiing
		Jet-skiing
●		Sailing
●		Sailboarding & wind-surfing
		SCUBA & snorkelling
		Canoeing
		Surfing
		Rowing
		Tourist boat trips/leisure barges
		Angling
		Other non-commercial fishing
●		Bathing & general beach recreation
		Terrestrial & intertidal-based recreation
●		Walking, including dog walking
		Bird-watching
		Sand-yachting
		4WD & trial-biking
		Car sand-racing
●		Horse-riding
		Rock-climbing
		Golf courses
		Clay-pigeon shooting
		Others
		Airborne recreation
		Overflying by light aircraft
		Radio-controlled model aircraft
		Others
		Wildfowling & hunting
		Wildfowling
		Other hunting-related activities
●		**Bait-collecting**
		Digging & pumping for lugworms & ragworms
		Hydraulic dredging for worms
		Others
		Commercial fisheries
		Fish-netting & trawling
		Fyke-netting for eels
		Fish traps & other fixed devices & nets
		Crustacea
		Molluscs – Hand-gathering
		Dredging
		Hydraulic dredging
●		**Cultivation of living resource**
		Saltmarsh grazing
		Sand dune grazing
		Agricultural land-claim
		Fish-farming
●		Shellfish farming
		Bottom & tray cultivation
		Suspended cultivation
		Crustacea farming
		Reeds for roofing
●		*Salicornia* picking
		Others
		Management & killing of birds & mammals
		Killing of mammals
		Killing of birds
		Adult fish-eating birds
		Adult shellfish-eating birds
●		Gulls
		Geese
		Wildlife habitat management
		Spartina control
		Habitat creation & restoration
		Marine
		Intertidal
		Terrestrial
		Habitat management
		Others

Features of human use

In 1989 there were few activities occurring within Traigh Cill-a-Rubha and most were not intensive. Leisure pursuits are concentrated around the small harbour and beach at Bowmore and include sailing, wind-surfing, bird-watching and horse-riding.

In addition sheep graze the saltmarsh, there is occasional bait-digging, and small patches of turf are cut sporadically. There is also trial cultivation of manilla clams *Tapes semidecussata*.

In 1989 there were proposals to build a road across the margin of the saltmarsh, and for a nature trail and interpretative facility. By 1992 this latter proposal had been withdrawn.

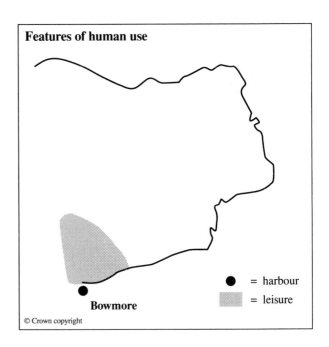

Further reading

Bignal, E.M., Curtis, D.J., & Matthews, J. 1988. Islay: land types, bird habitats and nature conservation. Part 1. Land types and birds on Islay. *Nature Conservancy Council, CSD Report*, No. 809.

Hiscock, K. 1983. Sublittoral survey of Jura and Islay. June 20th to July 3rd 1982. (Contractor: Oil Pollution Research Unit, Field Studies Council.) *Nature Conservancy Council, CSD Report*, No. 476.

Ogilvie, M.A. 1983. Wildfowl of Islay. *Proceedings of the Royal Society of Edinburgh*, 83B: 473-489.

Smith, S.M. 1982. The shores of Jura and Islay: marine flora and fauna. *Nature Conservancy Council, CSD Report*, No. 432.

Stroud, J.M., McKay, J., & Robertson, F. [1984]. *A survey of the intertidal invertebrates at the head of Loch Indaal, Isle of Islay, 20-24 January 1984, and the potential for shorebird feeding*. Unpublished report, Islay Natural History Trust and Department of Biological Science, University of Stirling.

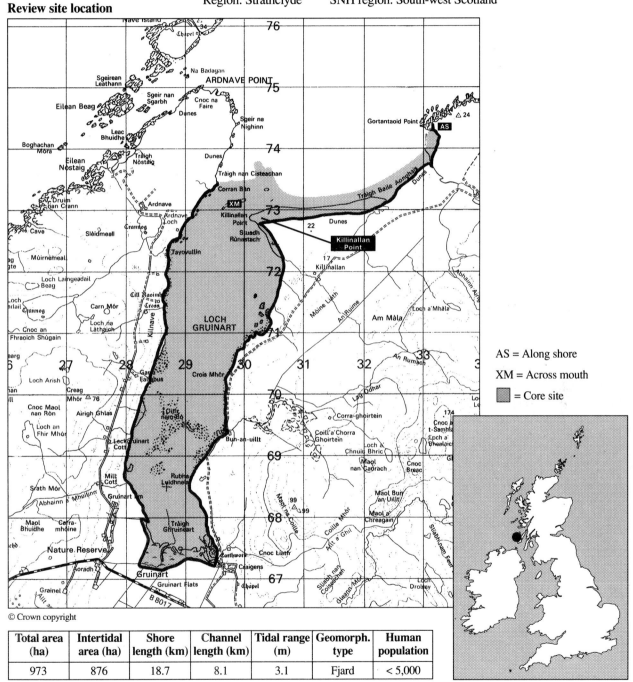

53   Loch Gruinart

Centre grid: NR2971   District: Argyll & Bute
Region: Strathclyde   SNH region: South-west Scotland

Review site location

AS = Along shore

XM = Across mouth

■ = Core site

© Crown copyright

Total area (ha)	Intertidal area (ha)	Shore length (km)	Channel length (km)	Tidal range (m)	Geomorph. type	Human population
973	876	18.7	8.1	3.1	Fjard	< 5,000

53.1

Description

Loch Gruinart lies on the northern shore of Islay in western Scotland, within the shelter of Ardnave Point. Loch Gruinart is a shallow estuary, and low tide exposes a wide sandflat with extensive lugworm beds. Towards the head of the loch the intertidal sandflats give way to mud and shingle. Some areas of the shingle are vegetated, and the flora contains northern elements of a shingle beach flora.

At the head of the loch there is one of the largest areas of saltmarsh in western Scotland, and the vegetation consists largely of mid-upper saltmarsh communities and shows transitions to grassland. The saltmarsh is used as a feeding and roosting area by large numbers of wintering waterfowl, which include a nationally important population of wintering light-bellied brent goose.

The estuary is used also as a feeding and roosting site by internationally important numbers of Greenland white-fronted geese and Greenland barnacle geese, which are particularly attracted by the extensive feeding areas provided by agricultural pasture surrounding the estuary.

The entrance to the estuary is narrowed by the high sand dunes at Killinallan Point. These dunes have developed on the shelf of a raised beach, and have a varied flora with mobile dunes, semi-fixed dunes, blow-outs, wet flushes and fixed dune vegetation which grades to grassland. The whole dune system is dynamic, accreting at the tip of Killinallan Point but eroding along the western shore of the estuary and at Traigh Baile Aonghais. There are also sand dunes on the western side of the estuary mouth at Ardnave.

Wildlife features

Coastal habitats

Subtidal	Saltmarsh	Sandflats	Mudflats	Sand dunes	Rocky shores	Shingle	Lowland grassland	Lagoon	Other
●	●	●	◍	●		●			

Area (ha)	97	51	825						

● = major habitat　　◍ = minor habitat

Birds

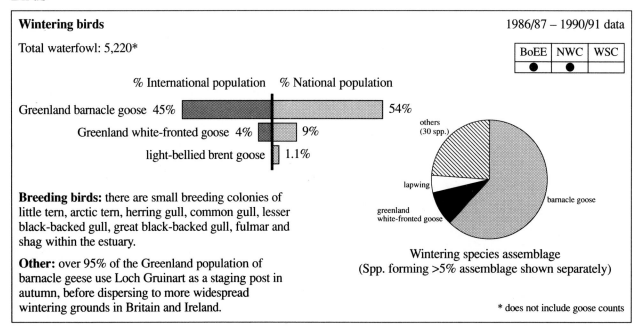

Wintering birds　　1986/87 – 1990/91 data

Total waterfowl: 5,220*

BoEE	NWC	WSC
●	●	

% International population　　% National population

Greenland barnacle goose 45% — 54%
Greenland white-fronted goose 4% — 9%
light-bellied brent goose — 1.1%

others (30 spp.)
lapwing
greenland white-fronted goose
barnacle goose

Wintering species assemblage
(Spp. forming >5% assemblage shown separately)

Breeding birds: there are small breeding colonies of little tern, arctic tern, herring gull, common gull, lesser black-backed gull, great black-backed gull, fulmar and shag within the estuary.

Other: over 95% of the Greenland population of barnacle geese use Loch Gruinart as a staging post in autumn, before dispersing to more widespread wintering grounds in Britain and Ireland.

* does not include goose counts

Additional wildlife features

Two nationally scarce plants maidenhair spleenwort *Asplenium trichomanes* and Ray's knotgrass *Polygonum oxyspermum* have recently been recorded in the dunes adjacent to the estuary.

Otters are present on Loch Gruinart, and the estuary and Nave Island are used by both common and grey seals.

Aquatic estuarine communities

Information unavailable.

Conservation status

● = designated   ◉ = proposed

	NCR	GCR	SSSI (B)	SSSI (G)	SSSI (M)	NNR	LNR	Ramsar	SPA	AONB	CWT	RSPB	ESA	NP	WWT	NT	NSA	HC	Other
	●	●	●					●	●			●							●
No.	1	1	1					1	1			1							2

The estuary lies within Gruinart Flats (3,170 ha) biological Site of Special Scientific Interest, which forms part of the Loch Gruinart-Loch Indaal Nature Conservation Review site. Loch Gruinart Flats has also been designated as a Special Protection Area and Ramsar site.

At Aoradh there is an RSPB reserve, and there is an agreement with landowners and occupiers for a goose sanctuary. Loch Gruinart is recognised by Argyll and Bute District Council as part of a Regional Scenic Coast.

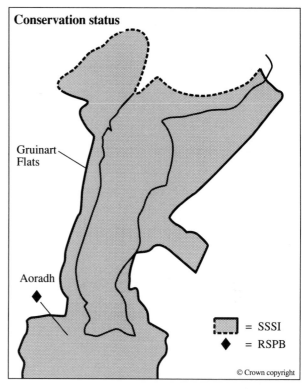

Conservation status

Gruinart Flats

Aoradh

▭ = SSSI
◆ = RSPB

© Crown copyright

At the head of Loch Gruinart lies one of the largest areas of saltmarsh in western Scotland. (Pat Doody, JNCC)

Human activities

Present   Proposed

Coast protection & sea defences ● (Present)
Linear defences
Training walls
Groynes
Brushwood fences
Spartina planting
Marram grass planting

Barrage schemes
Weirs & barrages for river management
Storm surge barrages
Water storage barrages & bunds
Leisure barrages
Tidal power barrages

Power generation
Thermal power stations
Import/export jetties (power generation)
Wind-power generation

Industrial, port & related development
Dock, port & harbour facilities
Manufacturing industries
Chemical industries
Ship & boat building
Others

Extraction & processing of natural gas & oil
Exploration
Production
Rig & platform construction
Pipeline construction
Pipeline installation
Import/export jetties & single-point moorings
Oil refineries
Mothballing of rigs & tankers

Military activities
Overflying by military aircraft
Others

Waste discharge ● (Present)
Domestic waste disposal
Sewage discharge & outfalls
Sewage treatment works
Rubbish tips
Industrial & agricultural waste discharge
Thermal discharges (power stations)
Dredge spoil
Accidental discharges
Aerial crop spraying
Waste incinerators
Others

Sediment extraction
Capital dredging
Maintenance dredging
Commercial estuarine aggregates extraction
Commercial terrestrial aggregates extraction
Non-commercial aggregates extraction ● (Present)
Hard-rock quarrying

Transport & communications
Airports & helipads
Tunnels, bridges & aqueducts
Causeways & fords
Road schemes
Ferries
Cables

Urbanisation
Land-claim for housing & car parks

Education & scientific research ● (Present) ● (Proposed)
Sampling, specimen collection & observation
Nature trails & interpretative facilities
Seismic studies & geological test drilling
Marine & terrestrial archaeology
Fossil collecting

Tourism & recreation
Infrastructure developments
  Marinas
  Non-marina moorings
  Dinghy & boat parks
  Caravan parks & chalets
  Leisure centres, complexes & piers
Aquatic-based recreation
  Power-boating & water-skiing
  Jet-skiing
  Sailing ● (Present)
  Sailboarding & wind-surfing ● (Present)
  SCUBA & snorkelling
  Canoeing
  Surfing
  Rowing
  Tourist boat trips/leisure barges
  Angling
  Other non-commercial fishing ● (Present)
  Bathing & general beach recreation ● (Present)
Terrestrial & intertidal-based recreation
  Walking, including dog walking ● (Present)
  Bird-watching ● (Present)
  Sand-yachting
  4WD & trial-biking
  Car sand-racing
  Horse-riding
  Rock-climbing
  Golf courses
  Clay-pigeon shooting
  Others
Airborne recreation
  Overflying by light aircraft
  Radio-controlled model aircraft
  Others

Wildfowling & hunting
Wildfowling
Other hunting-related activities

Bait-collecting
Digging & pumping for lugworms & ragworms
Hydraulic dredging for worms
Others

Commercial fisheries
Fish-netting & trawling
Fyke-netting for eels
Fish traps & other fixed devices & nets
Crustacea ● (Present)
Molluscs – Hand-gathering
    Dredging
    Hydraulic dredging

Cultivation of living resource
Saltmarsh grazing ● (Present)
Sand dune grazing ● (Present)
Agricultural land-claim
Fish-farming
Shellfish farming
  Bottom & tray cultivation ● (Present)
  Suspended cultivation
Crustacea farming
Reeds for roofing
Salicornia picking
Others

Management & killing of birds & mammals
Killing of mammals
Killing of birds
Adult fish-eating birds
Adult shellfish-eating birds
Gulls
Geese

Wildlife habitat management
Spartina control
Habitat creation & restoration
    Marine
    Intertidal
    Terrestrial
Habitat management ● (Present)

Others

Features of human use

Most activities involve exploitation of the natural resources, with saltmarsh and sand dune grazing by sheep and cattle, lobster- and crab-potting near the mouth of the estuary, and a small shellfishery cultivating manilla clams in trays. Leisure pursuits cover most of the estuary but are not intensive. These include sailing, wind-surfing, beach recreation and walking. Bird-watching is most active around Aoradh.

In 1989 there was a proposal to set up an information centre and bird hide at Gruinart Flats at the head of the estuary. By 1992 this had been built, to cater for an estimated 35,000 visitors annually.

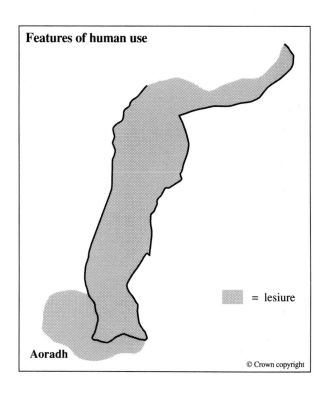

Further reading

Doarks, C., Hedley, S.M., Radley, G.P., & Woolven, S.C. 1991. *Sand dune survey of Great Britain. Site report No. 95, Killinallan*. Peterborough, Nature Conservancy Council. (Contract surveys, No. 201)

Doarks, C., Hedley, S.M., Radley, G.P., & Woolven, S.C. 1991. *Sand dune survey of Great Britain. Site report No. 96, Ardnave*. Peterborough, Nature Conservancy Council. (Contract surveys, No. 201)

Easterbee, N., Stroud, D.A., Bignall, E.M., & Dick, T.D. 1987. The arrival of Greenland barnacle geese at Loch Gruinart, Islay. *Scottish Birds, 14*: 175-170.

Ritchie, W., & Crofts, R. 1974. *Beaches of Islay, Jura and Colonsay*. Univeristy of Aberdeen, Department of Biology. Report to Countryside Commission for Scotland.

Smith, S.M. 1982. The shores of Jura and Islay: marine flora and fauna. *Nature Conservancy Council, CSD Report*, No. 432.

54	# Loch Crinan

Centre grid: NR7993 District: Argyll & Bute
Region: Strathclyde SNH region: South-west Scotland

Review site location

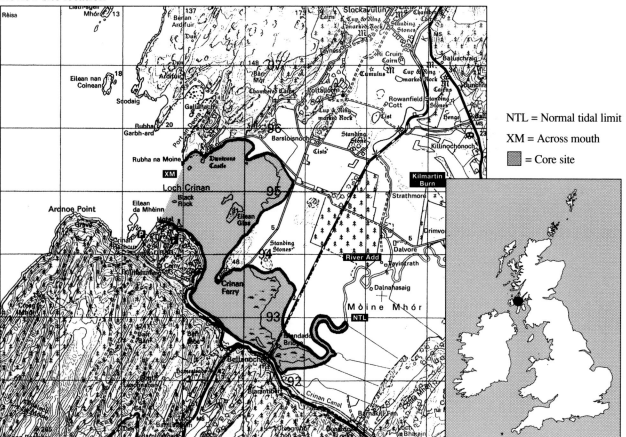

NTL = Normal tidal limit

XM = Across mouth

= Core site

© Crown copyright

Total area (ha)	Intertidal area (ha)	Shore length (km)	Channel length (km)	Tidal range (m)	Geomorph. type	Human population
280	168	15.3	6.2	3.7	Fjard	< 5,000

Description

Loch Crinan lies on the west coast of Scotland at the north-western end of the Crinan Canal. Loch Crinan once occupied all the low ground around it (now known as Moine Mhor), but today it is a fairly small estuary fed by the freshwaters of the River Add and Kilmartin Burn. The estuary is shallow from the deposited sediments of the River Add, but deepens quickly just outside the estuary mouth into the Sound of Jura. Water quality has been graded as class 1.

Much of the intertidal area is mudflat, with sand and gravel in the west and fine silt in the east. On the eastern shore near the mouth of the estuary there are extensive lugworm beds, and there are patches of algae. In the upper parts of the estuary there is a large area of saltmarsh which contains areas of low-mid and mid-upper saltmarsh vegetation, and freshwater transitions. The saltmarsh contains an interesting assemblage of plants, and Loch Crinan is one of the few sites in Britain where the transition from saltmarsh to raised bog can be seen.

The western shores of the estuary are a series of wooded hills, whereas to the east of the estuary there is an expanse of low moorland, which attracts wintering wildfowl.

Wildlife features

Coastal habitats

	Subtidal	Saltmarsh	Sandflats	Mudflats	Sand dunes	Rocky shores	Shingle	Lowland grassland	Lagoon	Other
	●	●	◉	●			◉			
Area (ha)	112	47	121							

● = major habitat   ◉ = minor habitat

Birds

Wintering birds   1984/85 data

Total waterfowl: 160

BoEE	NWC	WSC
		●

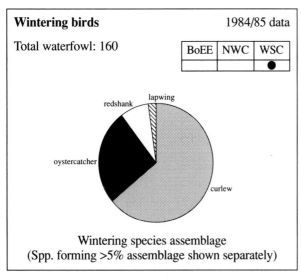

Wintering species assemblage
(Spp. forming >5% assemblage shown separately)

Aquatic estuarine communities

Soft substrate

1	2	3	4	5	6	7	8	9	10	11	12	13	14	15	16
												●		●	

Hard substrate

17	18	19	20	21	22	23	24	25	26	27	28	29	30	31	32	33

Additional wildlife features

Otters frequently use the estuary.

Conservation status

● = designated   ◉ = proposed

	NCR	GCR	SSSI (B)	SSSI (G)	SSSI (M)	NNR	LNR	Ramsar	SPA	AONB	CWT	RSPB	ESA	NP	WWT	NT	NSA	HC	Other
	●		●		●												●		●
No.	1		1		1												1		2

Much of the estuary lies within Moine Mhor biological Site of Special Scientific Interest (1,195 ha) which is a Nature Conservation Review site and partly a National Nature Reserve.

Loch Crinan is within the Knapdale National Scenic Area, and also lies within a Regional Scenic Area and Coastal Conservation Zone, as designated by Argyll District Council.

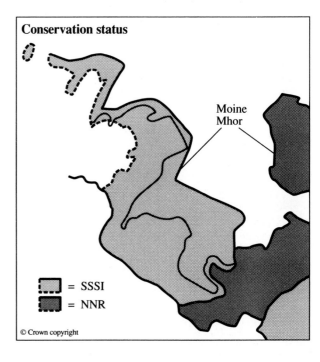

Conservation status

Moine Mhor

▨ = SSSI
▨ = NNR

© Crown copyright

Human activities

Coast protection & sea defences — ● (Present)
- Linear defences
- Training walls
- Groynes
- Brushwood fences
- *Spartina* planting
- Marram grass planting

Barrage schemes
- Weirs & barrages for river management
- Storm surge barrages
- Water storage barrages & bunds
- Leisure barrages
- Tidal power barrages

Power generation
- Thermal power stations
- Import/export jetties (power generation)
- Wind-power generation

Industrial, port & related development
- Dock, port & harbour facilities — ● (Present)
- Manufacturing industries
- Chemical industries
- Ship & boat building — ● (Present)
- Others

Extraction & processing of natural gas & oil
- Exploration
- Production
- Rig & platform construction
- Pipeline construction
- Pipeline installation
- Import/export jetties & single-point moorings
- Oil refineries
- Mothballing of rigs & tankers

Military activities
- Overflying by military aircraft
- Others

Waste discharge
- Domestic waste disposal
- Sewage discharge & outfalls — ● (Present)
- Sewage treatment works
- Rubbish tips
- Industrial & agricultural waste discharge
- Thermal discharges (power stations)
- Dredge spoil
- Accidental discharges
- Aerial crop spraying
- Waste incinerators
- Others

Sediment extraction
- Capital dredging
- Maintenance dredging
- Commercial estuarine aggregates extraction
- Commercial terrestrial aggregates extraction
- Non-commercial aggregates extraction
- Hard-rock quarrying

Transport & communications
- Airports & helipads
- Tunnels, bridges & aqueducts — ● (Present)
- Causeways & fords
- Road schemes
- Ferries
- Cables

Urbanisation
- Land-claim for housing & car parks

Education & scientific research
- Sampling, specimen collection & observation
- Nature trails & interpretative facilities
- Seismic studies & geological test drilling
- Marine & terrestrial archaeology
- Fossil collecting

Tourism & recreation
- Infrastructure developments
  - Marinas
  - Non-marina moorings — ● (Present)
  - Dinghy & boat parks
  - Caravan parks & chalets
  - Leisure centres, complexes & piers
- Aquatic-based recreation
  - Power-boating & water-skiing
  - Jet-skiing
  - Sailing — ● (Present)
  - Sailboarding & wind-surfing — ● (Present)
  - SCUBA & snorkelling
  - Canoeing — ● (Present)
  - Surfing
  - Rowing
  - Tourist boat trips/leisure barges
  - Angling — ● (Present)
  - Other non-commercial fishing
  - Bathing & general beach recreation — ● (Present)
- Terrestrial & intertidal-based recreation
  - Walking, including dog walking — ● (Present)
  - Bird-watching — ● (Present)
  - Sand-yachting
  - 4WD & trial-biking
  - Car sand-racing
  - Horse-riding
  - Rock-climbing
  - Golf courses
  - Clay-pigeon shooting
  - Others
- Airborne recreation
  - Overflying by light aircraft
  - Radio-controlled model aircraft
  - Others

Wildfowling & hunting — ● (Present)
- Wildfowling
- Other hunting-related activities

Bait-collecting — ● (Present)
- Digging & pumping for lugworms & ragworms
- Hydraulic dredging for worms
- Others

Commercial fisheries
- Fish-netting & trawling
- Fyke-netting for eels
- Fish traps & other fixed devices & nets
- Crustacea — ● (Present)
- Molluscs – Hand-gathering
  - Dredging
  - Hydraulic dredging

Cultivation of living resource
- Saltmarsh grazing — ● (Present)
- Sand dune grazing
- Agricultural land-claim
- Fish-farming
- Shellfish farming
  - Bottom & tray cultivation — ● (Present)
  - Suspended cultivation
- Crustacea farming
- Reeds for roofing
- *Salicornia* picking
- Others

Management & killing of birds & mammals
- Killing of mammals — ● (Present)
- Killing of birds
- Adult fish-eating birds
- Adult shellfish-eating birds
- Gulls — ● (Present)
- Geese

Wildlife habitat management
- *Spartina* control
- Habitat creation & restoration
  - Marine
  - Intertidal
  - Terrestrial
- Habitat management

Others

Features of human use

Leisure activities are not extensive, and are concentrated on the western shores of the estuary near the mouth. Canoeing, wind-surfing and sailing are generally not intensive, except during July when two sailing races are held, and boats often moor in Crinan and the Crinan Canal. In addition walking and bird-watching occur along the banks of the Crinan Canal.

Exploitation of the natural resources includes saltmarsh grazing by sheep and cows, and cultivation of manilla clams on an experimental basis over a small part of the intertidal area. Wildfowling occurs on a low level on the Poltalloch Estate from Duntrune Castle, and bait-digging and lobster- and crab-potting take place near the mouth of the estuary.

There are also harbour facilities and a small boat-building/repair yard near the entrance to the Crinan Canal.

Features of human use

Crinan

= leisure
● = harbour
▲ = industry

© Crown copyright

Categories of human use

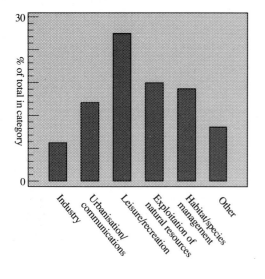

Further reading

Burd, F. 1987. *Saltmarsh survey of Great Britain. Scotland regional report - South-west.* Unpublished, Nature Conservancy Council.

McLusky, D.S. 1986. The intertidal ecology of three west of Scotland estuaries (Loch Crinan, Loch Gilp, West Loch Tarbert). *Bulletin of the Estuarine and Brackish Water Sciences Association, 43*: 15-25.

Wilkinson, M., & Roberts, C. 1974. Intertidal algae of the estuary of the River Add, Argyllshire. *Western Naturalist, 3*: 73-82.

Kentra Bay

Centre grid: NM6469 District: Lochaber
Region: Highland SNH region: North-west Scotland

Review site location

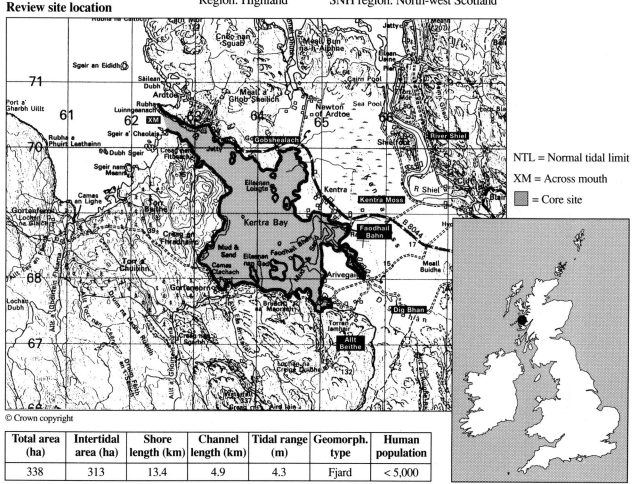

© Crown copyright

NTL = Normal tidal limit

XM = Across mouth

= Core site

Total area (ha)	Intertidal area (ha)	Shore length (km)	Channel length (km)	Tidal range (m)	Geomorph. type	Human population
338	313	13.4	4.9	4.3	Fjard	< 5,000

Description

Kentra Bay is a shallow sea loch which flows through a narrow mouth into the southern end of the Sound of Ardrishaig.

The estuary receives freshwater from a number of sources including Dig Bhan and Allt Beithe, which at low tide flow across one of the most extensive areas of intertidal flats in western Scotland. The inner flats are mud and sand, becoming more sandy towards the mouth of the estuary. There are also several small islands scattered over the Bay.

There are three main areas of saltmarsh in Kentra Bay. In the north of the estuary in the sandy bay at Gobshealach, there is a saltmarsh penetrated by tidal creeks with low and mid-marsh vegetation and a landward transition to

peatland on Kentra Moss. In the east where the Faodhail Bahn enters the estuary, there is a saltmarsh with narrow strips of mid-upper marsh and wider expanses of pioneer, low and mid-marsh communities. There is also extensive hummocking of the upper marsh turf, and a vertical transition of 2 to 3 metres from the Moss plateau to the saltmarsh turf. In the south of the estuary the largest area of saltmarsh stretches westwards from the Allt Beithe, and consists of mostly low and mid-marsh vegetation and is penetrated by narrow tidal creeks.

To the east of the estuary on low-lying ground between Kentra Bay and the River Shiel, there is an extensive area of raised mire, while the western, northern and southern shores of the estuary are bordered by steep, wooded slopes.

Wildlife features

Coastal habitats

	Subtidal	Saltmarsh	Sandflats	Mudflats	Sand dunes	Rocky shores	Shingle	Lowland grassland	Lagoon	Other
	●	●	●	●		●				
Area (ha)	25	41	272							

● = major habitat   ◉ = minor habitat

Birds

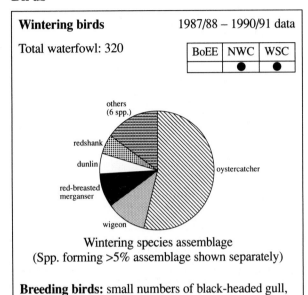

Wintering birds	1987/88 – 1990/91 data		

Total waterfowl: 320

	BoEE	NWC	WSC
		●	●

Wintering species assemblage
(Spp. forming >5% assemblage shown separately)

Breeding birds: small numbers of black-headed gull, arctic tern and redshank breed within the estuary.

Aquatic estuarine communities

Soft substrate

1	2	3	4	5	6	7	8	9	10	11	12	13	14	15	16
●			●									●			

Hard substrate

17	18	19	20	21	22	23	24	25	26	27	28	29	30	31	32	33
		●														

Additional wildlife features

Otters are present on the estuary.

Conservation status

● = designated   ◉ = proposed

	NCR	GCR	SSSI (B)	SSSI (G)	SSSI (M)	NNR	LNR	Ramsar	SPA	AONB	CWT	RSPB	ESA	NP	WWT	NT	NSA	HC	Other
	●		●														●		●
No.	1		1														1		1

Much of the estuary lies within Kentra Bay and Moss (820 ha) biological Site of Special Scientific Interest, of which Kentra Moss is a Nature Conservation Review site. Kentra Bay is also part of Morar, Moidart and Ardnamurchan National Scenic Area and is a Preferred Coastal Conservation Zone.

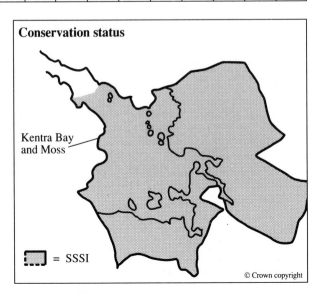

Conservation status

Kentra Bay and Moss

▨ = SSSI

© Crown copyright

Human activities

Coast protection & sea defences
Linear defences
Training walls
Groynes
Brushwood fences
Spartina planting
Marram grass planting

Barrage schemes
Weirs & barrages for river management
Storm surge barrages
Water storage barrages & bunds
Leisure barrages
Tidal power barrages

Power generation
Thermal power stations
Import/export jetties (power generation)
Wind-power generation

Industrial, port & related development
Dock, port & harbour facilities
Manufacturing industries
Chemical industries
Ship & boat building
Others

Extraction & processing of natural gas & oil
Exploration
Production
Rig & platform construction
Pipeline construction
Pipeline installation
Import/export jetties & single-point moorings
Oil refineries
Mothballing of rigs & tankers

Military activities
Overflying by military aircraft
Others

Waste discharge
● Domestic waste disposal
Sewage discharge & outfalls
Sewage treatment works
● ● Rubbish tips
Industrial & agricultural waste discharge
Thermal discharges (power stations)
Dredge spoil
Accidental discharges
Aerial crop spraying
Waste incinerators
Others

Sediment extraction
Capital dredging
Maintenance dredging
Commercial estuarine aggregates extraction
Commercial terrestrial aggregates extraction
Non-commercial aggregates extraction
Hard-rock quarrying

Transport & communications
Airports & helipads
Tunnels, bridges & aqueducts
Causeways & fords
Road schemes
Ferries
Cables

Urbanisation
Land-claim for housing & car parks

Education & scientific research
● Sampling, specimen collection & observation
Nature trails & interpretative facilities
Seismic studies & geological test drilling
Marine & terrestrial archaeology
Fossil collecting

Tourism & recreation
Infrastructure developments
  Marinas
  Non-marina moorings
  Dinghy & boat parks
  Caravan parks & chalets
  Leisure centres, complexes & piers
Aquatic-based recreation
  Power-boating & water-skiing
  Jet-skiing
● Sailing
  Sailboarding & wind-surfing
  SCUBA & snorkelling
  Canoeing
  Surfing
  Rowing
  Tourist boat trips/leisure barges
  Angling
  Other non-commercial fishing
  Bathing & general beach recreation
Terrestrial & intertidal-based recreation
  Walking, including dog walking
● Bird-watching
  Sand-yachting
  4WD & trial-biking
  Car sand-racing
  Horse-riding
  Rock-climbing
  Golf courses
  Clay-pigeon shooting
  Others
Airborne recreation
  Overflying by light aircraft
  Radio-controlled model aircraft
  Others

Wildfowling & hunting
Wildfowling
Other hunting-related activities

Bait-collecting
Digging & pumping for lugworms & ragworms
Hydraulic dredging for worms
Others

Commercial fisheries
Fish-netting & trawling
Fyke-netting for eels
Fish traps & other fixed devices & nets
Crustacea
Molluscs – Hand-gathering
            Dredging
            Hydraulic dredging

Cultivation of living resource
● Saltmarsh grazing
Sand dune grazing
Agricultural land-claim
Fish-farming
Shellfish farming
  Bottom & tray cultivation
  Suspended cultivation
Crustacea farming
Reeds for roofing
Salicornia picking
Others

Management & killing of birds & mammals
Killing of mammals
Killing of birds
Adult fish-eating birds
Adult shellfish-eating birds
Gulls
Geese

Wildlife habitat management
Spartina control
Habitat creation & restoration
  Marine
  Intertidal
  Terrestrial
Habitat management

Others

Features of human use

There are very few activities present on Kentra Bay.
Leisure pursuits include sailing from April to October in
the lower reaches of the estuary, and bird-watching.
Exploitation of the natural resources involves grazing the
saltmarsh by sheep and cattle, and sampling for botanical
studies and collection of cores for pollen analysis. Other
activities include very low-level sewage discharge, and a
rubbish tip at the southern end of Kentra Moss. In 1989
there was a proposal to extend the rubbish tip, which by
1992 had been refused.

Features of human use

Kentra
Moss

= leisure

© Crown copyright

Further reading

Bishop, G.M., & Holme, N.A. 1980. Survey of the littoral
zone of the coast of Great Britain. Final report - Part
1: the sediment shores - an assessment of their
conservation value. (Contractor: Scottish Marine
Biological Association/Marine Biological
Association.) *Nature Conservancy Council, CST
Report*, No. 326.

Howson, C. 1990. Surveys of Scottish sealochs: sealochs
of Arisaig and Moidart. *Nature Conservancy Council,
CSD Report*, No. 1,086.

Scott, K. 1984. *Saltmarsh survey of North-west Scotland.
Lochaber*. Inverness, Nature Conservancy Council.

Smith, S.M. 1978. Shores of west Inverness-shire and
north Argyll with emphasis on the Mollusca. *Nature
Conservancy Council, CSD Report*, No. 358.

56   Loch Moidart

Centre grid: NM6873   District: Lochaber
Region: Highland   SNH region: North-west Scotland

Review site location

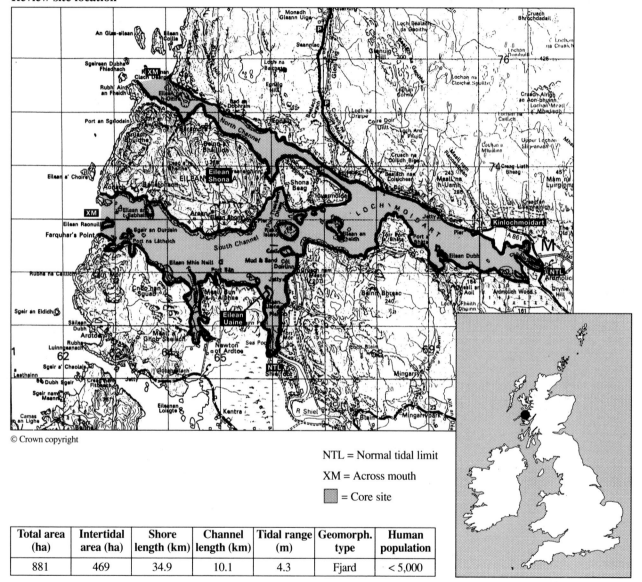

© Crown copyright

NTL = Normal tidal limit

XM = Across mouth

▓ = Core site

Total area (ha)	Intertidal area (ha)	Shore length (km)	Channel length (km)	Tidal range (m)	Geomorph. type	Human population
881	469	34.9	10.1	4.3	Fjard	< 5,000

Description

Loch Moidart is one of only two predominantly intertidal sea lochs in Lochaber, the other being the Kentra Bay review site to the south. The estuary is fed by the River Moidart which originates from the mountains to the east, and from the river that flows from Loch Shiel. The estuary flows into the Sound of Arisaig through two narrow mouths on either side of the island of Eilean Shona, and for the most part is surrounded by steep, rocky, wooded slopes.

At low tide large areas of the inner estuary are exposed as mudflat, and at the head of the estuary at Kinlochmoidart there is an area of saltmarsh. The vegetation is well developed around the edge of the loch head and lightly grazed, and there are also large detached islands of saltmarsh turf. There is also a small area of saltmarsh at the mouth of the River Shiel, between the island of Eilean Uaine and the coast, in the shelter of a small shingle bar. This area is heavily grazed.

Wildlife features

Coastal habitats	Subtidal	Saltmarsh	Sandflats	Mudflats	Sand dunes	Rocky shores	Shingle	Lowland grassland	Lagoon	Other
	●	●	◍	●		●	◍			
Area (ha)	412	24	445							

● = major habitat   ◍ = minor habitat

Birds

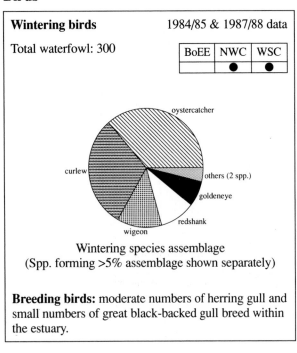

Wintering birds	1984/85 & 1987/88 data

Total waterfowl: 300

	BoEE	NWC	WSC
		●	●

Wintering species assemblage
(Spp. forming >5% assemblage shown separately)

Breeding birds: moderate numbers of herring gull and small numbers of great black-backed gull breed within the estuary.

Aquatic estuarine communities

Soft substrate

1	2	3	4	5	6	7	8	9	10	11	12	13	14	15	16
												●			

Hard substrate

17	18	19	20	21	22	23	24	25	26	27	28	29	30	31	32	33
		●		●												

Additional wildlife features

Otters are present on the estuary.

Conservation status

● = designated   ◍ = proposed

	NCR	GCR	SSSI (B)	SSSI (G)	SSSI (M)	NNR	LNR	Ramsar	SPA	AONB	CWT	RSPB	ESA	NP	WWT	NT	NSA	HC	Other
	●	●			●												●		●
No.	1	1			1												1		2

Much of the estuary is covered by Loch Moidart Site of Special Scientific Interest (799 ha), which is an SSSI for its biological and geological interest, and is also a Nature Conservation Review site and contains a Geological Conservation Review site. The estuary lies within of the Morar, Moidart and Ardnamurchan National Scenic Area, and is an Area of Great Landscape Value and a Preferred Coastal Conservation Zone.

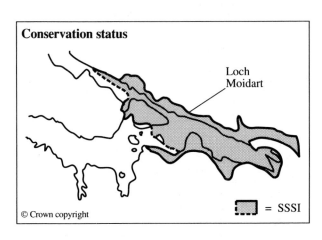

Conservation status

Loch Moidart

© Crown copyright

▭ = SSSI

Human activities

Present	Proposed	
●		**Coast protection & sea defences**
		Linear defences
		Training walls
		Groynes
		Brushwood fences
		Spartina planting
		Marram grass planting
		Barrage schemes
		Weirs & barrages for river management
		Storm surge barrages
		Water storage barrages & bunds
		Leisure barrages
		Tidal power barrages
		Power generation
		Thermal power stations
		Import/export jetties (power generation)
		Wind-power generation
		Industrial, port & related development
		Dock, port & harbour facilities
		Manufacturing industries
		Chemical industries
		Ship & boat building
		Others
		Extraction & processing of natural gas & oil
		Exploration
		Production
		Rig & platform construction
		Pipeline construction
		Pipeline installation
		Import/export jetties & single-point moorings
		Oil refineries
		Mothballing of rigs & tankers
●		**Military activities**
		Overflying by military aircraft
		Others
		Waste discharge
		Domestic waste disposal
●		Sewage discharge & outfalls
		Sewage treatment works
●		Rubbish tips
		Industrial & agricultural waste discharge
		Thermal discharges (power stations)
		Dredge spoil
		Accidental discharges
●		Aerial crop spraying
		Waste incinerators
		Others
		Sediment extraction
		Capital dredging
		Maintenance dredging
		Commercial estuarine aggregates extraction
		Commercial terrestrial aggregates extraction
●		Non-commercial aggregates extraction
		Hard-rock quarrying
		Transport & communications
		Airports & helipads
●		Tunnels, bridges & aqueducts
●		Causeways & fords
		Road schemes
		Ferries
		Cables
		Urbanisation
		Land-claim for housing & car parks
		Education & scientific research
●		Sampling, specimen collection & observation
●	●	Nature trails & interpretative facilities
		Seismic studies & geological test drilling
		Marine & terrestrial archaeology
		Fossil collecting

Present	Proposed	
		Tourism & recreation
		Infrastructure developments
●		Marinas
		Non-marina moorings
		Dinghy & boat parks
		Caravan parks & chalets
		Leisure centres, complexes & piers
		Aquatic-based recreation
●		Power-boating & water-skiing
		Jet-skiing
●		Sailing
		Sailboarding & wind-surfing
●		SCUBA & snorkelling
		Canoeing
		Surfing
		Rowing
		Tourist boat trips/leisure barges
●		Angling
		Other non-commercial fishing
		Bathing & general beach recreation
		Terrestrial & intertidal-based recreation
●		Walking, including dog walking
●		Bird-watching
		Sand-yachting
		4WD & trial-biking
		Car sand-racing
		Horse-riding
		Rock-climbing
		Golf courses
		Clay-pigeon shooting
		Others
		Airborne recreation
		Overflying by light aircraft
		Radio-controlled model aircraft
		Others
		Wildfowling & hunting
		Wildfowling
		Other hunting-related activities
		Bait-collecting
		Digging & pumping for lugworms & ragworms
		Hydraulic dredging for worms
		Others
		Commercial fisheries
		Fish-netting & trawling
		Fyke-netting for eels
		Fish traps & other fixed devices & nets
		Crustacea
●		Molluscs – Hand-gathering
		Dredging
		Hydraulic dredging
		Cultivation of living resource
●		Saltmarsh grazing
		Sand dune grazing
		Agricultural land-claim
	●	Fish-farming
		Shellfish farming
●		Bottom & tray cultivation
●		Suspended cultivation
		Crustacea farming
		Reeds for roofing
		Salicornia picking
		Others
		Management & killing of birds & mammals
		Killing of mammals
		Killing of birds
		Adult fish-eating birds
		Adult shellfish-eating birds
		Gulls
		Geese
		Wildlife habitat management
		Spartina control
		Habitat creation & restoration
		Marine
		Intertidal
		Terrestrial
●		Habitat management
		Others

Features of human use

There are few leisure activities on the estuary, and most are on a small scale. There are a small number of moorings and sailing is centred on the north and south channels on either side of Eilean Uaine, and at the mouth of the Shiel. Occasional windsurfing and canoeing also take place. A small number of bird-watchers and anglers use the estuary. The only industrial activity is the very occasional extraction of gravel from the riverbed.

Exploitation of the natural resources includes saltmarsh grazing, small-scale shellfish farming, hand-gathering of molluscs and research into manilla clams. There is also a nature trail along the south side of the loch.

In 1989 there were proposals for a halibut fish farm, and to provide an interpretative display along the nature trail.

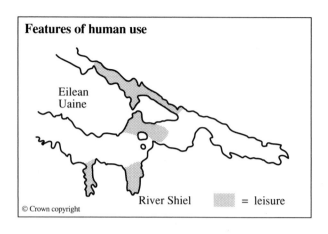

Features of human use

Eilean Uaine

© Crown copyright River Shiel = leisure

Categories of human use

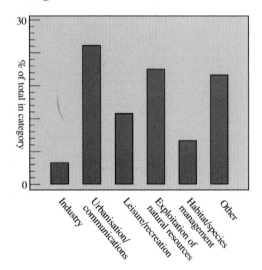

Further reading

Howson, C.M. 1990. Surveys of Scottish sealochs: sealochs of Arisaig and Moidart. *Nature Conservancy Council, CSD Report*, No. 1,086.

Scott, K. 1984. *Saltmarsh survey of North-west Scotland. Lochaber*. Inverness, Nature Conservancy Council.

Powell, H.T., Holme, N.A., Knight, S.J.T., Harvey, R., Bishop, G., & Bartrop, J. 1980. Survey of the littoral zone of the coast of Great Britain: 6. Report on the shores of North-west Scotland. (Contractor: Scottish Marine Biological Association, Intertidal Survey Unit.) *Nature Conservancy Council, CSD Report*, No. 289.

Wilkinson, M., & Scanlon, C. 1987. *Survey of Loch Moidart, 28-30th July 1987*. (Contractor: Heriot-Watt University, Edinburgh.) Unpublished report to the Nature Conservancy Council.

| 57 | **Traigh Mhor** |

Centre grid: NF7005   District: Barra
Region: Western Isles   SNH region: North-west Scotland

Review site location

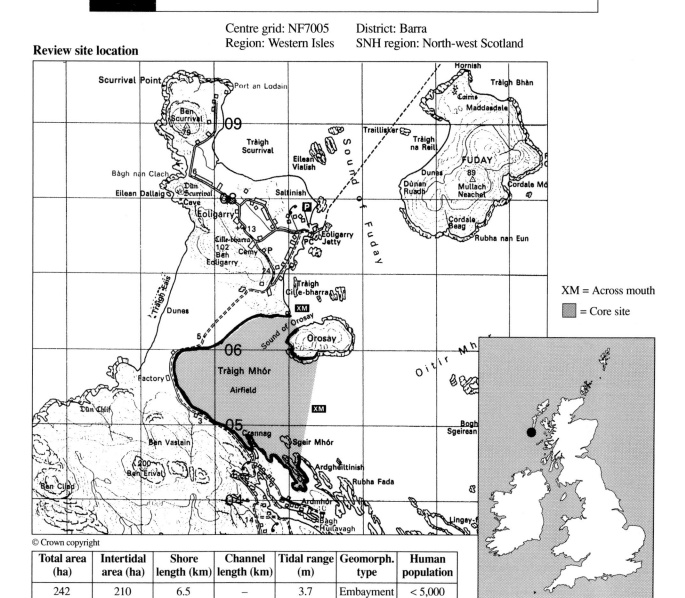

XM = Across mouth

■ = Core site

© Crown copyright

Total area (ha)	Intertidal area (ha)	Shore length (km)	Channel length (km)	Tidal range (m)	Geomorph. type	Human population
242	210	6.5	–	3.7	Embayment	< 5,000

Description

Traigh Mhor lies on the north-east tip of Barra, a small island in the south of the Outer Hebrides. The site includes the western shore of the islet of Orosay, and rocky shores at the southernmost tip of the estuary. At low tide Traigh Mhor is a vast sandflat with a profusion of intertidal banks of cockle shells. Along the beach there are a series of large-scale intertidal ripples and sandbars, that are probably related to local wave patterns, and on the western shore wave activity has caused undercutting and slumping of the stable machair on the coast edge, producing a 1-2 m vertical sand cliff.

To the west of Traigh Mhor lies the beach, dune and machair system of Eoligarry, which is bounded to the north and south by rocky hills. The machair extends from sea level up the southern slope of Ben Eoligary, and the dry machair plain is botanically varied. The high marram-covered dunes have spectacular blow-outs and dune slacks.

Wildlife features

Coastal habitats

	Subtidal	Saltmarsh	Sandflats	Mudflats	Sand dunes	Rocky shores	Shingle	Lowland grassland	Lagoon	Other
	●	◉	●		●	●				

| Area (ha) | 30 | | 210 | | | | | | | |

● = major habitat   ◉ = minor habitat

Birds

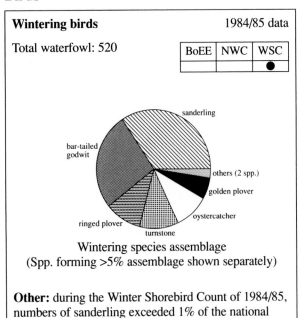

Wintering birds   1984/85 data

Total waterfowl: 520

	BoEE	NWC	WSC
			●

sanderling

bar-tailed godwit

others (2 spp.)

golden plover

oystercatcher

turnstone

ringed plover

Wintering species assemblage
(Spp. forming >5% assemblage shown separately)

Other: during the Winter Shorebird Count of 1984/85, numbers of sanderling exceeded 1% of the national population.

Aquatic estuarine communities

Soft substrate

1	2	3	4	5	6	7	8	9	10	11	12	13	14	15	16
									●			●			

Hard substrate

17	18	19	20	21	22	23	24	25	26	27	28	29	30	31	32	33

Conservation status

● = designated   ◉ = proposed

	NCR	GCR	SSSI (B)	SSSI (G)	SSSI (M)	NNR	LNR	Ramsar	SPA	AONB	CWT	RSPB	ESA	NP	WWT	NT	NSA	HC	Other
		●			●			◉	◉				●						
No.		1			1			1	1				1						

Traigh Mhor lies within the Eoligarry biological Site of Special Scientific Interest (449 ha), which also contains a Geological Conservation Review site. The area is also within the Machairs of the Uists and Benbecula and Barra Environmentally Sensitive Area, and is part of the West Sound of Barra proposed Special Protection Area and Ramsar site.

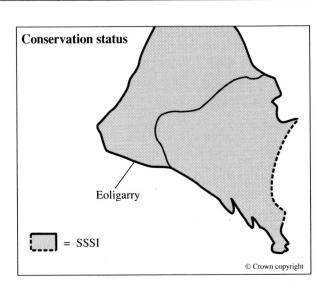

Conservation status

Eoligarry

▭ = SSSI

© Crown copyright

Human activities

Present **Proposed**

● Coast protection & sea defences
Linear defences
Training walls
Groynes
Brushwood fences
● *Spartina* planting
Marram grass planting

Barrage schemes
Weirs & barrages for river management
Storm surge barrages
Water storage barrages & bunds
Leisure barrages
Tidal power barrages

Power generation
Thermal power stations
Import/export jetties (power generation)
Wind-power generation

Industrial, port & related development
Dock, port & harbour facilities
Manufacturing industries
Chemical industries
Ship & boat building
Others

Extraction & processing of natural gas & oil
Exploration
Production
Rig & platform construction
Pipeline construction
Pipeline installation
Import/export jetties & single-point moorings
Oil refineries
Mothballing of rigs & tankers

Military activities
Overflying by military aircraft
Others

Waste discharge
Domestic waste disposal
Sewage discharge & outfalls
Sewage treatment works
Rubbish tips
Industrial & agricultural waste discharge
Thermal discharges (power stations)
Dredge spoil
Accidental discharges
Aerial crop spraying
Waste incinerators
Others

Sediment extraction
Capital dredging
Maintenance dredging
● Commercial estuarine aggregates extraction
Commercial terrestrial aggregates extraction
Non-commercial aggregates extraction
Hard-rock quarrying

Transport & communications
● Airports & helipads
Tunnels, bridges & aqueducts
Causeways & fords
Road schemes
Ferries
Cables

Urbanisation
Land-claim for housing & car parks

Education & scientific research
● Sampling, specimen collection & observation
Nature trails & interpretative facilities
Seismic studies & geological test drilling
Marine & terrestrial archaeology
Fossil collecting

Present **Proposed**

Tourism & recreation
Infrastructure developments
  Marinas
  Non-marina moorings
  Dinghy & boat parks
  Caravan parks & chalets
  Leisure centres, complexes & piers
Aquatic-based recreation
  Power-boating & water-skiing
  Jet-skiing
  Sailing
  Sailboarding & wind-surfing
  SCUBA & snorkelling
  Canoeing
  Surfing
  Rowing
  Tourist boat trips/leisure barges
  Angling
  Other non-commercial fishing
  Bathing & general beach recreation
Terrestrial & intertidal-based recreation
● Walking, including dog walking
  Bird-watching
  Sand-yachting
  4WD & trial-biking
  Car sand-racing
  Horse-riding
  Rock-climbing
  Golf courses
  Clay-pigeon shooting
  Others
Airborne recreation
● Overflying by light aircraft
  Radio-controlled model aircraft
  Others

Wildfowling & hunting
Wildfowling
Other hunting-related activities

Bait-collecting
● Digging & pumping for lugworms & ragworms
Hydraulic dredging for worms
Others

Commercial fisheries
Fish-netting & trawling
Fyke-netting for eels
Fish traps & other fixed devices & nets
Crustacea
● Molluscs – Hand-gathering
           Dredging
           Hydraulic dredging

Cultivation of living resource
● Saltmarsh grazing
● Sand dune grazing
Agricultural land-claim
Fish-farming
Shellfish farming
● Bottom & tray cultivation
  Suspended cultivation
Crustacea farming
Reeds for roofing
Salicornia picking
Others

Management & killing of birds & mammals
Killing of mammals
Killing of birds
Adult fish-eating birds
Adult shellfish-eating birds
Gulls
Geese

Wildlife habitat management
Spartina control
Habitat creation & restoration
  Marine
  Intertidal
● Terrestrial
Habitat management

Others

57.3

Features of human use

There are very few activities occurring on Traigh Mhor. Its main use is as an airfield for scheduled inter-island flights, and to maintain drainage conditions for the aircraft to land 200 m of the shore is embanked. In the south-west of the site some sediment extraction occurs, with removal of grit.

Most activities involve exploitation of the natural resources, with grazing on the sand dunes and on a very small area of saltmarsh, suspended cultivation of mussels, hand-gathering of molluscs, and digging for lugworms. The estuary is also used for geomorphological studies, and sand dunes in the west of the site are undergoing some restoration to prevent the sea breaching the dunes and effectively isolating the north of the island.

Further reading

Eleftheriou, A., & McIntyre, A.D. 1976. *The intertidal fauna of sandy beaches - a survey of the Scottish coast.* Aberdeen, Department of Agriculture and Fisheries for Scotland. (Scotland North West Region. Report No. 22.)

Farrow, G.E. 1974. On the ecology and sedimentation of the *Cardium* shell sands and transgressive shellbanks of Traigh Mhor, Island of Barra, Outer Hebrides. *Transactions of the Royal Society of Edinburgh, 69:* 203-230.

Fox, A.D., Ogilvie, M.A., Easterbee, N., & Bignal, E.M. East Greenland Barnacle Geese in Scotland, Spring 1988. *Scottish Birds, 16:* 1-10.

Powell, H.T., Holme, N.A., Knight, S.J.T., Harvey, R., Bishop, G., & Bartrop, J. 1979. Survey of the littoral zone of the coast of Great Britain. 3. Shores of the Outer Hebrides. (Contractor: Scottish Marine Biological Association/Marine Biological Association Intertidal Survey Unit.) *Nature Conservancy Council, CSD Report,* No. 272.

Stephen, A.C. 1930. Studies on the Scottish marine fauna. Additional observations on the fauna of the sandy and muddy areas of the tidal zone. *Transactions of the Royal Society of Edinburgh, 56:* 521-535.

58   Bagh nam Faoilean

Centre grid: NF7948   District: Benbecula
Region: Western Isles   SNH region: North-west Scotland

Review site location

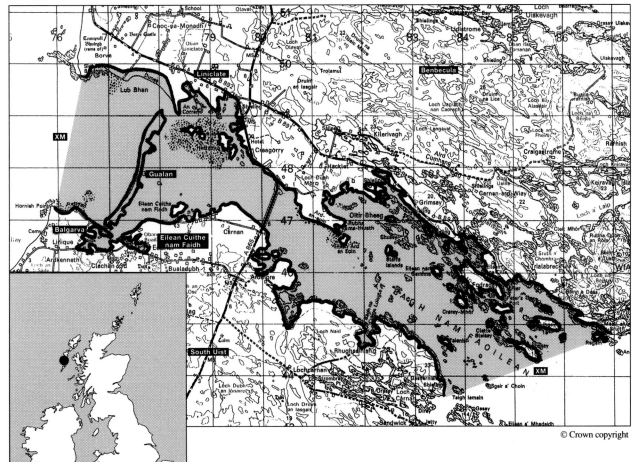

© Crown copyright

Total area (ha)	Intertidal area (ha)	Shore length (km)	Channel length (km)	Tidal range (m)	Geomorph. type	Human population
2,144	1,264	37.5	10.9	4.1	Fjard	< 5,000

XM = Across mouth

▨ = Core site

Description

Bagh nam Faoilean lies along the stretch of coast south of the island of Benbecula, separating it from South Uist, and is also known as the South Ford. The site is open to the sea to both the west and the east, and as a consequence is influenced by the Atlantic Ocean to the west and the Minch Channel to the east.

There are two main subtidal areas at the western and eastern extremities of the site. That in the east is characterised by many rocky outcrops. The aquatic estuarine communities within Bagh nam Faoilean are considered to be of significance, with a particularly rich example of the sand/muddy sand community, and areas of moderately exposed rocky shore community and sheltered rocky shore community that are considered to be of national importance.

In the west of the site there is the large, narrow, sand-capped spit of Gualan which projects across the width of the ford, and provides shelter from the Atlantic waves. Behind the spit is a large intertidal sandflat, which has patches of saltmarsh. The largest areas of saltmarsh are found within the small bay at Balgarva, in the shelter of Eilean Cuithe nam Faidh and at Liniclate on the northern shore, and there are smaller areas in the shelter of the Gualan spit. In the west of the site the gentle slopes have facilitated the development of machair, the dune grassland characteristic of the region, and on the northern shore near the mouth at Lub Bhan a small area of sand dunes has developed.

Bagh nam Faoilean supports fair numbers of wintering waterfowl and a number of breeding seabird colonies. There are also a variety of waders breeding on the lowland grassland adjacent to the site, including nationally important breeding populations of ringed plover.

The fjardic landscape of Bagh nam Faoilean, between Benbecula and South Uist. (Julian Bateson, English Nature)

Wildlife features

Coastal habitats

	Subtidal	Saltmarsh	Sandflats	Mudflats	Sand dunes	Rocky shores	Shingle	Lowland grassland	Lagoon	Other
	●	●	●	◉	●	●		●		
Area (ha)	880	35	1,229							

● = major habitat   ◉ = minor habitat

Birds

Wintering birds			1984/85 data

Total waterfowl: 2,160

	BoEE	NWC	WSC
			●

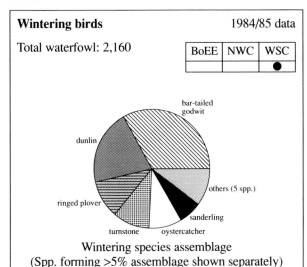

Wintering species assemblage
(Spp. forming >5% assemblage shown separately)

Breeding birds: small numbers of black-headed gull, herring gull, common gull, common tern, arctic tern and fulmar breed within the estuary. In addition moderate numbers of snipe, large numbers of oystercatcher, redshank, lapwing and dunlin, and nationally important numbers of ringed plover breed within the grasslands adjacent to the estuary.

Aquatic estuarine communities

Soft substrate

1	2	3	4	5	6	7	8	9	10	11	12	13	14	15	16
							●		●			●			

Hard substrate

17	18	19	20	21	22	23	24	25	26	27	28	29	30	31	32	33
	●	●														

Additional wildlife features

One Notable species of invertebrate has recently been recorded from the site, on the dunes at Borve.

There are a good number of otters on the estuary, and common seals often use the western parts of the site for pupping.

Conservation status

● = designated   ◉ = proposed

	NCR	GCR	SSSI (B)	SSSI (G)	SSSI (M)	NNR	LNR	Ramsar	SPA	AONB	CWT	RSPB	ESA	NP	WWT	NT	NSA	HC	Other
								◉	◉				●						
No.								1	1				1						

The western side of Bagh nam Faoilean lies within the Machairs of the Uists, Benbecula and Barra Environmentally Sensitive Area, and parts of the site lie within the South Uist Machair and Lochs proposed Ramsar site and Special Protection Area.

Human activities

Present	Proposed	Activity
●		**Coast protection & sea defences**
		Linear defences
		Training walls
		Groynes
		Brushwood fences
		Spartina planting
		Marram grass planting
		Barrage schemes
		Weirs & barrages for river management
		Storm surge barrages
		Water storage barrages & bunds
		Leisure barrages
		Tidal power barrages
		Power generation
		Thermal power stations
		Import/export jetties (power generation)
●		Wind-power generation
		Industrial, port & related development
		Dock, port & harbour facilities
		Manufacturing industries
		Chemical industries
		Ship & boat building
		Others
		Extraction & processing of natural gas & oil
		Exploration
		Production
		Rig & platform construction
		Pipeline construction
		Pipeline installation
		Import/export jetties & single-point moorings
		Oil refineries
		Mothballing of rigs & tankers
		Military activities
		Overflying by military aircraft
		Others
		Waste discharge
		Domestic waste disposal
		Sewage discharge & outfalls
		Sewage treatment works
		Rubbish tips
		Industrial & agricultural waste discharge
		Thermal discharges (power stations)
		Dredge spoil
		Accidental discharges
		Aerial crop spraying
		Waste incinerators
		Others
		Sediment extraction
		Capital dredging
		Maintenance dredging
●		Commercial estuarine aggregates extraction
		Commercial terrestrial aggregates extraction
●		Non-commercial aggregates extraction
		Hard-rock quarrying
		Transport & communications
		Airports & helipads
		Tunnels, bridges & aqueducts
●		Causeways & fords
		Road schemes
		Ferries
		Cables
		Urbanisation
		Land-claim for housing & car parks
		Education & scientific research
		Sampling, specimen collection & observation
		Nature trails & interpretative facilities
		Seismic studies & geological test drilling
		Marine & terrestrial archaeology
		Fossil collecting

Present	Proposed	Activity
		Tourism & recreation
		Infrastructure developments
		Marinas
		Non-marina moorings
		Dinghy & boat parks
		Caravan parks & chalets
		Leisure centres, complexes & piers
		Aquatic-based recreation
		Power-boating & water-skiing
		Jet-skiing
●		Sailing
		Sailboarding & wind-surfing
		SCUBA & snorkelling
		Canoeing
		Surfing
		Rowing
●		Tourist boat trips/leisure barges
●		Angling
		Other non-commercial fishing
		Bathing & general beach recreation
		Terrestrial & intertidal-based recreation
		Walking, including dog walking
●		Bird-watching
		Sand-yachting
		4WD & trial-biking
		Car sand-racing
		Horse-riding
		Rock-climbing
		Golf courses
		Clay-pigeon shooting
		Others
		Airborne recreation
		Overflying by light aircraft
		Radio-controlled model aircraft
		Others
●		**Wildfowling & hunting**
		Wildfowling
		Other hunting-related activities
		Bait-collecting
		Digging & pumping for lugworms & ragworms
		Hydraulic dredging for worms
		Others
		Commercial fisheries
		Fish-netting & trawling
		Fyke-netting for eels
		Fish traps & other fixed devices & nets
●		Crustacea
●		Molluscs – Hand-gathering
		Dredging
		Hydraulic dredging
		Cultivation of living resource
●		Saltmarsh grazing
●		Sand dune grazing
		Agricultural land-claim
		Fish-farming
		Shellfish farming
		Bottom & tray cultivation
		Suspended cultivation
		Crustacea farming
		Reeds for roofing
		Salicornia picking
		Others
		Management & killing of birds & mammals
●		Killing of mammals
		Killing of birds
		Adult fish-eating birds
		Adult shellfish-eating birds
●		Gulls
		Geese
		Wildlife habitat management
		Spartina control
		Habitat creation & restoration
		Marine
		Intertidal
●		Terrestrial
		Habitat management
		Others

Features of human use

Activities on Bagh nam Faoilean are not intensive.
Leisure pursuits include very infrequent sailing in the east
as there are listed anchorages just outside this area, and
bird-watching and occasional tourist boat-trips. The only
industrial activity is sediment extraction on either side of
the causeway, and sporadic sediment extraction by
crofters. Exploitation of the natural resources includes
heavy grazing of the saltmarsh, grazing of the sand dunes,
and wildfowling on the South Uist Estates for greylag
geese and ducks.

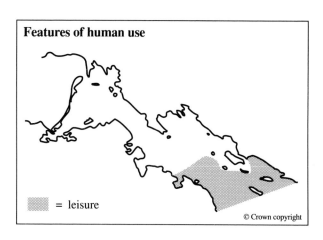

Features of human use

▨ = leisure

© Crown copyright

Categories of human use

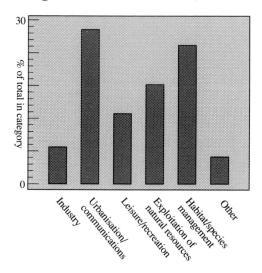

% of total in category

Industry
Urbanisation/communications
Leisure/recreation
Exploitation of natural resources
Habitat/species management
Other

Further reading

Bishop, G.M., & Holme, N.A. 1980. Survey of the littoral
zone of the coast of Great Britain. Final report – Part
1: the sediment shores – an assessment of their
conservation value. (Contractor: Scottish Marine
Biological Association/Marine Biological
Association.) *Nature Conservancy Council, CST
Report*, No. 326.

Buxton, N.E. 1982. Wintering waders on the Atlantic
shores of the Uists and Benbecula. *Scottish Birds*,
12: 106-113.

Fuller, R.J., Reed, T.M., Buxton, N.E., Webb, A.,
Williams, T.D., & Pienkowski, M.W. 1986.
Populations of breeding waders *Charadrii* and their
habitats on the crofting lands of the Outer Hebrides,
Scotland. *Biological Conservation*, *37*: 333-361.

Law, D., & Gilbert, D. 1986. *Saltmarsh survey of North-
west Scotland. The Western Isles.* Unpublished,
Nature Conservancy Council.

Powell, H.T., Holme, N.A., Knight, S.J.T., Harvey, R.,
Bishop, G., & Bartrop, J. 1979. Survey of the littoral
coast of Great Britain. 3. Report on the shores of the
Outer Hebrides. (Contractor: Marine Biological
Association/Scottish Marine Biological Association.)
Nature Conservancy Council, CST Report, No. 269.

59   Oitir Mhor

Centre grid: NF8158   District: Benbecula
Region: Western Isles   SNH region: North-west Scotland

Review site location

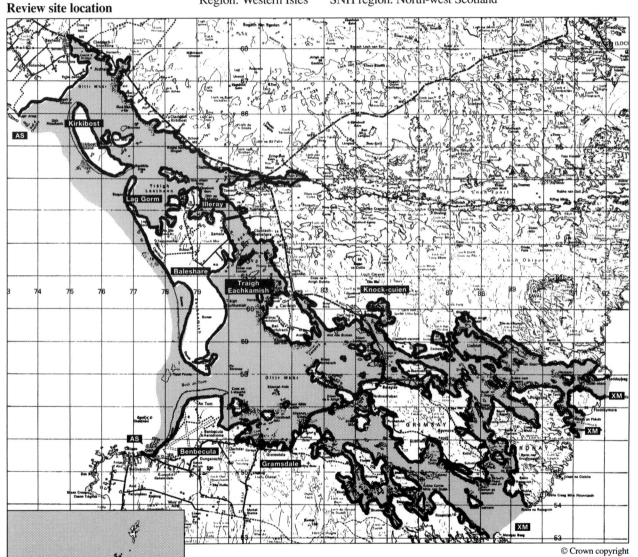

© Crown copyright

Total area (ha)	Intertidal area (ha)	Shore length (km)	Channel length (km)	Tidal range (m)	Geomorph. type	Human population
5,519	4,028	292.4	13.3	4.1	Fjard	< 5,000

XM = Across mouth

AS = Along shore

▓ = Core site

Description

Oitir Mhor separates the island of Benbecula from North Uist, and is influenced by the tides of the Atlantic to the west and by the Little Minch to the east. The western and eastern parts of the site contrast strongly, for in the west are the low-lying islands of Baleshare and Kirkibost which provide shelter from the Atlantic, and in the east there is a myriad of rocky outcrops and small, steep islands.

The aquatic estuarine communities within Oitir Mhor are considered to be of great interest, with a variable/reduced salinity mud community of high regional importance and a sheltered rocky shore community which has a free-living form of the brown alga *Ascophyllum nodosum*. Oitir Mhor is one of only two estuary sites where the *mackaii* variant of *Ascophyllum* occurs, although it is widespread in similar scattered sites in Scotland.

At low tide a large area of intertidal flats are exposed, which are predominantly sandy. There are many patches of saltmarsh scattered around the shores, with the largest areas at Illeray, Traigh Eachkamish and Lag Gorm on Baleshare, and in the small bays at Knock-cuien and Gramsdale. In addition, along the islands of Baleshare and Kirkibost lies one of the largest sand dune systems in West Scotland, supporting a range of dune vegetation from calcareous to acidic dune slack communities, often showing brackish influences. The dune slacks grade into machair, and the system has a particularly rich flora with amongst the highest number of plants species recorded on dune slack and wet machair in the Western Isles.

Oitir Mhor is of particular importance for wintering and breeding waders, with large numbers of waders breeding on the grasslands adjacent to the site. It is of international importance for its breeding population of ringed plover, and supports breeding colonies of a number of seabird species.

Wildlife features

Coastal habitats

	Subtidal	Saltmarsh	Sandflats	Mudflats	Sand dunes	Rocky shores	Shingle	Lowland grassland	Lagoon	Other
	●	●	●	◉	●	●	●	●		
Area (ha)	1,491	144	3,884							

● = major habitat   ◉ = minor habitat

Aquatic estuarine communities

Soft substrate

1	2	3	4	5	6	7	8	9	10	11	12	13	14	15	16
									●			●		●	

Hard substrate

17	18	19	20	21	22	23	24	25	26	27	28	29	30	31	32	33
		●		●												

Birds

Wintering birds — 1984/85 data

Total waterfowl: 2,030

BoEE	NWC	WSC
		●

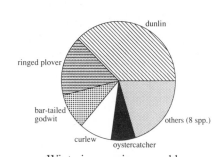

Wintering species assemblage
(Spp. forming >5% assemblage shown separately)

Breeding birds: there is a moderate-sized colony of black-headed gull, and small numbers of little tern, arctic tern, common gull and fulmar. In addition large number of oystercatcher, lapwing, dunlin, snipe, redshank and ringed plover breed within the grasslands adjacent to the estuary. The numbers of ringed plover exceed 1% of the international breeding population.

Other: during the Winter Shorebird Count of 1984/85, numbers of wintering ringed plover exceeded 1% of the national population.

Additional wildlife features

Otters are present on the estuary, and common seals are often seen on the eastern shores. Small numbers of common seals pup here.

Conservation status

● = designated   ◉ = proposed

	NCR	GCR	SSSI (B)	SSSI (G)	SSSI (M)	NNR	LNR	Ramsar	SPA	AONB	CWT	RSPB	ESA	NP	WWT	NT	NSA	HC	Other
	●		●					◉	◉				●						
No.	1		1					1	1				1						

A small part of Oitir Mhor is covered by Baleshare and Kirkibost biological Site of Special Scientific Interest (1,466 ha), which is also a Nature Conservation Review site. The western part of the site also lies within the Machairs of the Uists, Benbecula, Barra and Vatersay Environmentally Sensitive Area.

Oitir Mhor lies within the proposed Baleshare and Kirkibost Special Protection Area and Ramsar site.

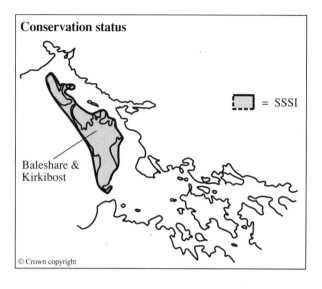

Conservation status

Baleshare & Kirkibost

⬚⬚⬚ = SSSI

© Crown copyright

The aquatic estuarine communities of Oitir Mhor are considered to be of great interest. (Pat Doody, JNCC)

Human activities

Coast protection & sea defences ● *(Present)*
Linear defences
Training walls
Groynes
Brushwood fences
Spartina planting
Marram grass planting

Barrage schemes
Weirs & barrages for river management
Storm surge barrages
Water storage barrages & bunds
Leisure barrages
Tidal power barrages

Power generation
Thermal power stations
Import/export jetties (power generation)
Wind-power generation

Industrial, port & related development
Dock, port & harbour facilities ● *(Present)*
Manufacturing industries
Chemical industries
Ship & boat building
Others

Extraction & processing of natural gas & oil
Exploration
Production
Rig & platform construction
Pipeline construction
Pipeline installation
Import/export jetties & single-point moorings
Oil refineries
Mothballing of rigs & tankers

Military activities
Overflying by military aircraft ● *(Present)*
Others

Waste discharge
Domestic waste disposal
Sewage discharge & outfalls ● *(Present)*
Sewage treatment works
Rubbish tips
Industrial & agricultural waste discharge
Thermal discharges (power stations)
Dredge spoil
Accidental discharges
Aerial crop spraying
Waste incinerators
Others

Sediment extraction
Capital dredging
Maintenance dredging
Commercial estuarine aggregates extraction
Commercial terrestrial aggregates extraction ● *(Present)*
Non-commercial aggregates extraction ● *(Present)*
Hard-rock quarrying

Transport & communications
Airports & helipads ● *(Present)*
Tunnels, bridges & aqueducts
Causeways & fords ● *(Present)*
Road schemes
Ferries
Cables

Urbanisation
Land-claim for housing & car parks

Education & scientific research
Sampling, specimen collection & observation ● *(Present)*
Nature trails & interpretative facilities
Seismic studies & geological test drilling
Marine & terrestrial archaeology
Fossil collecting

Tourism & recreation
Infrastructure developments
  Marinas
  Non-marina moorings ● *(Present)*
  Dinghy & boat parks
  Caravan parks & chalets
  Leisure centres, complexes & piers
Aquatic-based recreation
  Power-boating & water-skiing
  Jet-skiing
  Sailing ● *(Present)*
  Sailboarding & wind-surfing
  SCUBA & snorkelling
  Canoeing
  Surfing
  Rowing
  Tourist boat trips/leisure barges
  Angling ● *(Present)*
  Other non-commercial fishing ● *(Present)*
  Bathing & general beach recreation
Terrestrial & intertidal-based recreation
  Walking, including dog walking ● *(Present)*
  Bird-watching
  Sand-yachting
  4WD & trial-biking
  Car sand-racing
  Horse-riding ● *(Present)*
  Rock-climbing
  Golf courses
  Clay-pigeon shooting
  Others
Airborne recreation
  Overflying by light aircraft ● *(Present)*
  Radio-controlled model aircraft
  Others

Wildfowling & hunting
Wildfowling ● *(Present)*
Other hunting-related activities

Bait-collecting
Digging & pumping for lugworms & ragworms
Hydraulic dredging for worms
Others

Commercial fisheries
Fish-netting & trawling
Fyke-netting for eels
Fish traps & other fixed devices & nets
Crustacea ● *(Present)*
Molluscs – Hand-gathering ● *(Present)*
  Dredging
  Hydraulic dredging

Cultivation of living resource
Saltmarsh grazing ● *(Present)*
Sand dune grazing ● *(Present)*
Agricultural land-claim
Fish-farming ● *(Present)*
Shellfish farming
  Bottom & tray cultivation ● *(Present)*
  Suspended cultivation
Crustacea farming
Reeds for roofing
Salicornia picking ● *(Present)*
Others

Management & killing of birds & mammals
Killing of mammals ● *(Present)*
Killing of birds
Adult fish-eating birds
Adult shellfish-eating birds
Gulls ● *(Present)*
Geese

Wildlife habitat management
Spartina control
Habitat creation & restoration
  Marine
  Intertidal
  Terrestrial
Habitat management

Others

Features of human use

Exploitation of the natural resources are the predominant activities present, and include grazing over the saltmarsh and most of the sand dunes, salmon fish farms, cultivation of mussels, and algal cutting for the alginate industry. Winkles are also gathered by hand, lobster- and crab-potting occurs, and wildfowlers shoot over Baleshare. The two small harbour facilities at Eileanan Glasa and Garth Eilean Mor are used by fishing craft.

Recreational activity is not intensive over the site, and includes sailing in the east and south where there is a small number of moorings, horse-riding at Benbecula, and walking and bird-watching.

In addition there is an airport at Benbecula to the south-west of Oitir Mhor, which is the focus for aircraft.

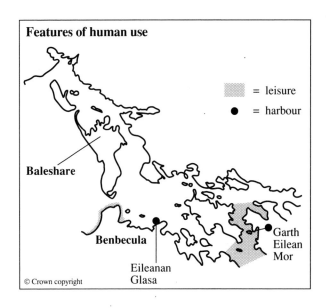

Features of human use

= leisure
● = harbour

Baleshare
Benbecula
Eileanan Glasa
Garth Eilean Mor

© Crown copyright

Categories of human use

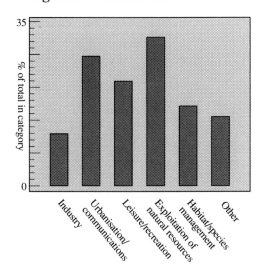

Further reading

Bishop, G.M., & Holme, N.A. 1980. Survey of the littoral zone of the coast of Great Britain. Final report- Part 1: The sediment shores – an assessment of their conservation value. (Contractor: Scottish Marine Biological Association/Marine Biological Association.) *Nature Conservancy Council, CST Report*, No. 326.

Buxton, N.E. 1982. Preliminary estimates of the number of waders wintering in the Outer Hebrides, Scotland. *Wader Study Group*, 35: 6-7.

Buxton, N.E. 1982. Wintering waders on the Atlantic shores of the Uists and Benbecula. *Scottish Birds*, 12: 106-113.

Fuller, R.J., Reed, T.M., Buxton, N.E., Webb, A., Williams, T.D., & Pienkowski, M.W. 1986. Populations of breeding waders *Charadrii* and their habitats on the crofting lands of the Outer Hebrides, Scotland. *Biological Conservation*, 37: 333-361.

Law, D., & Gilbert, D. 1986. *Saltmarsh survey of North-west Scotland. The Western Isles.* Unpublished, Nature Conservancy Council.

Powell, H.T., Holme, N.A., Knight, S.J.T., Harvey, R., Bishop, G.M., & Bartrop, J. 1979. Survey of the littoral zone of the coast of Great Britain. 3. Report on the shores of the Outer Herbrides. (Contractor: Marine Biological Association/Scottish Marine Biological Association.) *Nature Conservancy Council, CST report*, No. 272.

60 Traigh Valley

Centre grid: NF7875 District: North Uist
Region: Western Isles SNH region: North-west Scotland

Review site location

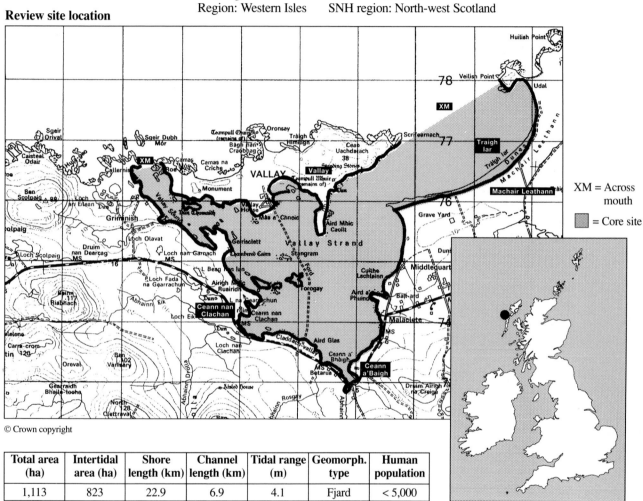

XM = Across mouth

▨ = Core site

© Crown copyright

Total area (ha)	Intertidal area (ha)	Shore length (km)	Channel length (km)	Tidal range (m)	Geomorph. type	Human population
1,113	823	22.9	6.9	4.1	Fjard	< 5,000

Description

Traigh Valley, also known as Valley Strand, lies on the north-west coast of North Uist in the Outer Hebrides. It is separated from the Oronsay review site to the east by the peninsula of Machair Leathann. The island of Valley protects the site from the open sea, and shelters a large intertidal sandflat which drains almost completely at low tide. In a small bay on the south of Valley there is an area of saltmarsh, with largely mid-upper saltmarsh vegetation and grassland transition communities, and on the southern shore of the site at Ceann a'Baigh and Ceann nan Clachan there are smaller, narrow strips of saltmarsh vegetation, marked by small cliffs caused by erosion.

In addition there are stretches of bare shingle along the shores of Traigh Valley, and on either side of the western and eastern mouths of the site there are patches of rocky shore.

To the east of the site the narrow, sandy beach of Traigh Iar extends along the Machair Leathann peninsula. Here the extensive system of dune and machair vegetation along the Machair Leathann spit is highly dynamic. The exposed foredunes along the spit are subject to erosion and are retreating, with only the small spit at the south-western end of Traigh Iar showing signs of accretion.

Traigh Valley supports breeding populations of several species of wader, which includes an internationally important breeding population of ringed plover.

Wildlife features

Coastal habitats

	Subtidal	Saltmarsh	Sandflats	Mudflats	Sand dunes	Rocky shores	Shingle	Lowland grassland	Lagoon	Other
	●	●	●	◉	●	●	●	●		
Area (ha)	290	15	808							

● = major habitat ◉ = minor habitat

Birds

Wintering birds: Traigh Vallay is not a regularly counted site, but Buxton (1982) recorded large numbers of ringed plover and bar-tailed godwit wintering on the estuary, along with smaller numbers of oystercatcher, grey plover and dunlin.

Breeding birds: large numbers of lapwing, moderate numbers of oystercatcher and small numbers of ringed plover, dunlin and redshank are known to breed on the grasslands adjacent to the estuary. Large numbers of breeding waders have been recorded on Machair Leathann and Sollas, which lie between the Traigh Vallay and Oronsay review sites, and the ringed plover survey of 1984 recorded a breeding population of international importance.

Aquatic estuarine communities

Soft substrate

1	2	3	4	5	6	7	8	9	10	11	12	13	14	15	16
												●			

Hard substrate

17	18	19	20	21	22	23	24	25	26	27	28	29	30	31	32	33
				●												

Additional wildlife features

Otters regularly use the estuary.

Conservation status

● = designated ◉ = proposed

	NCR	GCR	SSSI (B)	SSSI (G)	SSSI (M)	NNR	LNR	Ramsar	SPA	AONB	CWT	RSPB	ESA	NP	WWT	NT	NSA	HC	Other
			●										●				●		
No.			1										1				1		

Vallay (307 ha) has been designated as a biological Site of Special Scientific Interest. Vallay Strand is a National Scenic Area and the estuary forms part of the Machairs of the Uists, Benbecula, Barra and Vatersay Environmentally Sensitive Area.

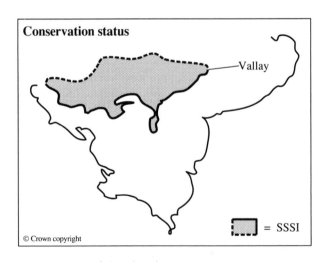

Conservation status

Vallay

© Crown copyright

▨ = SSSI

Human activities

Coast protection & sea defences
Linear defences
Training walls
Groynes
Brushwood fences
Spartina planting
Marram grass planting

Barrage schemes
Weirs & barrages for river management
Storm surge barrages
Water storage barrages & bunds
Leisure barrages
Tidal power barrages

Power generation
Thermal power stations
Import/export jetties (power generation)
Wind-power generation

Industrial, port & related development *(Present ●)*
Dock, port & harbour facilities
Manufacturing industries
Chemical industries
Ship & boat building
Others

Extraction & processing of natural gas & oil
Exploration
Production
Rig & platform construction
Pipeline construction
Pipeline installation
Import/export jetties & single-point moorings
Oil refineries
Mothballing of rigs & tankers

Military activities
Overflying by military aircraft
Others

Waste discharge
Domestic waste disposal
Sewage discharge & outfalls
Sewage treatment works
Rubbish tips
Industrial & agricultural waste discharge
Thermal discharges (power stations)
Dredge spoil
Accidental discharges
Aerial crop spraying
Waste incinerators
Others

Sediment extraction
Capital dredging
Maintenance dredging
Commercial estuarine aggregates extraction
Commercial terrestrial aggregates extraction
Non-commercial aggregates extraction
Hard-rock quarrying

Transport & communications
Airports & helipads
Tunnels, bridges & aqueducts
Causeways & fords *(Present ●)*
Road schemes
Ferries
Cables

Urbanisation
Land-claim for housing & car parks

Education & scientific research
Sampling, specimen collection & observation
Nature trails & interpretative facilities
Seismic studies & geological test drilling
Marine & terrestrial archaeology
Fossil collecting

Tourism & recreation
Infrastructure developments
  Marinas
  Non-marina moorings
  Dinghy & boat parks
  Caravan parks & chalets
  Leisure centres, complexes & piers
Aquatic-based recreation
  Power-boating & water-skiing
  Jet-skiing
  Sailing
  Sailboarding & wind-surfing
  SCUBA & snorkelling
  Canoeing
  Surfing
  Rowing
  Tourist boat trips/leisure barges
  Angling
  Other non-commercial fishing
  Bathing & general beach recreation
Terrestrial & intertidal-based recreation *(Present ●)*
  Walking, including dog walking
  Bird-watching
  Sand-yachting
  4WD & trial-biking
  Car sand-racing
  Horse-riding
  Rock-climbing
  Golf courses
  Clay-pigeon shooting
  Others
Airborne recreation
  Overflying by light aircraft
  Radio-controlled model aircraft
  Others

Wildfowling & hunting *(Present ●)*
Wildfowling
Other hunting-related activities

Bait-collecting
Digging & pumping for lugworms & ragworms
Hydraulic dredging for worms
Others

Commercial fisheries
Fish-netting & trawling
Fyke-netting for eels
Fish traps & other fixed devices & nets
Crustacea *(Present ●)*
Molluscs – Hand-gathering
        Dredging
        Hydraulic dredging

Cultivation of living resource *(Present ● ●)*
Saltmarsh grazing
Sand dune grazing
Agricultural land-claim
Fish-farming
Shellfish farming
  Bottom & tray cultivation
  Suspended cultivation
Crustacea farming
Reeds for roofing
Salicornia picking
Others

Management & killing of birds & mammals
Killing of mammals
Killing of birds
Adult fish-eating birds
Adult shellfish-eating birds
Gulls
Geese

Wildlife habitat management
Spartina control
Habitat creation & restoration
    Marine
    Intertidal
    Terrestrial
Habitat management

Others

Features of human use

There are very few activities occurring on Traigh Vallay.
There is a small pier near Griminish in the west for
mooring fishing boats, and lobster and crab potting occur
in the west channel, but not intensively. The saltmarsh
and sand dunes are lightly grazed, and wildfowling occurs
from September to February.

The only leisure activity on Traigh Vallay is walking, for
tourists walk across the ford to Vallay Island.

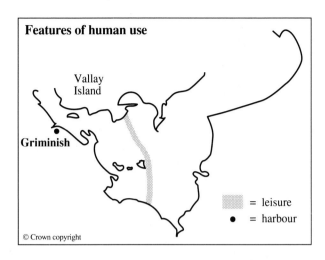

Further reading

Buxton, N.E. 1982. Wintering waders on the Atlantic
shores of the Uists and Benbecula. *Scottish Birds, 12*:
106-113.

Crawford, I. 1989. *National sand dune vegetation survey.
Site report No. 66, Middlequarter, North Uist.*
Peterborough, Nature Conservancy Council. (Contract
Surveys, No. 116).

Crawford, I. 1989. *National sand dune vegetation survey.
Site report No. 67, Sollas, North Uist.* Peterborough,
Nature Conservancy Council. (Contract Surveys, No.
117).

Eleftheriou, A. 1970. *Report on the general biological
survey at North Uist.* Aberdeen, Department of
Agriculture and Fisheries for Scotland.

Eleftheriou, A., & McIntyre, A.D. 1976. *The intertidal
fauna of sandy beaches – a survey of the Scottish
coast.* Aberdeen, Department of Agriculture and
Fisheries for Scotland (Scottish Fisheries Research
Report, No. 6).

Fuller, R.J., Reed, T.M., Buxton, N.E., Webb, A.,
Williams, T.D., & Pienkowski, M.W. 1986.
Populations of breeding waders *Charadrii* and their
habitats on the crofting lands of the Outer Hebrides,
Scotland. *Biological Conservation, 37*: 333-361.

Law, D., & Gilbert, D. 1986. *Saltmarsh survey of
North-west Scotland. The Western Isles.* Unpublished,
Nature Conservancy Council.

Oronsay

Centre grid: NF8575 District: North Uist
Region: Western Isles SNH region: North-west Scotland

Review site location

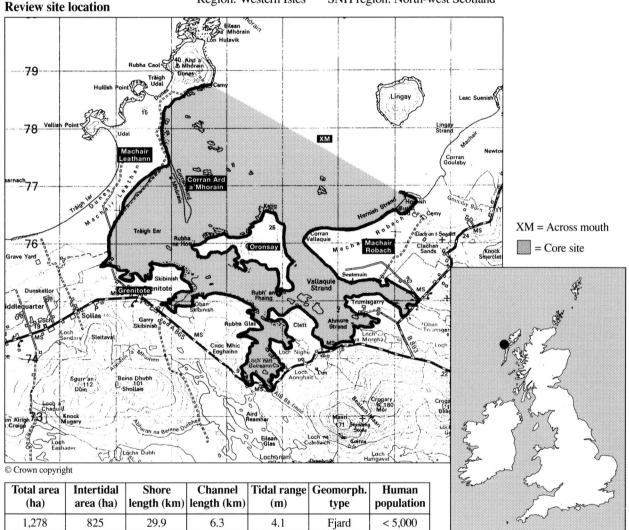

© Crown copyright

XM = Across mouth

= Core site

Total area (ha)	Intertidal area (ha)	Shore length (km)	Channel length (km)	Tidal range (m)	Geomorph. type	Human population
1,278	825	29.9	6.3	4.1	Fjard	< 5,000

Description

Oronsay lies on the north coast of North Uist in the Outer Hebrides, and is separated from the Traigh Valley review site by the peninsula of Machair Leathann. The island of Oronsay lies in the centre of the site. Much of Oronsay is a vast, intertidal sandflat, sheltered and well protected from serious wave attack.

Along the inner shores lie various strips of shingle, and there is a small area of mature saltmarsh at Grenitote in the south-west. To the east of the estuary mouth lies Machair Robach, an important coastal site in the Western Isles for it is the most dynamic and representative dune and machair area in the Uists and demonstrates the effects

of severe wind erosion on mature high machair plateau, with deep blow-outs and ridge retreat. The vegetation is also of importance for it shows a range of vegetation communities, with dune slacks, wet machair and a particularly species-rich uncultivated machair. The site also supports a wide diversity of moss species.

There is a further area of sand dune along the narrow tongue of Corran Ard a'Mhorain, a small peninsula running south-east from Machair Leathann, which at high water forms a strip of marram-covered dunes only a few metres wide. This peninsula is rapidly eroding.

Wildlife features

Coastal habitats

	Subtidal	Saltmarsh	Sandflats	Mudflats	Sand dunes	Rocky shores	Shingle	Lowland grassland	Lagoon	Other
	●	◉	●	◉	●			●		
Area (ha)	453	6	819							

● = major habitat   ◉ = minor habitat

Birds

Wintering birds: Oronsay is not a regularly counted site, but Buxton (1982) recorded a large flock of ringed plover and bar-tailed godwit.

Breeding birds: there are small breeding colonies of little tern and arctic tern on the estuary. Small numbers of lapwing, snipe and redshank are known to breed within the site, and a further 480 pairs of breeding waders have been recorded on Machair Leathann and Sollas, which lie between the Vallay Strand and Oronsay review sites. The ringed plover survey recorded a breeding population adjacent to the site that exceeded 1% of the international ringed plover population.

Aquatic estuarine communities

Soft substrate

1	2	3	4	5	6	7	8	9	10	11	12	13	14	15	16
												●			

Hard substrate

17	18	19	20	21	22	23	24	25	26	27	28	29	30	31	32	33

Additional wildlife features

Otters are present on the estuary.

Conservation status

● = designated   ◉ = proposed

	NCR	GCR	SSSI (B)	SSSI (G)	SSSI (M)	NNR	LNR	Ramsar	SPA	AONB	CWT	RSPB	ESA	NP	WWT	NT	NSA	HC	Other
		●			●			◉	◉				●				●		
No.		1			1			1	1				1				1		

Part of the site lies within the Machairs Robach and Newton (758 ha) Site of Special Scientific Interest, which has been designated for its biological and geomorphological interest, and contains the Machairs Robach Newton and North Uist Geological Conservation Review site. The site is also part of the Machairs of the Uists and Benbecula, Barra and Vatersay Environmentally Sensitive Area, and Vallaquie Strand is a National Scenic Area. Part of the site lies within the West Sound of Harris proposed Ramsar site and Special Protection Area.

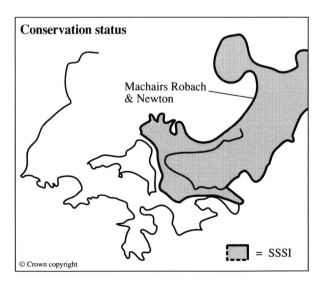

Conservation status

Machairs Robach & Newton

© Crown copyright

▨ = SSSI

Human activities

Present Proposed

		Coast protection & sea defences
		Linear defences
		Training walls
		Groynes
		Brushwood fences
		Spartina planting
	●	Marram grass planting

		Barrage schemes
		Weirs & barrages for river management
		Storm surge barrages
		Water storage barrages & bunds
		Leisure barrages
		Tidal power barrages

		Power generation
		Thermal power stations
		Import/export jetties (power generation)
		Wind-power generation

		Industrial, port & related development
		Dock, port & harbour facilities
		Manufacturing industries
		Chemical industries
		Ship & boat building
		Others

		Extraction & processing of natural gas & oil
		Exploration
		Production
		Rig & platform construction
		Pipeline construction
		Pipeline installation
		Import/export jetties & single-point moorings
		Oil refineries
		Mothballing of rigs & tankers

		Military activities
		Overflying by military aircraft
		Others

		Waste discharge
		Domestic waste disposal
		Sewage discharge & outfalls
		Sewage treatment works
		Rubbish tips
		Industrial & agricultural waste discharge
		Thermal discharges (power stations)
		Dredge spoil
		Accidental discharges
		Aerial crop spraying
		Waste incinerators
		Others

		Sediment extraction
		Capital dredging
		Maintenance dredging
		Commercial estuarine aggregates extraction
●		Commercial terrestrial aggregates extraction
		Non-commercial aggregates extraction
		Hard-rock quarrying

		Transport & communications
		Airports & helipads
		Tunnels, bridges & aqueducts
●		Causeways & fords
		Road schemes
		Ferries
		Cables

		Urbanisation
		Land-claim for housing & car parks

		Education & scientific research
●		Sampling, specimen collection & observation
		Nature trails & interpretative facilities
		Seismic studies & geological test drilling
●		Marine & terrestrial archaeology
		Fossil collecting

Present Proposed

		Tourism & recreation
		Infrastructure developments
		Marinas
		Non-marina moorings
		Dinghy & boat parks
		Caravan parks & chalets
		Leisure centres, complexes & piers
		Aquatic-based recreation
		Power-boating & water-skiing
		Jet-skiing
		Sailing
		Sailboarding & wind-surfing
		SCUBA & snorkelling
		Canoeing
		Surfing
		Rowing
		Tourist boat trips/leisure barges
		Angling
		Other non-commercial fishing
		Bathing & general beach recreation
		Terrestrial & intertidal-based recreation
		Walking, including dog walking
		Bird-watching
		Sand-yachting
		4WD & trial-biking
		Car sand-racing
		Horse-riding
		Rock-climbing
		Golf courses
		Clay-pigeon shooting
		Others
		Airborne recreation
		Overflying by light aircraft
		Radio-controlled model aircraft
		Others

		Wildfowling & hunting
●		Wildfowling
		Other hunting-related activities

		Bait-collecting
		Digging & pumping for lugworms & ragworms
		Hydraulic dredging for worms
		Others

		Commercial fisheries
		Fish-netting & trawling
		Fyke-netting for eels
		Fish traps & other fixed devices & nets
		Crustacea
		Molluscs – Hand-gathering
		Dredging
		Hydraulic dredging

		Cultivation of living resource
●		Saltmarsh grazing
●		Sand dune grazing
		Agricultural land-claim
		Fish-farming
		Shellfish farming
		Bottom & tray cultivation
		Suspended cultivation
		Crustacea farming
		Reeds for roofing
		Salicornia picking
		Others

		Management & killing of birds & mammals
●		Killing of mammals
		Killing of birds
		Adult fish-eating birds
		Adult shellfish-eating birds
●		Gulls
		Geese

		Wildlife habitat management
		Spartina control
		Habitat creation & restoration
		Marine
	●	Intertidal
		Terrestrial
		Habitat management

		Others

Features of human use

There are very few activities occurring on Oronsay.
Exploitation of the natural resources includes heavy
grazing of the saltmarsh and moderate grazing of the sand
dunes, and wildfowlers shoot over part of the site in
winter mainly for greylag geese. Terrestrial archaeology
occurs at Udal and there has been some research into
greylag geese.

In 1989 consent had been granted for small-scale sand
extraction on Machair Robach, and there was some
control of rabbits, rats and greylag geese. In 1989 there
was a proposal to restore the dunes, by planting marram
grass in the blow-outs in Machair Robach.

Further reading

Buxton, N.E. 1982. Wintering waders on the Atlantic
shores of the Uists and Benbecula. *Scottish Birds*, *12*:
106-113.

Crawford, I.C. 1989. *National sand dune vegetation
survey. Site report, No. 68, Grenetote, North Uist.*
Peterborough, Nature Conservancy Council. (Contract
surveys, No. 118.)

Eleftheriou, A. 1970. *Report on the general biological
survey at North Uist.* Aberdeen, Department of
Agriculture and Fisheries for Scotland.

Eleftheriou, A., & McIntyre, A.D. 1976. *The intertidal
fauna of sandy beaches – a survey of the Scottish
coast.* Aberdeen, Department of Agriculture and
Fisheries for Scotland. (Scottish Fisheries Research
Report, No. 6.)

Fuller, R.J., Reed, T.M., Buxton, N.E., Webb, A.,
Williams, T.D., & Pienkowski, M.W. 1986.
Populations of breeding waders *Charadrii* and their
habitats on the crofting lands of the Outer Hebrides,
Scotland. *Biological Conservation*, *37*: 333-361.

Law, D. & Gilbert, D. 1986. *Saltmarsh survey of North-
west Scotland, The Western Isles.* Unpublished, Nature
Conservancy Council.

<table>
<tr><td>**62**</td><td colspan="2">## Scarista</td></tr>
</table>

Centre grid: NF9992   District: Harris
Region: Western Isles   SNH region: North-west Scotland

Review site location

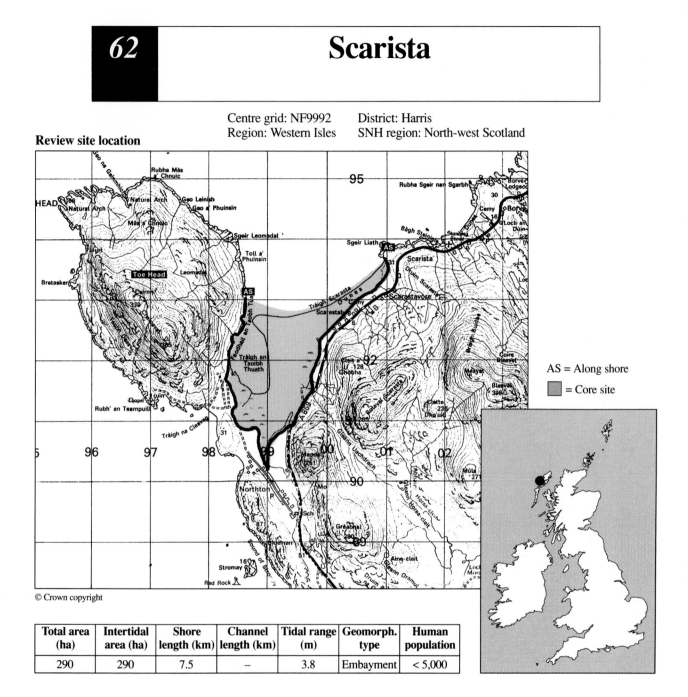

AS = Along shore
= Core site

© Crown copyright

Total area (ha)	Intertidal area (ha)	Shore length (km)	Channel length (km)	Tidal range (m)	Geomorph. type	Human population
290	290	7.5	–	3.8	Embayment	< 5,000

Description

Scarista lies on the south-west coast of the Isle of Harris in the Outer Hebrides, sheltered between Toe Head and the mainland. At low water the site is a large beach of intertidal shell sand which grades into saltmarsh and brackish water fen on the shores in the upper reaches of the estuary. Behind this fringing saltmarsh there is an unusual zone of calcareous machair, with both wet and dry machair, parts of which are cultivated on a rotational basis, and this area supports a diversity of plant species. On the sand dunes the vegetation merges from dry machair into acid moorland.

Wildlife features

Coastal habitats

	Subtidal	Saltmarsh	Sandflats	Mudflats	Sand dunes	Rocky shores	Shingle	Lowland grassland	Lagoon	Other
	◍	●	●	◍	●	◍				
Area (ha)		40	250							

● = major habitat   ◍ = minor habitat

Birds

> **Wintering birds:** Scarista is not a regularly counted site.
>
> **Breeding birds:** there are small breeding colonies of black-headed gull, little tern and arctic tern and a moderate-sized breeding colony of common gull within the site.

Additional wildlife features

Otters regularly use the estuary.

Aquatic estuarine communities

Soft substrate

1	2	3	4	5	6	7	8	9	10	11	12	13	14	15	16
												●			

Hard substrate

17	18	19	20	21	22	23	24	25	26	27	28	29	30	31	32	33

Conservation status

● = designated   ◍ = proposed

	NCR	GCR	SSSI (B)	SSSI (G)	SSSI (M)	NNR	LNR	Ramsar	SPA	AONB	CWT	RSPB	ESA	NP	WWT	NT	NSA	HC	Other
	●	●			●												●		●
No.	1	3			1												1		1

The estuary lies within the Northton Bay Site of Special Scientific Interest (415 ha), which was designated for its biological and geological interest and contains three Geological Conservation Review sites: Scarista, Chaipaval Pegmatite and Borve. Scarista is a National Scenic Area and is a preferred Coastal Conservation Zone.

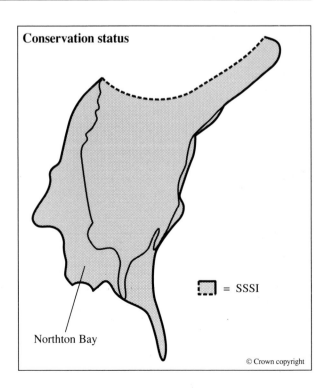

Conservation status

◻ = SSSI

Northton Bay

© Crown copyright

Human activities

Present	Proposed	Activity
●		**Coast protection & sea defences**
		Linear defences
		Training walls
		Groynes
		Brushwood fences
		Spartina planting
		Marram grass planting
		Barrage schemes
		Weirs & barrages for river management
		Storm surge barrages
		Water storage barrages & bunds
		Leisure barrages
		Tidal power barrages
		Power generation
		Thermal power stations
		Import/export jetties (power generation)
		Wind-power generation
		Industrial, port & related development
		Dock, port & harbour facilities
		Manufacturing industries
		Chemical industries
		Ship & boat building
		Others
		Extraction & processing of natural gas & oil
		Exploration
		Production
		Rig & platform construction
		Pipeline construction
		Pipeline installation
		Import/export jetties & single-point moorings
		Oil refineries
		Mothballing of rigs & tankers
		Military activities
		Overflying by military aircraft
		Others
		Waste discharge
		Domestic waste disposal
●		Sewage discharge & outfalls
		Sewage treatment works
		Rubbish tips
		Industrial & agricultural waste discharge
		Thermal discharges (power stations)
		Dredge spoil
		Accidental discharges
		Aerial crop spraying
		Waste incinerators
		Others
		Sediment extraction
		Capital dredging
		Maintenance dredging
		Commercial estuarine aggregates extraction
●		Commercial terrestrial aggregates extraction
●		Non-commercial aggregates extraction
		Hard-rock quarrying
		Transport & communications
●		Airports & helipads
		Tunnels, bridges & aqueducts
		Causeways & fords
		Road schemes
		Ferries
		Cables
		Urbanisation
		Land-claim for housing & car parks
		Education & scientific research
		Sampling, specimen collection & observation
		Nature trails & interpretative facilities
		Seismic studies & geological test drilling
		Marine & terrestrial archaeology
		Fossil collecting

Present	Proposed	Activity
		Tourism & recreation
		Infrastructure developments
		Marinas
		Non-marina moorings
		Dinghy & boat parks
		Caravan parks & chalets
		Leisure centres, complexes & piers
		Aquatic-based recreation
		Power-boating & water-skiing
		Jet-skiing
		Sailing
		Sailboarding & wind-surfing
		SCUBA & snorkelling
		Canoeing
		Surfing
		Rowing
		Tourist boat trips/leisure barges
		Angling
		Other non-commercial fishing
●		Bathing & general beach recreation
		Terrestrial & intertidal-based recreation
●		Walking, including dog walking
		Bird-watching
		Sand-yachting
●		4WD & trial-biking
		Car sand-racing
		Horse-riding
		Rock-climbing
●		Golf courses
		Clay-pigeon shooting
		Others
		Airborne recreation
		Overflying by light aircraft
		Radio-controlled model aircraft
		Others
		Wildfowling & hunting
		Wildfowling
		Other hunting-related activities
		Bait-collecting
		Digging & pumping for lugworms & ragworms
		Hydraulic dredging for worms
		Others
		Commercial fisheries
		Fish-netting & trawling
		Fyke-netting for eels
		Fish traps & other fixed devices & nets
		Crustacea
		Molluscs – Hand-gathering
		Dredging
		Hydraulic dredging
		Cultivation of living resource
●		Saltmarsh grazing
●		Sand dune grazing
		Agricultural land-claim
		Fish-farming
		Shellfish farming
		Bottom & tray cultivation
		Suspended cultivation
		Crustacea farming
		Reeds for roofing
		Salicornia picking
		Others
		Management & killing of birds & mammals
●		Killing of mammals
		Killing of birds
		Adult fish-eating birds
		Adult shellfish-eating birds
		Gulls
		Geese
		Wildlife habitat management
		Spartina control
		Habitat creation & restoration
		Marine
		Intertidal
		Terrestrial
●		Habitat management
		Others

Features of human use

In 1989 there were very few activities occurring on
Scarista. Sand extraction occurs both commercially and
non-commercially but on a very small scale, and the
beach has been used in the past for landing aircraft.
Leisure activities are widespread but not at all intensive,
and include beach recreation, bird-watching and trial-
biking. In addition the saltmarsh and the sand dunes are
grazed. The sand dunes suffer very serious erosion by
rabbits, and so rabbit traps and fences have been erected
in an attempt to minimise this.

Further reading

Buxton, N.E. 1981. Wader populations of the soft shores
of Lewis and Harris, Outer Hebrides in 1979. *Wader
Study Group Bulletin*, *32*: 29-33

Buxton, N.E. 1982. Preliminary estimates of the number
of waders wintering in the Outer Hebrides, Scotland.
Wader Study Group Bulletin, *35*: 6-7.

Fuller, R.J., Reed, T.M., Buxton, N.E., Webb, A.,
Williams, T.D., & Pienkowski, M.W. 1986.
Populations of breeding waders *Charadrii* and their
habitats on the crofting lands of the Outer Hebrides,
Scotland. *Biological Conservation*, *37*: 333-361.

Law, D., & Gilbert, D. 1986. *Saltmarsh survey of North-
west Scotland. The Western Isles*. Unpublished, Nature
Conservancy Council.

Centre grid: NG0798   District: Harris
Region: Western Isles   SNH region: North-west Scotland

Review site location

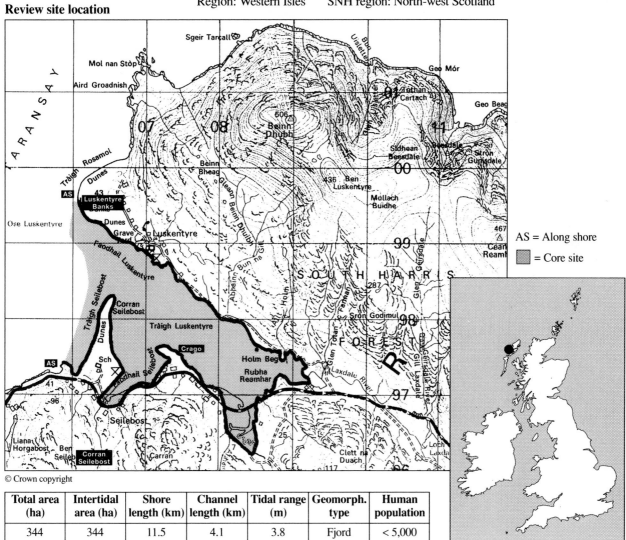

© Crown copyright

Total area (ha)	Intertidal area (ha)	Shore length (km)	Channel length (km)	Tidal range (m)	Geomorph. type	Human population
344	344	11.5	4.1	3.8	Fjord	< 5,000

Description

Traigh Luskentyre lies on the south-west coast of the island of Harris in the Outer Hebrides. At low water a wide sandflat is exposed in this sheltered inlet, which is partly protected by the island of Taransay to the north-west. The intertidal flats shows distinct zonation from open shell-sand beach and sandflat through saltmarsh, dunes and machair to rough pasture. There are two main saltmarshes on the southern shore: an area of mid-upper saltmarsh vegetation in the shelter of Corran Seilebost which is dissected by numerous channels, creeks and pans, and the other is sheltered in the small bay to the east of Crago, and is marked by a 1 metre high erosion cliff.

The site is of particular note for its geomorphology. The northward pointing peninsula of Corran Seilebost contains a variety of beach, dune and machair landforms, and is a dynamic spit with vegetation that is representative of Harris dune and machair. Further east is Crago, a north-west pointing promontory which is partly covered by blown sand. In addition there are both erosional and depositional landforms at Luskentyre Banks to the north. The entire system of Luskentyre Banks, Corran Seilebost and the intertidal flats are thought to be the remains of a much larger area of machair which has been fragmented by postglacial flooding.

Wildlife features

Coastal habitats

	Subtidal	Saltmarsh	Sandflats	Mudflats	Sand dunes	Rocky shores	Shingle	Lowland grassland	Lagoon	Other
	◍	●	●	◍	●	●				
Area (ha)		32	312							

● = major habitat ◍ = minor habitat

Birds

Wintering birds: Traigh Luskentyre is not a regularly counted site, but Buxton (1982) considered the site to be of regional importance for wintering waders in the Outer Hebrides.

Breeding birds: small numbers of black-headed gull, arctic tern and fulmar breed within the estuary.

Additional wildlife features

Otters regularly use the estuary, and the river supports a good salmon fishery.

Aquatic estuarine communities

Soft substrate

1	2	3	4	5	6	7	8	9	10	11	12	13	14	15	16
			●									●		●	

Hard substrate

17	18	19	20	21	22	23	24	25	26	27	28	29	30	31	32	33

Conservation status

● = designated ◍ = proposed

	NCR	GCR	SSSI (B)	SSSI (G)	SSSI (M)	NNR	LNR	Ramsar	SPA	AONB	CWT	RSPB	ESA	NP	WWT	NT	NSA	HC	Other
		●			●												●		●
No.		1			1												1		1

The estuary falls within Luskentyre Banks and Saltings Site of Special Scientific Interest (1,172 ha), which has been designated for its biological and geomorphological interest and contains a Geological Conservation Review site. The estuary also lies within a preferred Coastal Conservation Area and a National Scenic Area.

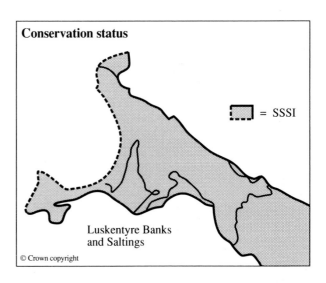

Conservation status

▢ = SSSI

Luskentyre Banks and Saltings

© Crown copyright

Human activities

Present | Proposed

● Coast protection & sea defences
Linear defences
Training walls
Groynes
Brushwood fences
Spartina planting
Marram grass planting

● Barrage schemes
Weirs & barrages for river management
Storm surge barrages
Water storage barrages & bunds
Leisure barrages
Tidal power barrages

Power generation
Thermal power stations
Import/export jetties (power generation)
Wind-power generation

Industrial, port & related development
Dock, port & harbour facilities
Manufacturing industries
Chemical industries
Ship & boat building
Others

Extraction & processing of natural gas & oil
Exploration
Production
Rig & platform construction
Pipeline construction
Pipeline installation
Import/export jetties & single-point moorings
Oil refineries
Mothballing of rigs & tankers

Military activities
Overflying by military aircraft
Others

Waste discharge
Domestic waste disposal
● Sewage discharge & outfalls
Sewage treatment works
Rubbish tips
Industrial & agricultural waste discharge
Thermal discharges (power stations)
Dredge spoil
Accidental discharges
Aerial crop spraying
Waste incinerators
Others

Sediment extraction
Capital dredging
Maintenance dredging
Commercial estuarine aggregates extraction
● (Present) ● (Proposed) Commercial terrestrial aggregates extraction
Non-commercial aggregates extraction
Hard-rock quarrying

Transport & communications
Airports & helipads
Tunnels, bridges & aqueducts
● Causeways & fords
Road schemes
Ferries
Cables

Urbanisation
Land-claim for housing & car parks

Education & scientific research
Sampling, specimen collection & observation
Nature trails & interpretative facilities
Seismic studies & geological test drilling
Marine & terrestrial archaeology
Fossil collecting

Tourism & recreation
Infrastructure developments
  Marinas
  Non-marina moorings
  Dinghy & boat parks
  Caravan parks & chalets
  Leisure centres, complexes & piers
Aquatic-based recreation
  Power-boating & water-skiing
  Jet-skiing
  Sailing
  Sailboarding & wind-surfing
  SCUBA & snorkelling
  Canoeing
  Surfing
  Rowing
  Tourist boat trips/leisure barges
  ● Angling
  Other non-commercial fishing
  ● Bathing & general beach recreation
Terrestrial & intertidal-based recreation
  Walking, including dog walking
  Bird-watching
  Sand-yachting
  4WD & trial-biking
  Car sand-racing
  Horse-riding
  Rock-climbing
  Golf courses
  Clay-pigeon shooting
  Others
Airborne recreation
  Overflying by light aircraft
  Radio-controlled model aircraft
  Others

Wildfowling & hunting
Wildfowling
Other hunting-related activities

Bait-collecting
Digging & pumping for lugworms & ragworms
Hydraulic dredging for worms
Others

Commercial fisheries
Fish-netting & trawling
Fyke-netting for eels
Fish traps & other fixed devices & nets
Crustacea
Molluscs – Hand-gathering
            Dredging
            Hydraulic dredging

Cultivation of living resource
● Saltmarsh grazing
● Sand dune grazing
Agricultural land-claim
Fish-farming
Shellfish farming
  Bottom & tray cultivation
  Suspended cultivation
Crustacea farming
Reeds for roofing
Salicornia picking
Others

Management & killing of birds & mammals
Killing of mammals
Killing of birds
Adult fish-eating birds
Adult shellfish-eating birds
Gulls
Geese

Wildlife habitat management
Spartina control
Habitat creation & restoration
    Marine
    Intertidal
    Terrestrial
Habitat management

Others

Features of human use

In 1989 there were very few activities occurring on the estuary. Leisure pursuits were not intensive and included beach recreation, angling and bird-watching. Exploitation of the natural resource included grazing of the saltmarsh and the sand dunes, and the only industrial activity present was small-scale sand extraction from the dunes. In 1989 there was a proposal to continue this sand extraction outside the SSSI.

Further reading

Angus, I.S. 1979. The macrofauna of intertidal sand in the Outer Hebrides. *Proceedings of the Royal Society of Edinburgh, 77B*: 155-171.

Buxton, N.E. 1981. Wader populations of the soft shores of Lewis and Harris, Outer Hebrides in 1979. *Wader Study Group Bulletin, 32*: 29-33.

Buxton, N.E. 1982. Preliminary estimates of the number of waders wintering in the Outer Hebrides, Scotland. *Wader Study Group Bulletin, 32*: 29-33.

Buxton, N.E. 1982. Wintering waders of Lewis and Harris. *Scottish Birds, 12*: 38-43.

Fuller, R.J., Reed, T.M., Buxton, N.E., Webb, A., Williams, T.D., & Pienkowski, M.W. 1986. Populations of breeding waders and *Charadrii* and their habitats on the crofting lands of the Outer Hebrides, Scotland. *Biological Conservation, 37*: 333-361.

Harris, T., & Ritchie, W. 1989. *Dune and machair erosion in the Luskentyre area: a preliminary survey.* (Contractor: Department of Geography, University of Aberdeen.) Unpublished report to Nature Conservancy Council.

Law, D., & Gilbert, D. 1986. *Saltmarsh survey of North-west Scotland. The Western Isles.* Inverness, Nature Conservancy Council.

Powell, H.T., Holme, N.A., Knight, S.J.T., Harvey, R., Bishop, G., & Bartop, J. 1979. Survey of the littoral zone of the coast of Great Britain. 3: Report on the shores of the Outer Hebrides. (Contractor: Marine Biological Association/Scottish Marine Biological Association.) *Nature Conservancy Council, CST Report*, No. 269.

Camus Uig

Centre grid: NB0433 District: Isle of Lewis
Region: Western Isles SNH region: North-west Scotland

Review site location

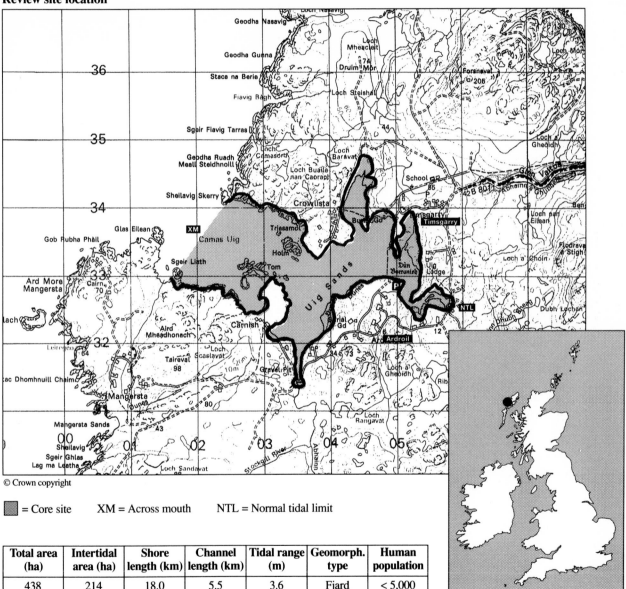

© Crown copyright

■ = Core site XM = Across mouth NTL = Normal tidal limit

Total area (ha)	Intertidal area (ha)	Shore length (km)	Channel length (km)	Tidal range (m)	Geomorph. type	Human population
438	214	18.0	5.5	3.6	Fjard	< 5,000

Description

Camus Uig lies on the north-west shores of the Isle of Lewis in the Outer Hebrides. The innermost parts of this sheltered bay are exposed as sandflats at low water, across which flow two large rivers, dividing the sand into three main areas. There is also a small area of saltmarsh at Timsgarry which is moderately grazed.

To the north and west of Ardroil, large areas of blown sand have accumulated which now support machair vegetation. There are also long stretches of rocky shores on either side of the estuary mouth.

Wildlife features

Coastal habitats

Subtidal	Saltmarsh	Sandflats	Mudflats	Sand dunes	Rocky shores	Shingle	Lowland grassland	Lagoon	Other
●	◉	●	◉	●	●				

| Area (ha) | 224 | 10 | 204 | | | | | | |

● = major habitat   ◉ = minor habitat

Aquatic estuarine communities

Soft substrate

1	2	3	4	5	6	7	8	9	10	11	12	13	14	15	16
		●	●									●		●	

Hard substrate

17	18	19	20	21	22	23	24	25	26	27	28	29	30	31	32	33

Additional wildlife features

The invertebrate fauna recently recorded on the site includes one Notable species. In addition otters regularly use the site.

Birds

> **Wintering birds:** Camus Uig is not a regularly counted site.

Conservation status

● = designated   ◉ = proposed

	NCR	GCR	SSSI (B)	SSSI (G)	SSSI (M)	NNR	LNR	Ramsar	SPA	AONB	CWT	RSPB	ESA	NP	WWT	NT	NSA	HC	Other
																	●		●
No.																	1		1

Camus Uig lies within a National Scenic Area and a preferred Coastal Conservation Zone.

Human activities

Coast protection & sea defences
Linear defences
Training walls
Groynes
Brushwood fences
Spartina planting
Marram grass planting

Barrage schemes
Weirs & barrages for river management
Storm surge barrages
Water storage barrages & bunds
Leisure barrages
Tidal power barrages

Power generation
Thermal power stations
Import/export jetties (power generation)
Wind-power generation

Industrial, port & related development
Dock, port & harbour facilities
Manufacturing industries
Chemical industries
Ship & boat building
Others

Extraction & processing of natural gas & oil
Exploration
Production
Rig & platform construction
Pipeline construction
Pipeline installation
Import/export jetties & single-point moorings
Oil refineries
Mothballing of rigs & tankers

Military activities
Overflying by military aircraft
Others

Waste discharge
Domestic waste disposal
Sewage discharge & outfalls
Sewage treatment works
Rubbish tips
Industrial & agricultural waste discharge
Thermal discharges (power stations)
Dredge spoil
Accidental discharges
Aerial crop spraying
Waste incinerators
Others

Sediment extraction
Capital dredging
Maintenance dredging
Commercial estuarine aggregates extraction
Commercial terrestrial aggregates extraction
Non-commercial aggregates extraction
Hard-rock quarrying

Transport & communications
Airports & helipads
Tunnels, bridges & aqueducts
Causeways & fords
Road schemes
Ferries
Cables

Urbanisation
Land-claim for housing & car parks

Education & scientific research
Sampling, specimen collection & observation
Nature trails & interpretative facilities
Seismic studies & geological test drilling
Marine & terrestrial archaeology
Fossil collecting

Tourism & recreation
Infrastructure developments
  Marinas
  Non-marina moorings
  Dinghy & boat parks
  Caravan parks & chalets
  Leisure centres, complexes & piers
Aquatic-based recreation
  Power-boating & water-skiing
  Jet-skiing
  Sailing
  Sailboarding & wind-surfing
  SCUBA & snorkelling
  Canoeing
  Surfing
  Rowing
  Tourist boat trips/leisure barges
  Angling (Present ●)
  Other non-commercial fishing
  Bathing & general beach recreation (Present ●)
Terrestrial & intertidal-based recreation
  Walking, including dog walking
  Bird-watching
  Sand-yachting (Present ●)
  4WD & trial-biking
  Car sand-racing
  Horse-riding
  Rock-climbing
  Golf courses
  Clay-pigeon shooting
  Others
Airborne recreation
  Overflying by light aircraft
  Radio-controlled model aircraft
  Others

Wildfowling & hunting
Wildfowling
Other hunting-related activities

Bait-collecting
Digging & pumping for lugworms & ragworms
Hydraulic dredging for worms
Others

Commercial fisheries
Fish-netting & trawling
Fyke-netting for eels
Fish traps & other fixed devices & nets
Crustacea
Molluscs – Hand-gathering
    Dredging
    Hydraulic dredging

Cultivation of living resource
Saltmarsh grazing (Present ●)
Sand dune grazing (Present ●)
Agricultural land-claim
Fish-farming
Shellfish farming
  Bottom & tray cultivation
  Suspended cultivation
Crustacea farming
Reeds for roofing
Salicornia picking
Others

Management & killing of birds & mammals
Killing of mammals
Killing of birds
Adult fish-eating birds
Adult shellfish-eating birds
Gulls
Geese

Wildlife habitat management
Spartina control
Habitat creation & restoration
  Marine
  Intertidal
  Terrestrial
Habitat management

Others

Features of human use

There are very few activities occurring on Camus Uig. In summer beach recreation is not intensive. A single craft is used for sand-yachting and angling occurs for sea trout and salmon. The saltmarsh and sand dunes are grazed by sheep.

Further reading

Angus, I.S. 1979. The macrofauna of intertidal sand in the Outer Hebrides. *Proceedings of the Royal Society of Edinburgh, 77B*: 155-171.

Buxton, N.E. 1981. Wader populations of the soft shores of Lewis and Harris, Outer Hebrides in 1979. *Wader Study Group Bulletin, 32*: 29-33.

Buxton, N.E. 1982. Preliminary estimates of the number of waders wintering in the Outer Hebrides. *Wader Study Group Bulletin, 35*: 6-7.

Buxton, N.E. 1982. Wintering coastal waders of Lewis and Harris. *Scottish Birds, 12*: 38-43.

Fuller, R.J., Reed, T.M., Buxton, N.E., Webb, A., Williams, T.D., & Pienkowski, M.W. 1986. Populations of breeding waders *Charadrii* and their habitats on the crofting lands of the Outer Hebrides, Scotland. *Biological Conservation, 37*: 333-361.

65 Laxdale Estuary

Centre grid: NG0798   District: Isle of Lewis
Region: Western Isles   SNH region: North-west Scotland

Review site location

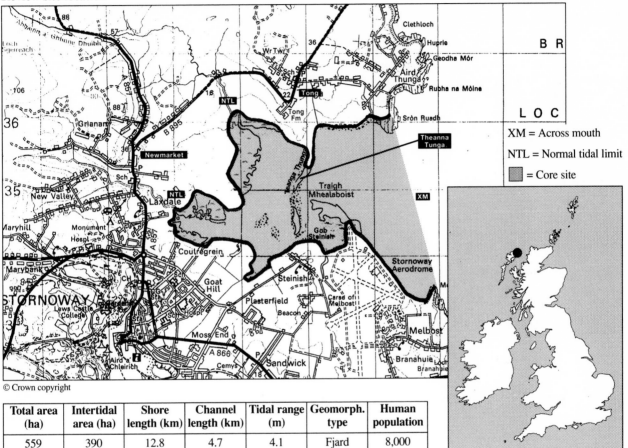

XM = Across mouth

NTL = Normal tidal limit

▨ = Core site

© Crown copyright

Total area (ha)	Intertidal area (ha)	Shore length (km)	Channel length (km)	Tidal range (m)	Geomorph. type	Human population
559	390	12.8	4.7	4.1	Fjard	8,000

Description

The Laxdale Estuary lies on the eastern coast of the Isle of Lewis in the Outer Hebrides, in close proximity to Stornoway. The estuary is the confluence of two rivers, the Laxdale and Abhainn a'Ghlinne Dhuibh, and has one of the largest areas of tidal flats and saltmarsh in the Western Isles. Saltmarshes and mudflats lie in the shelter of two spits which extend into the estuary, while beyond these spits the intertidal flats are predominantly sandy.

Extending southwards into the main channel is Theanna Tunga, a shingle spit covered with blown sand. The shingle is derived from cliffs to the north of the site. The spit is now suffering erosion, although in places there is accretion, and at the end of Theanna Tunga there is a small grass-covered island. On the southern shore of the estuary is a sand spit. The extension of the airfield in 1983 removed an area of intertidal flats, thereby altering the

coastal configuration and changing sediment distribution. As a result the spit is growing northwards but eroding at its southern end.

In the innermost bay within the shelter of these spits saltmarshes have developed where the rivers flow into the bay. The largest area of saltmarsh is in the northernmost bay that stretches from Tong to Newmarket, where there is an area of largely mid-upper saltmarsh vegetation. The seaward edge of this saltmarsh is marked by a 1 metre high erosion cliff.

In addition the estuary supports aquatic estuarine communities of both soft and hard substrates, and the exposed rocky shore and moderately exposed rocky shore communities are considered to be of national importance.

Wildlife features

Coastal habitats

	Subtidal	Saltmarsh	Sandflats	Mudflats	Sand dunes	Rocky shores	Shingle	Lowland grassland	Lagoon	Other
	●	●	●	●	●	●	◉			
Area (ha)	169	96	294							

● = major habitat   ◉ = minor habitat

Birds

Wintering birds   1987/88 – 1990/91 data

Total waterfowl: 570

BoEE	NWC	WSC
	●	

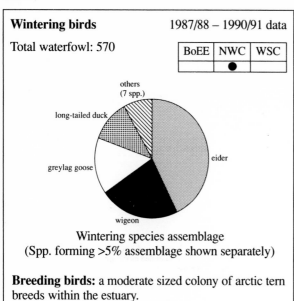

others (7 spp.)
long-tailed duck
greylag goose
eider
wigeon

Wintering species assemblage
(Spp. forming >5% assemblage shown separately)

Breeding birds: a moderate sized colony of arctic tern breeds within the estuary.

Aquatic estuarine communities

Soft substrate

1	2	3	4	5	6	7	8	9	10	11	12	13	14	15	16
			●									●			

Hard substrate

17	18	19	20	21	22	23	24	25	26	27	28	29	30	31	32	33
●	●															

Conservation status

● = designated   ◉ = proposed

	NCR	GCR	SSSI (B)	SSSI (G)	SSSI (M)	NNR	LNR	Ramsar	SPA	AONB	CWT	RSPB	ESA	NP	WWT	NT	NSA	HC	Other
			●																●
No.			1																3

Much of the estuary lies within the Tong Saltings biological Site of Special Scientific Interest (417 ha), and the Ministry of Defence own land north of the airfield.

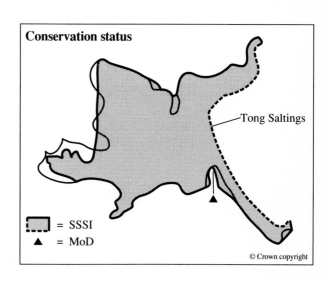

Conservation status

Tong Saltings

▨ = SSSI
▲ = MoD

© Crown copyright

Human activities

Present	Proposed	Activity
●		**Coast protection & sea defences**
		Linear defences
		Training walls
		Groynes
		Brushwood fences
		Spartina planting
		Marram grass planting
		Barrage schemes
		Weirs & barrages for river management
		Storm surge barrages
		Water storage barrages & bunds
		Leisure barrages
		Tidal power barrages
		Power generation
		Thermal power stations
		Import/export jetties (power generation)
		Wind-power generation
●		**Industrial, port & related development**
		Dock, port & harbour facilities
		Manufacturing industries
		Chemical industries
		Ship & boat building
		Others
	●	**Extraction & processing of natural gas & oil**
		Exploration
		Production
		Rig & platform construction
		Pipeline construction
		Pipeline installation
		Import/export jetties & single-point moorings
		Oil refineries
		Mothballing of rigs & tankers
●		**Military activities**
●		Overflying by military aircraft
		Others
		Waste discharge
		Domestic waste disposal
●		Sewage discharge & outfalls
		Sewage treatment works
●		Rubbish tips
		Industrial & agricultural waste discharge
		Thermal discharges (power stations)
		Dredge spoil
		Accidental discharges
		Aerial crop spraying
		Waste incinerators
		Others
		Sediment extraction
		Capital dredging
		Maintenance dredging
		Commercial estuarine aggregates extraction
●		Commercial terrestrial aggregates extraction
		Non-commercial aggregates extraction
		Hard-rock quarrying
●		**Transport & communications**
		Airports & helipads
●		Tunnels, bridges & aqueducts
		Causeways & fords
		Road schemes
		Ferries
		Cables
		Urbanisation
		Land-claim for housing & car parks
		Education & scientific research
		Sampling, specimen collection & observation
		Nature trails & interpretative facilities
		Seismic studies & geological test drilling
		Marine & terrestrial archaeology
		Fossil collecting

Present	Proposed	Activity
		Tourism & recreation
		Infrastructure developments
●		Marinas
		Non-marina moorings
		Dinghy & boat parks
		Caravan parks & chalets
		Leisure centres, complexes & piers
		Aquatic-based recreation
		Power-boating & water-skiing
		Jet-skiing
		Sailing
		Sailboarding & wind-surfing
●		SCUBA & snorkelling
		Canoeing
		Surfing
		Rowing
		Tourist boat trips/leisure barges
		Angling
●		Other non-commercial fishing
		Bathing & general beach recreation
		Terrestrial & intertidal-based recreation
●	●	Walking, including dog walking
●		Bird-watching
		Sand-yachting
●		4WD & trial-biking
●		Car sand-racing
●		Horse-riding
		Rock-climbing
		Golf courses
		Clay-pigeon shooting
		Others
		Airborne recreation
●		Overflying by light aircraft
		Radio-controlled model aircraft
		Others
		Wildfowling & hunting
		Wildfowling
		Other hunting-related activities
		Bait-collecting
		Digging & pumping for lugworms & ragworms
		Hydraulic dredging for worms
●		Others
		Commercial fisheries
		Fish-netting & trawling
		Fyke-netting for eels
		Fish traps & other fixed devices & nets
		Crustacea
		Molluscs – Hand-gathering
		Dredging
		Hydraulic dredging
●		**Cultivation of living resource**
●		Saltmarsh grazing
		Sand dune grazing
		Agricultural land-claim
		Fish-farming
		Shellfish farming
		Bottom & tray cultivation
		Suspended cultivation
		Crustacea farming
		Reeds for roofing
●		*Salicornia* picking
		Others
		Management & killing of birds & mammals
		Killing of mammals
		Killing of birds
		Adult fish-eating birds
		Adult shellfish-eating birds
		Gulls
		Geese
		Wildlife habitat management
		Spartina control
		Habitat creation & restoration
		Marine
	●	Intertidal
		Terrestrial
		Habitat management
		Others

Features of human use

Leisure activities are numerous but generally low-key, and include moorings at Tong pier, canoeing, beach recreation, walking and bird-watching. Trial-biking and sand-racing occur on the north end of the spit, the saltmarsh and intertidal flats.

Exploitation of the natural resources includes light grazing of the saltmarsh and sand dunes, mussel collection for bait, and turf-cutting for horticulture. In 1989 there was a lease for a shellfishery on the shore at Tong but by 1992 this had not been taken up.

Industrial activity includes a small harbour for fishing boats at Tong pier, and shingle extraction from the north of the spit (1-2 ha).

In 1989 there were proposals for marram grass planting to stabilise the dunes near the airport, and for a walkway from Laxdale to Sandwick.

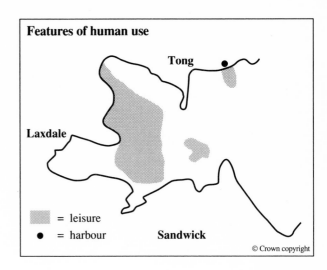

Categories of human use

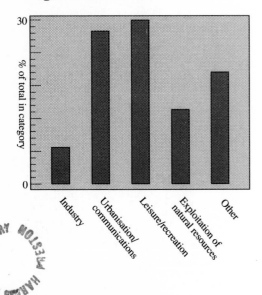

HARRIS PUBLIC LIBRARY PRESTON

Further reading

Buxton, N.E. 1981. Wader populations of the soft shores of Lewis and Harris, Outer Hebrides in 1979. *Wader Study Group Bulletin, 32*: 29-33.

Buxton, N.E. 1982. Wintering coastal waders of Lewis and Harris, *Scottish Birds, 12*: 38-43.

Buxton, N.E. 1982. Preliminary estimates of waders wintering in the Outer Hebrides, Scotland. *Wader Study Group Bulletin, 35*: 6-7.

Fuller, R.J. 1986. Populations of breeding waders *Charadrii* and their habitats on the crofting lands of the Outer Hebrides, Scotland. *Biological Conservation, 37*: 333-361.

Law, D., & Gilbert, D. 1986. *Saltmarsh survey of North-west Scotland. The Western Isles*. Inverness, Nature Conservancy Council.

Powell, H.T., Holme, N.A., Knight, S.J.T., Harvey, R., Bishop, G., & Bartrop, J. 1979. Survey of the littoral zone of the coast of Great Britain. 3. Report on the shores of the Outer Hebrides (Contractor: Marine Biological Association/Scottish Marine Biological Association). *Nature Conservancy Council, CST report*, No. 272.